Designing Inclusive Assessment in Schools

Written by teachers and teacher educators, this book presents practice-focused ideas and provocative questions to help teachers plan for inclusive curriculum and assessment within key learning areas in school education.

Providing content on specific disciplines including geography, history, mathematics, science, English, and the Arts, this book supports teachers with hands-on examples for creating inclusive assessment practices in schools. There are additional sections on interdisciplinary perspectives delivering practical strategies for assessing students who use English as an additional language, being inclusive in relation to gender and sexual diversity, using a variety of technologies to promote inclusivity, and applying inclusive assessment in rural, regional, and remote contexts. Each chapter is designed around problems encountered by teachers, practical responses, and recommendations for practice. The authors address Australian Indigenous perspectives, gender and diversity, rural and remote school systems, and translanguaging for multicultural contexts.

Engaging and easy to read, this book is essential reading for pre- and in-service teachers seeking to make an impactful contribution to inclusive education in their classrooms.

James P. Davis is an Associate Professor in STEM and Entrepreneurial Education, Academic Lead Engagement (Research) in the School of Teacher Education and Leadership, as well as the Lead for the QUT STEM Education Research Group. James is also a former Program Leader for Engagement and Learning in the QUT Centre for Inclusive Education, and a current executive committee member of the Australian Teacher Education Association (ATEA).

Sarah Adams is a Lecturer in Geography Education, School of Teacher Education and Leadership, Queensland University of Technology, Australia.

Catherine Challen is a Senior Lecturer in Maths Education, School of Teacher Education and Leadership, Queensland University of Technology, Australia.

Theresa Bourke is a Professor and Head of School at the Queensland University of Technology, Australia. She is the current President of the Australian Teacher Education Association (ATEA).

Designing Inclusive Assessment in Schools

A Guide to Disciplinary and Interdisciplinary Practice

Edited by James P. Davis, Sarah Adams, Catherine Challen and Theresa Bourke

LONDON AND NEW YORK

Designed cover image: Getty

First published 2025
by Routledge
4 Park Square, Milton Park, Abingdon, Oxon OX14 4RN

and by Routledge
605 Third Avenue, New York, NY 10158

Routledge is an imprint of the Taylor & Francis Group, an informa business

© 2025 selection and editorial matter, James P. Davis, Sarah Adams, Catherine Challen and Theresa Bourke; individual chapters, the contributors

The right of James P. Davis, Sarah Adams, Catherine Challen and Theresa Bourke to be identified as the authors of the editorial material, and of the authors for their individual chapters, has been asserted in accordance with sections 77 and 78 of the Copyright, Designs and Patents Act 1988.

All rights reserved. No part of this book may be reprinted or reproduced or utilised in any form or by any electronic, mechanical, or other means, now known or hereafter invented, including photocopying and recording, or in any information storage or retrieval system, without permission in writing from the publishers.

Trademark notice: Product or corporate names may be trademarks or registered trademarks, and are used only for identification and explanation without intent to infringe.

British Library Cataloguing-in-Publication Data
A catalogue record for this book is available from the British Library

ISBN: 9781032728735 (hbk)
ISBN: 9781032728711 (pbk)
ISBN: 9781003463184 (ebk)

DOI: 10.4324/9781003463184

Typeset in Times New Roman
by KnowledgeWorks Global Ltd.

Contents

List of figures and tables   *vii*
List of contributors   *viii*
Foreword   *xi*

Introduction   1

1 **Inclusive assessment in action**   3
SARAH ADAMS, CATHERINE CHALLEN, JAMES P. DAVIS,
AND THERESA BOURKE

PART I
Disciplinary practices   13

2 **Unlocking history for all: Achieving inclusivity in the history classroom through Assessment for Learning (AfL)**   15
DEBORAH HENDERSON, DANIELLE GORDON, AND MARK MATHER

3 **Designing inclusive Assessment for Learning in English Language Arts**   27
JULIE ARNOLD AND MICHAEL HOLDEN

4 **Daily Discourse: Empowering every student in mathematics through Assessment for Learning**   39
CATHERINE CHALLEN AND SARAH STRONG

5 **Supporting children's spatial understanding through technology: The importance of dialogical exchange analysed through inclusive research**   50
FRANCESCA GRANONE AND GLENN KNUDSEN

vi Contents

6   A place for all: Inclusive practices in Arts assessment   62
    TRICIA CLARK-FOOKES

7   Learning and assessment in school science: Assistive
    technologies for diverse learners   73
    NICHOLAS K. TEH AND JAMES P. DAVIS

8   Inclusive practice and geographical assessment: Practical
    tips to increase task accessibility   83
    SARAH ADAMS, THERESA BOURKE, REECE MILLS,
    AND ASHLEE DREW

PART II
Interdisciplinary practices   95

9   Indigenous perspectives in assessment: Applying
    a place-based approach   97
    DANIELLE ARMOUR, ANTOINETTE COLE, AMY THOMSON, DANIEL
    KIWA MCKINNON, REN PERKINS, AND MARNEE SHAY

10 Queer(y)ing primary assessment: Bodies, genders,
    and sexuality diversity   109
    LISA VAN LEENT AND MICHELLE JEFFRIES

11 Embracing translanguaging in designing inclusive
    assessments with learners of English as an additional
    language or dialect   119
    RONAN KELLY AND MARIA STEWART

12 Spotlighting rural and remote inclusive assessment:
    Systemic perspectives from the field   129
    SARAH JAMES AND TRACEY SEMPOWICZ

PART III
Future practice   139

13 Inclusive classroom assessment and social justice   141
    KAREN DOOLEY, ANNETTE WOODS, AND MARTIN MILLS

    Index   *149*

List of figures and tables

Figures

3.1	Conceptualising inclusive Assessment for Learning as an event, occasion, and invitation	28
5.1	The drawing after the introduction of the number sequence	54
8.1	Task 1 written by the pre-service teacher	85
8.2	Task 2 written by the pre-service teacher	86
8.3	Task 3 written by the pre-service teacher	87
8.4	Task 1 rewritten to overcome some barriers	89
8.5	Task 2 rewritten to overcome some barriers	89
8.6	Task 3 rewritten to overcome some barriers	91
9.1	Indigenous place-based assessment conceptual framework informed by custodianship and sustainability	101

Tables

2.1	Student learning considerations before and after the unit's final assessment	23
7.1	Guided checklist to making appropriate adjustments	77
9.1	Cross-curriculum priorities for assessment	104

List of contributors

Sarah Adams is a lecturer at the Queensland University of Technology, Australia where she teaches geography and prior to this, was a geography teacher in Queensland for over ten years.

Danielle Armour is a Kamilaroi woman and senior lecturer at the University of Queensland, Australia and has over 20 years' experience in Indigenous education.

Julie Arnold is a Lecturer in English curriculum, pedagogy and assessment at the Queensland University of Technology, Australia and Vice President of the English Teachers Association of Queensland.

Theresa Bourke is Head of School and Professor at Queensland University of Technology, Australia and researches professional standards, professionalism, accreditation processes, and diversity in education.

Catherine Challen is a senior lecturer in mathematics education at the Queensland University of Technology, Australia.

Tricia Clark-Fookes is an experienced classroom educator and curriculum writer who currently holds the position Senior Lecturer specialising in Arts curriculum and pedagogy at the Queensland University of Technology, Australia.

Antoinette Cole, a proud Torres Strait Islander descendant with maternal connections to Boigu and Erub (Darnley Island) in the Torres Strait, is an HDR candidate, Research Assistant, and Teaching Assistant at the University of Queensland, Australia and has demonstrated outstanding service within and beyond the Catholic Education community for almost 30 years, showing integrity as a formidable leader.

James P. Davis is Associate Professor in STEM and Entrepreneurial Education and leads the STEM Education Research Group at the Queensland University of Technology, Australia.

Karen Dooley is a Professor of Education, Queensland University of Technology, Australia, and researches in areas related to social justice and education, in particular in conditions of linguistic and cultural difference and economic disparity.

List of contributors ix

Ashlee Drew is an early-career secondary school teacher (Australia) who has a special interest in making the geography curriculum accessible and engaging.

Danielle Gordon taught History in secondary schools for 12 years and is a Lecturer at the Queensland University of Technology, Australia.

Francesca Granone is an Associate Professor in the Department of Early Childhood Education at the University of Stavanger, Norway, and she spearheads two research projects employing inclusive research methods to enhance children's technological and mathematical competencies.

Deborah Henderson is an Associate Professor at Queensland University of Technology, Australia, and is a Past President of the History Teachers' Association of Australia (HTAA), and Life Member of the Australian Curriculum Studies Association (ACSA).

Michael Holden is a PhD Candidate and Graduate Teaching Fellow at Queen's University in Ontario, Canada and a Sessional Instructor at the University of Calgary in Alberta, Canada.

Sarah James is a Senior Lecturer and Academic Lead Professional Experience at the Queensland University of Technology, Australia whose research focuses on initial teacher education and delves into literacy, mentoring, and early career teacher retention in rural areas.

Michelle Jeffries (she/her) is a post-doctoral research fellow at the Queensland University of Technology, Australia and is passionate about schools as inclusive and welcoming spaces for gender and sexuality-diverse students, teachers, and families.

Ronan Kelly is a Lecturer and the study area coordinator for Teaching English to Speakers of Other Languages (TESOL) in the School of Teacher Education and Leadership at the Queensland University of Technology, Australia.

Glenn Knudsen is a co-researcher at the University of Stavanger, Norway, and he uniquely enhances two projects with his expertise in mathematics, specifically related to autism spectrum disorder.

Mark Mather is a Master of Teaching Graduate from the Queensland University of Technology, Australia, and is now a teacher of Humanities and English at Trinity College Beenleigh, Queensland.

Daniel Kiwa McKinnon (Ngāti Rangitihi, Puketapu, Pākehā) is a recent PhD graduate, casual academic and secondary school teacher living and learning on Quandamooka Country.

Martin Mills is a Professor of Education, Queensland University of Technology, Australia, and researches in areas related to social justice and education.

Reece Mills is an Associate Professor in Education at the Queensland University of Technology, Australia whose research aims to create socially and environmentally sustainable futures.

Ren Perkins is a Lecturer at Griffith University, Australia, and is a member of the Australian Association for Research in Education and The National Aboriginal and Torres Strait Islander Higher Education Consortium.

Tracey Sempowicz is a Lecturer in the School of Education and Tertiary Access at the University of the Sunshine Coast, Australia who works in the areas of Inclusive Education and Professional Practice.

Marnee Shay is an Aboriginal (Wagiman) educator with 20 years of experience in teaching, leadership and research, and is an Associate Professor and Principal Research Fellow in the School of Education at the University of Queensland in Australia.

Maria Stewart is a School Improvement Professional in the Education Authority Northern Ireland, an Associate Lecturer in St Mary's University College Belfast, and is a convenor of the Northern Ireland branch of NALDIC (National Association of Language Development in the Curriculum).

Sarah Strong leads the STEM cohort of the High Tech High Teacher Residency Program, USA, and is the author of the book Dear Math, and multiple publications about project-based learning and student-centred assessment in math.

Nicholas K. Teh is a secondary school science, mathematics, and special education teacher, and a tutor in STEM and entrepreneurial education at the Queensland University of Technology, Australia.

Amy Thomson is a Mandandanji woman and a current Doctorate of Philosophy student enrolled in the School of Education at the University of Queensland, Australia and is currently working as a senior research assistant and has previously worked as a secondary English and Music teacher.

Lisa van Leent is an academic at Queensland University of Technology, Australia and is interested in research related to diverse bodies, genders, and sexualities in education.

Annette Woods is a professor at the Queensland University of Technology, Australia, and researches in the areas of literacies, curriculum, pedagogy and assessment, and social justice education.

Foreword

Creating inclusive teacher education: Assessment as a tool of social justice

I write this foreword on Boonwurrung lands of the Eastern Kulin Nations in Naarm (Melbourne, Australia). I take this opportunity to pay my respects to their Elders past and present and thank them for caring for Country. I write at a time known as Waring season or wombat season. A time where the days start to grow shorter and nights are cooler here in the southern part of Australia. I share this context with you the reader, as being grounded in and knowing place and season is an important element that underpins the construct of this volume. Written by teachers for teachers, this book presents context-specific strategies to help address the needs of diverse students, and an invitation to consider adaptations for a wide range of contexts.

While the collective authors focus on the topic of assessment, it is assessment that is *for* learning that is the highlight and that makes this collection unique in exploring what it means to construct inclusive assessment. Acknowledging, understanding, and knowing the specific context from which one's learning, teaching, and assessment occurs is a key theme across the chapters, with the authors acknowledging and meeting the diversity of people, place, and perspectives as essential in creating an inclusive teaching workforce.

I also write from the position of a Dean of a School of Education and acknowledge the increasing diversity of our pre-service teachers, who in turn will teach an increasingly diverse student cohort. We, as a teaching profession, need to find new and better ways to enable all students to demonstrate their learning and build their understanding. Authentic and inclusive assessment is positioned as the key to meet the needs of *all* learners, underpinned by the notion that educators know their students, and know how they learn and this applies to teacher educators as well. It is here that teacher educators demonstrate their agency in responding to a myriad of ways in which assessment *for* learning can occur, often set against increasing regulated standards.

The volume contributes to expanding the notion of what authentic and inclusive education can look like and importantly positions assessment as a tool for greater social justice. While assessment conversations can often be centred on thinking about criterion-based rubrics and discussing penalty marks for lateness, this volume takes a more open and dare I say inclusive lens to thinking about how assessment can be considered and enacted, thus lifting the field and profession as a whole. The authors collectively and individually push the boundaries of what inclusive assessment means and provide examples of new ways of thinking about assessing pre-service teachers. I particularly enjoyed the representation of inclusion that embraces notions of diversity of all people, their bodies, sexualities, places, and practices.

Combined, this book represents the complex, collective learning of pre-service teachers, teachers, and teacher educators who engage with the design of inclusive assessment in schools. Many of the chapters appropriately focus on pre-service teachers to explain ways in which developing an understanding of learner complexity and diversity may be developed as a professional capability. Other chapters focus on teachers who offer practice-based insights into their understandings of complex localised contexts where inclusive assessment is performed.

Overall, the authors both challenge and empower readers to reflect deeply on current practices and consider new frameworks, structures, and pedagogies to reimagine what inclusive assessment can look like for all learners. A variety of strategies and approaches are encouraged from adopting universal principles of design to exploring integrating assistive technologies and real-world place-based examples.

Initial teacher education is always under intense scrutiny. Here is an example of teacher educators taking their expertise and scholarly knowledge to apply to an increasingly important field for the profession. I know this volume will contribute greatly to enhancing the profession.

Professor Simone White
Dean of the School of Education, RMIT University
3rd May 2024

Introduction

1 Inclusive assessment in action

*Sarah Adams, Catherine Challen,
James P. Davis, and Theresa Bourke*

Complexity, diversity, and continuous change

The capabilities of teachers for designing inclusive assessment in schools are grounded in a practical and often intuitive understanding of complexity in localised and dynamic contexts. Complexity thinking (Davis & Sumara, 2005) in education enables an understanding of learners as diverse individuals connected with localised contexts and comprised of behavioural and biological sub-systems. Such learners grow their knowledge individually where they may be a part of a community, connected to their place or Indigenous country, mediated through technologies, engaging through embodied experiences, and learning at the level of bodily sub-systems that encompass diverse identities and neurodiversity. This book represents the complex, collective learning of pre-service teachers, teachers, and teacher educators who engage with the design of inclusive assessment in schools. Many of the chapters focus on pre-service teachers to explain ways in which an intuitive understanding of learner complexity and diversity may be developed as a professional capability. Other chapters focus on teachers who offer practice-based insights into their understanding of complex localised contexts where inclusive assessment is performed.

We adopt complexity thinking as a way of describing and explaining the diversity of the authors' responses in this book, who were invited to share their practical experiences with designing inclusive assessment in schools. As you read this book, we invite you to consider the complexity of this field and your own understanding of inclusive assessment as a complex field of practice in constant disequilibrium and change. Features evidencing complexity include the self-organising nature of this book where autonomous authors write, and where their collective knowledge converges despite diversity in their disciplines or contexts. Complexity is evident in the bottom-up approach of authors' responses that are not aligned centrally or ideologically throughout the book, yet they achieve a pragmatic coherence with ideas that are closely connected. Such pragmatic coherence enables us to illustrate not only the complexity of designing inclusive assessment but also the commonalities across a diverse body of professional pre-service teachers, teachers, and teacher educators.

DOI: 10.4324/9781003463184-2

Broadening inclusion and contextualising systems

The chapters in this book simultaneously recognise the diversity of learners and learning conditions, and converge around commonalities, including a shared perspective on inclusive education as a fundamental human right. The United Nations (UN) Convention on the Rights of Persons with Disabilities (CRPD) defines inclusion as 'a process of systemic reform embodying changes and modifications in content, teaching methods, approaches, structures and strategies in education to overcome barriers with a vision serving to provide all students of the relevant age range with an equitable and participatory learning experience and environment that best corresponds to their requirements and preferences' (United Nations, 2016, paragraph 11). The desire to create equitable experiences for all learners in schools has emerged as a core value for many countries in response to research showing that students with disabilities thrive academically, emotionally, and socially when educated with their non-disabled peers (Hehir et al., 2016).

The notion of inclusive education has moved beyond assurances for students with disabilities to include students of different genders, those from ethnically, culturally, and linguistically diverse backgrounds, and students presenting with a wide range of cognitive, social, and behavioural characteristics (Cerna et al., 2021). Authentic inclusive education meets the needs of *all* learners through classroom and system-level supports, underpinned by the notion that educators know their students, and know how they learn. It is through this knowledge that educators can systematically remove barriers to access and participation through flexible and creative assessment approaches that ascertain what and how a diverse range of students learn.

Collective learning

The authors of this book assert that there is no single solution to effective inclusive assessment. Inclusive education is portrayed as an ongoing iterative and systemic process, involving a professional ethos contingent upon educators' adeptness in navigating classroom heterogeneity and problem-solving endeavours. Realising this ambition necessitates input from diverse stakeholders including families, communities, and, notably, students themselves. Written by teachers for teachers, this book presents context-specific strategies to help address the needs of diverse students and an invitation to consider adaptations for a wide range of contexts. The authors both challenge and empower readers to reflect deeply on current practices and consider new frameworks, structures, and pedagogies to reimagine assessment for all learners.

Central to this discourse is the imperative for change and a belief in its feasibility. Legislative and policy directives in many countries now oblige schools to provide inclusive learning opportunities for all students. Nevertheless, there remains an undeniable tension between the principles of inclusive education and entrenched institutional structures, like assessment, originally conceived without due consideration for learner diversity. School leaders and teachers have embraced the call for solutions, developing collective efficacy as they create solutions and learn together.

Recommendations

Drawing from the various chapters of this book, the authors suggest the following recommendations for addressing inclusive assessment in schools:

- Adopt Assessment for Learning (AfL) principles to enable differentiation of pedagogy for fostering student engagement.
- Create agency and build growth mindset capabilities among students through practices involving self-assessment checklists, graphic organisers, developing glossaries, use of exemplars, exit slips, multi-modal learning and assessment, and being flexible with classroom space design to accommodate different pedagogies.
- Enable students to visualise and celebrate their learning progression with meaningful alignment of formative and summative assessment.
- Integrate assistive technologies in both formative and summative assessment; for example, the C-pen, or applications of generative AI.
- Adjust assessment to incorporate frameworks such as Universal Design for Learning (UDL) to inform project-based or inquiry-based learning.
- Promote student engagement with AfL practices such as Daily Discourse (DD), students co-constructing and sharing success criteria, self and peer assessment, and making adjustments for specific student needs.
- Connect students' learning to real-world scenarios. This bridging technique helps build student capabilities for transferring their knowledge and skills to broader contexts and, ultimately, assessment contexts.
- Communicate in ways and with language that is inclusive for students with diverse identities or neurodiversity.
- Promote student agency and autonomy by giving students choices through multi-mode assessment.
- Design and simplify assessment task sheets that are linguistically, visually, and procedurally aligned with students' needs.
- Adopt culturally responsive curriculum to support inclusion.
- Incorporate Indigenous place-based education (PBE) in curriculum to building a sense of identity, place, and belonging for all.
- Consult with Indigenous community members to ensure protocols are followed and the knowledge taught is accurate when planning curriculum with Country/Indigenous knowledge and cultural practices.
- Develop knowledge of trauma-informed approaches to support inclusivity with assessment items.
- Represent diversity of gender, families, bodies, and sexualities as they exist in society.
- Promote translanguaging in designing inclusive assessment for students with English as an additional language or dialect (EAL/D), because multi-lingual students think in multiple languages simultaneously.

Chapter summaries

Part I – Disciplinary practices

Chapter 2. Unlocking history for all: Achieving inclusivity in the history classroom through Assessment for Learning (AfL)

Henderson et al. outline a case study of practice related to a pre-service teacher's assessment practices whilst on professional experience. AfL is foregrounded as a classroom pedagogy that encourages inclusivity, student learning, and engagement. The pre-service teacher adjusted their teaching through differentiation to account for students' achievement levels, used entry point strategies to hook, engage, and motivate student interest as well as scaffolding techniques to ensure accessibility of first- and second-order historical concepts. Other inclusive strategies included graphic organisers, self-assessment checklists, simulations, glossaries, exemplars, exit slips, and multiple modes for sources as well as using the space in the classroom differently, for example campfires (teacher-led instruction), watering holes (collaborative activities), or caves (independent study). Students could move between the different spaces freely. For most students, there were improvements in their learning.

Chapter 3. Designing inclusive Assessment for Learning in English Language Arts

Arnold and Holden's chapter is focused on designing assessment for learning in English Language Arts in Canada and Australia where AfL is seen as an event, occasion, and invitation, each with implications for designing inclusive assessment. Vignettes from three teachers are outlined. In the Australian vignette, AfL practices such as co-constructing and sharing success criteria and peer assessment are used as ways to centre inclusive practices and promote learner agency. In the Canadian vignettes, for the kindergarten teacher, differentiating instruction to the children's needs was very important; making the correct adjustments so all could succeed as well as extending those who had average reading levels. Once again, a level of agency was involved in the learning process. For the secondary teacher in Canada, inviting the students into the assessment process was achieved by occasioning inclusive practices through the UDL framework and using project-based learning and inquiry-based tasks. Students experienced multiple opportunities to express thoughts, feelings, and ideas in diverse ways.

Chapter 4. Daily Discourse: Empowering every student in mathematics through Assessment for Learning

Challen and Strong feature an American-based study of 700 students in a financially under-resourced school, focused on a pedagogical routine known as DD. This AfL discourse-based approach specifically allows teachers to orchestrate productive mathematical discussions to improve problem-solving and reasoning skills for culturally and linguistically diverse students. To develop an inclusive classroom, students need to feel like capable contributors to maths discussions and feel safe and supported to share their incorrect and incomplete ideas. Teachers reinforce the need for all students to participate, listen to each other, and accept different points of view. If this is not the case, maths anxiety can result where students lose their sense of belonging in a class that does not value the myriad of ways in which students can be mathematical; in other words, the focus is merely on procedural fluency, speedy calculations, memorising, and applying formulas to find the correct answer. The ultimate result is disengagement from the discipline. In sum, DD is posited as an AfL routine based on a notice/wonder approach that requires little preparation and minimal changes to the classroom setup while promoting inclusivity and reducing anxiety.

Chapter 5. Supporting children's spatial understanding through technology: The importance of dialogical exchange analysed through inclusive research

Granone and Knudsen present a Norwegian-based study about observation (assessment) in early childhood education and care (ECEC) in the discipline of mathematics using technology. In Norway, all children are included in mainstream classes regardless of their neurodiversity but unfortunately a recent report claimed that inclusive provision remains at an unsatisfactory standard, especially in mathematics and technology. A unique stance in this chapter and relatively new in ECEC in Norway, is the inclusion of a co-researcher and co-author who has autism spectrum disorder (ASD). This inclusive research method actively engages individuals with neurodiversity to allow a better understanding of the difficulties children may encounter in activities. Specifically, this chapter highlights the different points of view between the two researchers while preparing a play activity with a coding toy (a robotic car called Rugged Robot) for a group of children aged 3–5 and how this can affect the observation/assessment instrument produced. Findings reveal that the activity enhanced spatial orientation. However, insights from the co-researcher highlighted that some children, rather than focusing on the spatial aspect of the activity could be distracted by the numerical sequencing. The co-researcher also argued for dialogical exchange alongside observation as an effective pedagogy.

Chapter 6. A place for all: Inclusive practices in Arts assessment

In this chapter, Clark-Fookes frames curriculum and assessment as opportunities for inclusion by presenting a range of authentic approaches in arts education. As art communicates by feeling more than words it allows a broad range of people to understand regardless of culture, age, and ability. That said, exclusivity based in Eurocentric perspectives persists as do the tensions with the performative and accountability regimes prevalent in the assessment agenda in education today. This chapter presents both formative and summative approaches to assessment to navigate these tensions. For formative assessment specifically two practices are outlined – resisting criteria compliance and assisting all students to access and apply feedback productively. Regarding summative assessment, it is important that the valued features of arts practice and arts knowledge are prioritised. This can be difficult when what is valued is compartmentalised in criteria sheets. Qualifiers are posited as a mechanism that allow for multiple ways to achieve standards of creativity, thus fostering inclusion. Other mechanisms outlined for inclusivity in the Arts are developing optimism (students are well prepared for assessment), differentiation practices including providing students with a choice of texts (script, musical score, performance, artwork, film, etc.), adjusting physical processes, for example, using tactile resources for students with a visual disability, using assistive technologies such as magnifiers or generative AI, and embedding enabling constraints.

Chapter 7. Learning and assessment in school science: Assistive technologies for diverse learners

Teh and Davis's chapter is focused on the discipline of science and concentrates on planning, teaching, and assessing using assistive technologies to cater for the needs of diverse learners especially in formative and summative assessments. The categories from the Nationally Consistent Collection of Data on School Students and Disability (NCCD) framework, namely cognitive, social-emotional, physical, and sensory disabilities, are outlined and labelled as barriers to learning which result in an uneven playing field for learners with disabilities. After defining what assistive technologies are, a range are outlined from simple tools, for example pencil grips, to adaptive educational software such as DreamBox Learning which supports learners with dyslexia. Then a three-phase adjustment process is outlined alongside an adjustment guide checklist which consists of a set of reflective questions to prompt planning and actions to increase accessibility in science learning for all students. The phases include identification of learners who may need adjustments and collecting data related to those students. Then, the category of adjustment is determined in relation to the NCCD framework. There is a future focus in this chapter that accounts for developments in AI and virtual and augmented realities in terms of formative and summative assessments.

Chapter 8. Inclusive practice and geographical assessment: Practical tips to increase task accessibility

Adams et al. use Graham et al.'s (2018) model of visual, procedural, and linguistic complexities as a heuristic tool to examine the level of inclusiveness of a geography task design developed by a pre-service teacher in a Masters of Teaching course at the Queensland University of Technology. While it was found that all three complexities were evident and acted as barriers to learning for students, these were easy to 'design out' with targeted tweaking of the assessment tasks. Such tweaking included, for example, visually, laying the tasks out with ample use of white space and consistency in font type/size and using visual cues such as underlining, bold, or italics for emphasis. In terms of linguistic and procedural accessibility, this related to, for example, using the correct cognitive verbs so students could achieve the set task and ensuring the complexity of the task aligned with the rubrics. Adams et al. added to Graham et al.'s (2018) model by including structural and gender-based barriers which also should be considered if assessments in geography are inclusive for all.

Part II – Interdisciplinary practices

Chapter 9. Indigenous perspectives in assessment: Applying a place-based approach

This chapter by Armour et al. aims to give educators tools for grounding curriculum on Country and to embed Indigenous knowledges and perspectives in curriculum and assessment. PBE is foregrounded as an approach to not only meet policy and curriculum requirements but more importantly to harness the collective benefit of Indigenous ways of knowing, being, and doing to better prepare young people and future generations as custodians and stewards of the land. In this chapter, the authors consider models of PBE in relation to assessment *for*, *of*, and *as* learning from and with Country. Following Spillman et al. (2023), the authors conceptualise Indigenous approaches to place-based assessment where Country is always at the centre along with Culture and Peoples. Additionally, the cross-curriculum priority of sustainability as inseparable from Indigenous worldviews due to relationship with Country is part of the conceptualisation. An example of how Indigenous placed-based approaches to assessment can be applied in science and at multi-grade levels is detailed. This example and others using PBE come from a strengths-based approach, which is not about measurement or ranking but rather is about supporting *all* students to understand the world around them.

Chapter 10. Queer(y)ing primary assessment: Bodies, genders, and sexuality diversity

In this chapter, van Leent and Jeffries argue for queer(y)ing primary school assessment practices. They pose a series of questions for socially just assessment practices including are children with diverse bodies, genders, and sexualities included in assessments as visible identities? Are non-binary, trans, and queer identities represented in literature, assessment scenarios, images in books, and on worksheets? Are adjustments made for these children and do teachers acknowledge the knowledge these children bring? These writers suggest ways in which assessments can be queered including deconstructing normative representations of gender and sexuality and reconstructing them through a queer lens so that all identities are recognised and asking students how they might best be able to demonstrate their learning rather than using prescribed assessment tasks. That said, the authors following Thomas-Reid (2021), point out that suggesting ways for queer(y)ing assessment can be counterproductive by establishing new regulatory regimes. They do, however, list things that teachers should think about in their own assessment practices/designs, what should be thought about in high-stakes testing regimes, and give ideas for the reporting of assessment data, so it is not just about males/females. In conclusion, they maintain that by engaging queer theory in assessment practices, assumptions are challenged, bias is dismantled, and space is created that celebrates the diversity of human identities.

Chapter 11. Embracing translanguaging in designing inclusive assessments with learners of English as an additional language or dialect

In this chapter by Kelly and Stewart, it is argued that all assessments operate in the bounds of a monolingual ideology which potentially excludes EAL/D learners so that their true abilities are only partially represented. This has implications for the validity and fairness of assessments for EAL/D learners who are often positioned in narratives of deficit and failure. Translanguaging as a theory and pedagogic approach is offered as a pathway for teachers to design inclusive school-based assessments for EAL/D learners. These assessments are translingual offering flexible choices across languages and modes. Following Angelo and Hudson (2020), the authors advocate for a spiral curriculum where oral language-based activities are used first, then literacy activities progressing to in-depth curriculum area learning and finally summative assessment tasks. Having a progressive transmodal sequence allows EAL/D learners to demonstrate their ability across various modes. Machine translation, partnering with families and bilingual teachers, using conceptual scoring models, and generative AI are also put forward as mechanisms to support EAL/D students to engage with translingual assessments. Using these approaches makes assessment inclusive for EAL/D learners.

Chapter 12. Spotlighting rural and remote inclusive assessment: Systemic perspectives from the field

James and Sempowicz explore the complexity of key systemic issues impacting inclusive assessment in rural and remote (RR) contexts from the perspectives of two principals. Recognising that inclusivity is about continuous change and adaptability within the limitations of complex systems and resourcing, this chapter accesses interviews with two school leaders to consider the issues faced by RR administrators as they strive to ensure quality education and assessment outcomes for all students. Teachers and administrators at the frontline of school systems are responsible for making inclusivity policies happen and are faced with realities that are not reflected in policy, theory, or most textbooks on inclusive education. This chapter reveals pragmatic challenges for delivering inclusive assessment practices, which include teacher shortages, the need for professional learning, the importance of effective leadership, teacher expertise and efficacy, cultural competence, and diversity in Indigenous communities. These challenges highlight the theory–practice interface where reality on the ground often challenges policy due to the systemic limitations in which teaching work is performed.

Part III – Future practice

The book concludes by considering future practice in Dooley et al.'s chapter titled *Inclusive classroom assessment and social justice*.

References

Angelo, D., & Hudson, C. (2020). From the periphery to the centre: Securing the place at the heart of the TESOL field for First Nations learners of English as an Additional Language/Dialect. *TESOL in Context, 29*(1), 5–35. https://doi.org/10.21153/tesol2020vol29no1art1421

Cerna, L., Mezzanotte, C., Rutigliano, A., Brussino, O., Santiago, P., Borgonovi, F., & Guthrie, C. (2021). *Promoting inclusive education for diverse societies: A conceptual framework* [OECD Education Working Paper No. 260].

Davis, B., & Sumara, D. (2005). *Complexity and education: Inquiries into learning, teaching, and research*. Routledge.

Graham, L., Tancredi, H., Willis, J., & McGraw, K. (2018). Designing out barriers to student access and participation in secondary school assessment. *Australian Educational Researcher, 45*, 103–124. https://doi.org/10.1007/s13384-018-0266-y

Hehir, T., Grindal, T., Freeman, B., Lamoreau, R., Borquaye, Y., & Burke, S. (2016). *A summary of the evidence on inclusive education*. Abt Associates.

Spillman, D., Wilson, B., Nixon, M., & McKinnon, K. (2023). 'New localism' in Australian schools: Country as Teacher as a critical pedagogy of place. *Curriculum Perspectives, 43*(2), 103–114. https://doi.org/10.1007/s41297-023-00201-2

Thomas-Reid, M. (2021). Queer pedagogical theory. In *Oxford Research Encyclopaedia of Education*. https://doi.org/10.1093/acrefore/9780190264093.013.1398

United Nations (UN). (2016). *General comment no. 4 (2016). Article 24: Right to inclusive education*. United Nations. https://www.ohchr.org/Documents/HRBodies/CRPD/GC/RighttoEducation/CRPD-C-GC-4.doc

Part I
Disciplinary practices

2 Unlocking history for all

Achieving inclusivity in the history classroom through Assessment for Learning (AfL)

Deborah Henderson, Danielle Gordon, and Mark Mather

Introduction

Sources of evidence are the basis of all historical knowledge and important tools for accessing the past. A recurring theme in research into adolescent thinking and understanding in history is the critical role of source-based inquiry in engaging young people in learning about the past and fostering their disciplinary knowledge and reasoning skills (Lee, 2004, 2005, 2011). Yet engaging *all* students in meaningful inquiry-based learning and historical thinking is complex and something teachers find challenging. This is because it requires students to understand the uses and limitations of sources as items of evidence about the past. It also requires students to use the second-order historical concepts (or meta-concepts around which history is constructed) to produce historical accounts of past events and processes. Sheehan (2013) contends that while the development of historical thinking is necessary for students to make sense of the past and participate as active and informed citizens in society, historical thinking is not a natural process. It requires 'systematic instruction in the methodologies and vocabulary of the discipline' (Sheehan, 2013, p. 69). A compounding factor in this process is that students with language and/or attentional difficulties are present in most Australian classrooms, and there is limited research on how their learning needs can be identified, better understood, and addressed in ways that enable them to access and participate in the taught curriculum (Tancredi et al., 2023). Hence, it is critical that teachers interpret curriculum documents, and plan for teaching, learning, and assessment in ways that engage diverse learners in the classroom.

In this chapter, we explore an approach to engaging all learners in source-based historical inquiry through Assessment for Learning (AfL) that fosters active learning in the classroom. Our chapter focuses on AfL rather than 'formative assessment' as formative assessment is defined in such diverse ways that the term itself has become generalised and does not include the characteristic identified as 'helping learning' (Wiliam, 2011, p. 10). Moreover, the Assessment Reform Group and other researchers (Klenowski, 2009; Stobart, 2008) prefer the term AfL which can be defined as 'the process of seeking and interpreting evidence for use by learners and their teachers to decide where the learners are in their learning, where they need to go and how best to get there' (Broadfoot et al., 2002, pp. 2–3). We contend that AfL has the potential to create an inclusive classroom environment whereby all students have access to history disciplinary knowledge and understanding. First, we draw from the literature on AfL, followed by selected international research studies on adolescent thinking and reasoning about the past. Then, to illustrate how AfL approaches can be utilised to create an inclusive classroom, we explore three vignettes from a qualitative case study of a pre-service teacher's planning and practice to support student engagement in historical inquiry in a Grade 8 classroom. Using backward design (Wiggins & McTighe, 2005) and metacognitive practices (Flavell, 1977), Mark, our pre-service teacher and co-author, purposefully drew from AfL to plan ways to meet his students where they were in their learning and provide feedback to develop their historical thinking. To highlight Mark's use of AfL as a form of situational classroom interaction that encourages student learning through teacher feedback, we draw from Stobart's (2008) theorisation of AfL processes as follows:

1 The active involvement of pupils in their own learning.
2 The provision of effective feedback to pupils.
3 Adjusting teaching to take account of the results of assessment.
4 The need for pupils to be able to assess themselves.
5 A recognition of the profound influence that assessment has on the motivation and self-esteem of pupils, both of which are crucial influences on learning.

(Stobart, 2008, pp. 145–146)

Here, AfL is foregrounded as a form of assessment that is embedded in the daily learning process to foster students' engagement and enhance the quality of classroom interactions through feedback and guidance. This contrasts with summative forms of assessment (assessment *of* learning) that are designed to measure 'how much' a student has learned after a unit or course has reached its completion (Kennedy & Henderson, 2024, p. 118).

Creating inclusivity with AfL

One way to create an inclusive classroom during historical inquiry is to plan for and implement AfL practices as classroom pedagogy in flexible and creative ways. This is because AfL emphasises learning as an active and social process whereby the individual makes meaning by building on what is already known (Stobart, 2008). Understanding how to embed AfL practices in the history classroom benefits both teachers and students (Lee et al., 2020) because its priority is to promote students' learning. In this context, Klenowski (2009) emphasises AfL as part of the everyday practice of students and teachers as they seek, reflect upon, and respond to information arising from dialogue, demonstration, and observation to enhance ongoing learning. Furthermore, Wiliam (2011) reminds us that because learning is invisible and we cannot assume students learn what they are taught, teachers must plan for and implement AfL strategies in their classrooms to ascertain how students are progressing in their learning as a part of their everyday pedagogical practice. Indeed, the Australian Institute for Teaching and School Leadership (AITSL) Standard 5.1 describes Highly Accomplished Teachers in terms of performing at a level where they can develop and apply a comprehensive range of assessment strategies to diagnose student learning needs (AITSL, 2022).

Although interest in AfL is well established, and it is generally accepted that it remains one of the most important factors influencing student learning (Wiliam, 2011), AfL remains under-researched in discipline-specific contexts despite the evidence of its efficacy. For example, researchers advocate that implementing AfL as a pedagogical practice for inclusion avoids excluding students whose differentiated work isolates them from the wider classroom community (Allan, 2006; Florian & Beaton, 2018). Other researchers, such as Warnich and Lubbe (2019), argue that AfL integrates enjoyment, holds educational value, and removes student anxiety. They encourage pre-service teachers to 'make time for experimenting with creative, engaging yet effective formative assessment techniques amidst the constraints of a full syllabus ... to bring History to life in the classroom' (Warnich & Lubbe, 2019, p. 112).

Given AITSL's (2022) advocacy in Standard 5.1, it might be assumed that AfL is integral to teachers' pedagogical practices as a means of ascertaining what students know (knowledge and understanding) and can do (skills) in the history classroom. However, DeLuca et al. (2018) found that many students have not experienced historical inquiry through AfL practices and, as a result, they remain heavily reliant on their teacher's guidance. These researchers suggest that 'students need to be explicitly taught about AfL concepts, terminology, and use over time' (DeLuca et al., 2018, p. 91). Notwithstanding such advocacy, a recent scoping review by Arnold (2022) highlights a dearth in current AfL research, notably concerning student learning in humanities classrooms. Before examining three vignettes which illustrate how Mark planned for and utilised AfL to create an inclusive history classroom, we draw from the research on developing adolescent thinking in history.

Historical thinking and reasoning

Effective teaching and learning encompass ways of thinking and doing that are representative of how disciplinary experts reason and work within a particular knowledge domain (Darling-Hammond & Bransford, 2005). This approach advocates for history teaching and learning that represent it as an evidentiary form of knowledge and makes explicit the processes through which historians make sense of the past in ways that are accessible to learners (Shemilt, 2018). Concomitantly, there is considerable support for immersing students in this discipline-centred approach in the history education literature, because, as a discipline, history has its own methods and procedures that make it different from other ways of understanding human experiences (Seixas et al., 2015). Moreover, this emphasis is reflected in the aims of the *Australian Curriculum: History 7–10* (Australian Curriculum, Assessment and Reporting Authority [ACARA], 2023) (henceforth, the *Australian Curriculum*), which requires teachers to engage their students in learning experiences that foster mastery of historical inquiry processes, the development of conceptual understanding, and the acquisition of skills.

Research on developing adolescents' historical thinking relevant to the curriculum's aims is concerned with historical literacy (Lee, 2004, 2011; Taylor & Young, 2003). This approach emphasises historical thinking as a process that involves conceptual understandings, skills, and attitudes which mediate students' awareness of the nature and purposes of history and how adolescent learners situate themselves in relation to others in time. A focus on historical thinking around first-order and second-order concepts (Seixas, 2006, 2017) also informs the teaching of history in Australian classrooms. First-order concepts, also referred to as substantive concepts, are concerned with the subject matter being investigated, such as feudalism or nationalism. Second-order concepts, or procedural concepts, are the big ideas or structures unique to history that contribute to the development of historical knowledge and understanding. The current version (v9.0) of the *Australian Curriculum* (ACARA, 2023) identifies six such concepts: evidence, perspectives, interpretations and contestability, continuity and change, cause and effect, and significance. In this chapter, we contend that AfL fosters such discipline-specific forms of knowledge, understanding, and thinking.

Significant to fostering AfL approaches in the inclusive history classroom are those empirical studies which demonstrate that progression in language literacy and disciplinary literacy are complementary. This is notable because so many sources from the past are written (often translated) and require student reading and comprehension in the initial phases of engagement. The limited research available suggests that while reading and writing can assist with mastery of content, some literature emphasises the high cognitive demand it places on students owing to sources including antiquated vocabulary and unfamiliar writing conventions (De La Paz, 2005).

Related challenges to reading and writing in the history classroom include limited contextual knowledge of an event or period and lack of understanding about how history is produced (that it is not transmitted factual knowledge, but rather that it is constructed and contested). Nokes (2011) contends that students find analysing historical documents burdensome because of the comprehension challenges involved and a lack of familiarity with how historians work. He also emphasises the difficulties students encounter during historical analysis when they try to synthesise information from multiple texts. Similarly, Stahl et al.'s (1996) study noted that even when provided with contradictory information, students still relied on their initial understanding of an event gleaned from the first texts they encountered. Monte-Sano and De La Paz (2012) emphasise the role of the teachers and contend that fostering students' capacities to read and write historically is shaped by the nature and quality of the inquiry tasks that teachers design and structure for their students.

Despite these challenges, engaging students in source work is critical to teaching history. In what follows, Mark writes in first person to convey his decision-making for pedagogical practice and his reflections on how the students responded, while we deploy Stobart's (2008, p. 145) five 'deceptively simple' factors to analyse three selected vignettes from the case study of Mark's practice during his final practicum. Table 2.1, provided after the vignettes, illustrates the positive impact of such AfL strategies on the learning outcomes of six students in the summative assessment task scheduled at the end of the unit.

Designing accessible and inclusive history classrooms through AfL: Three vignettes and discussion

Sunshine High (pseudonym) is a co-educational Catholic secondary school situated in a new urban region in Southeast Queensland, Australia. The Index of Community Socio-Educational Advantage (ICSEA[1]) (ACARA, 2020) value was 1019 in 2022, indicating an average level of educational advantage for attending students when considered in comparison with other schools throughout Australia. The Grade 8 students (aged from 12–14 years) in the history class selected, reflected the school's ICSEA profile and included several students identified in the Nationally Consistent Collection of Data on School Students with Disability (NCCD) (Education Services Australia, 2022) lists. Such lists are designed to aid schools in understanding the needs of students with a disability and how they can be appropriately supported.

Through these lists I was able to familiarise myself with each student's level of achievement before planning what I would teach them during my placement; thus, I could plan to adjust my teaching to take account of these results by addressing barriers to learning through differentiation in personalised ways (Stobart, 2008). Given these factors, I aimed to utilise AfL to create an inclusive classroom whereby all students are involved with meaningful historical inquiry and source work in the designated topic on Medieval Europe (c. 590 – c. 1500) from the curriculum. The first phase of planning for the five-week in-depth inquiry on the topic involved 'backward mapping' (Wiggins & McTighe, 2005) in two stages. First, I backward mapped from the *Australian Curriculum*'s statement of what students should know (knowledge and understanding) and do (skills) by the end of Grade 8 history as specified in the achievement standard. Second, this process was repeated with specific reference to the summative examination timetabled for the end of the unit to ensure that in preparing students for their assessment task, I was also designing learning experiences that fostered their authentic active involvement in their own learning (Stobart, 2008) during their inquiry.

In the second phase of unit planning, I drew from a range of AfL strategies such as entry points (Gardner, 1991), to 'hook', engage, and motivate student interest in the topic by accommodating their different learning styles; differentiation (Moorhouse, 2018), to meet the needs of the varying ability levels of students; and scaffolding (Lee & Shemilt, 2003), to ensure that the first-order and second-order concepts associated with the topic were accessible and readily understood. Other inclusive teaching strategies included graphic organisers, 'chunking guides' (Monte-Sano & De La Paz, 2012) (dividing tasks and processes into linked segments or 'chunks' to make learning more manageable), history-specific primary and secondary source engagement techniques such as TADPOLE[2] and TEEL[3] analysis, puzzles, quizzes, videos, artwork, and simulations. In what follows, I draw from three different vignettes to illustrate my use of AfL as a pedagogical practice to create an inclusive classroom.

Vignette 1. Engaging with sources: TADPOLE and TEEL analysis

Each source I selected for students to respond to was provided in multiple modes so that every student could be active in their learning (Stobart, 2008) and not hampered by their level of literacy (De La Paz, 2005). Sources were provided physically (in hard copy), projected onto the classroom wall, read aloud by me before students engaged with the learning task, and online for students to access on their own devices. This enabled students to engage with each source in their own manner and at their own pace. I encouraged students to highlight, shape (break into sub-sections), and engage with each source as they preferred. Given the nature of the unit's content, definitions and glossaries were also provided so that the distinctive vocabulary of the Medieval period, such as 'serf', 'joust', and 'fealty', were accessible (Nokes, 2011), as were prompting questions to foster inquiry (Lee, 2004, 2005).

Learning tasks ranged from completing a TADPOLE source investigation which contained a series of prompts that required students to identify the type, author, date, purpose, opinion/fact, language, and evidence contained in each source, to crafting a TEEL analysis of a source. The latter required students to craft a paragraph response that followed an explicitly taught, defined, and logical structure, commencing with a topic sentence, followed by an explanation, then by an example or evidence to support the topic. A linking sentence completes this sequenced approach to analysing a source by placing it in the context of the topic and its reliability, or otherwise, as an item of evidence about the past. Effective AfL helps students to 'be clearer about what is to be learned and what achieving it would look like' (Stobart, 2008, p. 153). Accordingly, students were provided with exemplars of how their TEEL analysis could be constructed and I also workshopped how inquiry questions could be phrased (Seixas, 2017). To foster learner autonomy during each activity (Stobart, 2008), I made clear to students they could decide to share the 'products' of their learning with their peers verbally, handwritten, typed, as a PowerPoint, or on a poster or collage. Because the completed 'products' of student learning were of varying modes and quality, I modified my language in individual feedback and in the lessons that followed, for example, specifying 'craft a TEEL analysis', rather than 'write a paragraph'. As the unit progressed, students overcame their initial reluctance to participate and this routine of foregrounding a specific strategy led to increased student confidence and participation, and enabled students to gradually internalise the AfL practices to build greater autonomy (DeLuca et al., 2018).

Assessing and providing constructive feedback (Stobart, 2008) on student source analysis indicated that student content knowledge was strong, and while the utilisation of historical skills was initially lacking, it developed throughout the unit. I also observed students enjoying engaging with sources and discussing and/or producing their work in groups. Such evidence of increasing student autonomy enabled me to adjust my daily pedagogical practices based on their work (Stobart, 2008), and I decided to provide students with more AfL opportunities to work with sources in groups, through a 'campfires, caves, and watering holes' strategy.

Vignette 2. Working with sources – Campfires, caves, and watering holes

'Campfires, caves, and watering holes' is a way of utilising learning spaces in the classroom to accommodate several pedagogies, practices, and student preferences at once. The 'campfire' is a space where students learn more directly from the teacher; the 'watering hole' is where students can work collaboratively by sharing information and producing shared findings; and the 'cave' is a private space for individual work. Students are encouraged to travel between these allocated spaces in the classroom as desired. This practice requires students to be actively involved in their learning as they make decisions about how to engage and work with sources. Both individual and group activities were accommodated; all groups were given the task to 'craft a TEEL analysis on this source'. I found this to be a useful way of creating an inclusive classroom, and as students had developed the capacity to access a source in their preferred mode, the need for teacher-led whole-class discussions and explanations was reduced.

I was able to orbit the classroom more frequently, with increased opportunities to provide 'conference' feedback (Shemilt, 2018). This was beneficial for those students who were reluctant to participate in groups. Additionally, this facilitated student extension and student chunking simultaneously (Seixas, 2017). For example, students AA and AC (see Table 2.1), both of whom had language difficulties, regularly gravitated towards the 'campfire', where I could provide scaffolds, chunks, and prompting questions. On the other hand, students V and E (neurotypical students), in the 'watering hole', often requested extension and enrichment activities. The latter were prepared in advance and included self-assessment activities through reflections and criteria checklists, to prompt student engagement with the historical thinking concepts of interpretation and contestability (Seixas, 2017). This interactive approach (Stobart, 2008) allowed for AfL to be embedded in the day-to-day classroom practices with the result of 'continuing adaptation of the learning, particularly through feedback and guidance' (Stobart, 2008, p. 147). Moreover, it was a positive approach to ensuring that the three concepts central to the national guidelines for including all students in learning, namely 'on the same basis', 'consultation', and 'reasonable adjustments' (ACARA, 2017; Kennedy & Henderson, 2024, pp. 67–68), were met.

Vignette 3. Vicariously engaging with the past – Classroom re-enactments

In response to a formal classroom task designed to assess where students were in their understanding of a significant event in Medieval Europe, I realised I needed to adjust my teaching to take account of the results (Stobart, 2008). These results indicated that some students did not understand the hierarchical structure of feudal society and had not fully grasped the first-order concept of feudalism and its significance (a second-order concept). Rather than repeat my practice of using a diagram to illustrate the 'pyramid' structure of societal rankings and status during this time, a proactive approach, where a teacher uses previous AfL results to anticipate misconceptions and change teaching practices, was taken (Stobart, 2008). Accordingly, I devised a simulation (historical re-enactment) to help students understand the rigid nature of society at this time.

The simulation I designed identified a set of student roles to reflect the structure of Medieval society and how it shaped how peoples' lives were regulated. The roles I created included the Pope, the King, four lords, 12 knights, and several serfs. The simulation was designed so that students self-selected their roles to facilitate and enhance their continued involvement in their learning (Stobart, 2008). To set the scene for the students' re-enactment of a 'typical day' in Medieval society according to their selected role, I designed the following scenario for the class. At the beginning of the day, the lords had to swear fealty to the King, and the King would then present them with land in return. The serfs would provide the lords with food, who in turn would use the food to garner the services of the knights, while the Pope was required to stand apart and aloof from such interactions.

In what followed, it seemed that the students were authentically engaging with the rigid structure of Medieval society through such imaginative learning. As Lee (2004) contends, such experiences allow students to connect their tacit knowledge (here on Medieval society) with a deeper understanding of historical content and skills through imagination. For example, one lord joined forces with another to take the food from a third. The fourth lord realised that he had more knights than the King and decided to take the throne. The King appealed to the Pope who declared his neutrality by decrying 'I do not have to help; I am the Pope!' The two lords who had allied themselves together decided to settle how they would distribute their conquered wealth with a trial by combat, drawing upon their knowledge from previous learning to do so. Serfs, who were bound to the land, produced less food when their lord did not treat them with kindness. Knights would often find themselves switching allegiance as prospects became more appealing elsewhere.

My observations indicated that student engagement was high. At the lesson's conclusion, I used exit slips and strategic questioning to assess student knowledge of the first-order concept of 'feudalism' and the second-order concept of 'significance' formatively with encouraging results. This positive outcome of utilising AfL as a pedagogical approach in the history classroom was further reinforced following the in-depth study's summative assessment task results, as evidenced in Table 2.1 for six students.

Unlocking history for all 23

Table 2.1 Student learning considerations before and after the unit's final assessment

Pseudonym	NCCD list and learning considerations	Previous summative assessment result	Medieval Europe summative assessment result
B	Autism spectrum disorder (ASD); social anxiety disorder (SAD); attention-deficit/hyperactivity disorder (ADHD)	C+	A−
Y	Autism spectrum disorder (ASD); Generalised anxiety *Suggested adjustments:* Provide scaffolding and technology aid Provide extra time to complete tasks, and give access to class notes Keep instructions short and clear and different modes (on the board) Model tasks Conference	C−	C+
AA	Specific language impairment (SLI): Developmental language disorder (DLD) *Suggested adjustments:* Breakdown tasks and provide alternate formats Conference frequently Provide scaffolding and prompts Encourage dot-points Simplify instructions Use visuals as much as possible	D	C
AC	Developmental language disorder (DLD); anxiety *Suggested adjustments:* Reduce length and complexity of work Multimodal formats Visual aids Clear verbal and visual instructions Chunk tasks Avoid verbal responses	C−	C
V	Neurotypical	B	A
E	Neurotypical Often requires extension	A	A+

Conclusion

A focus on inclusion provides recognition that some individuals and groups need special attention if they are to benefit from schooling in the same way as their peers. In this chapter, we have argued that AfL practices can be used to include *all* students in meaningful learning in the history classroom whilst also enhancing learner autonomy. The vignettes of AfL as pedagogical practice from Mark's history classroom during a source-based inquiry into life in Medieval Europe indicate that this approach had a positive impact on engaging and including students in their learning. In this history classroom, students were able to develop their knowledge and understanding of the past through authentic inquiry-based source work.

Researchers such as Lee (2004, 2005, 2011) contend that source-base inquiry constitutes the main building block for developing students' capacity to think in time and reason historically. Shemilt (2018) argues that specific strategies are required to help students engage with sources critically, whilst Taylor and Young (2003) emphasise that understanding the discipline-specific language of history is essential for students to develop historical thinking and reasoning. Mark's explicit use of AfL practices to foster student thinking and reasoning about the past was evident in the TEEL analysis and the associated language expectations around this strategy (DeLuca et al., 2018). AfL was also employed to foster student engagement with sources via a 'campfires, caves, and watering holes' approach, and through the use of simulation to reenact an aspect of life in the past. Collectively, these approaches together with the other strategies discussed, provided inclusive ways through which the diverse learners in this Grade 8 history class engaged in thinking and reasoning about the past. While implementing AfL practices to enhance learner autonomy is considered by some to be challenging for teachers in classrooms with diverse learners (see Kennedy & Henderson, 2024, pp. 62–75), its impact on the nature and quality of student learning is significant (Wiliam, 2011), as evidenced in the discussion of three vignettes from Mark's classroom practice.

Notes

1. Schools in Australia are given an ICSEA score (mean = 1,000, standard deviation = 100). ICSEA is a calculation of the relative affluence of the school community (ACARA, 2020) and is accessed from www.myschool.edu.au
2. TADPOLE is an acronym for a specific approach to guide student analysis of a primary or secondary source in the history classroom.
3. TEEL is an acronym for a strategy to guide students in writing an analysis of a primary and/or secondary source in a paragraph.

References

Allan, J. (2006). The repetition of exclusion. *International Journal of Inclusive Education*, *10*(2–3), 121–133.

Arnold, J. (2022). Prioritising students in Assessment for Learning: A scoping review of research on students' classroom experience. *Review of Education*, *10*(3), e3366. https://doi.org/10.1002/rev3.3366\

Australian Curriculum, Assessment and Reporting Authority (ACARA). (2017). *Students with disability*. https://www.australiancurriculum.edu.au/resources/student-diversity/students-with-disability

Australian Curriculum, Assessment and Reporting Authority (ACARA). (2020). *Guide to understanding ICSEA*. https://www.myschool.edu.au/media/1820/guide-to-understanding-icsea-values.pdf

Australian Curriculum, Assessment and Reporting Authority (ACARA). (2023). *Australian Curriculum: History 7–10*. Version 9.0. https://v9.australiancurriculum.edu.au/f-10-curriculum/learning-areas/history-7-10/year-7_year-8_year-9_year-10?view=quick&detailed-content-descriptions=0&hide-ccp=0&hide-gc=0&side-by-side=1&strands-start-index=0&subjects-start-index=0

Australian Institute for Teaching and School Leadership (AITSL). (2022). *Australian Professional Standards for Teachers*. https://www.aitsl.edu.au/docs/default-source/national-policy-framework/australian-professional-standards-for-teachers.pdf

Broadfoot, P. M., Daugherty, R., Gardner, J., Harlen, W., James, M., & Stobart, G. (2002). *Assessment for learning: 10 principles*. University of Cambridge School of Education.

Darling-Hammond, L., & Bransford, J. (Eds.). (2005). *Preparing teachers for a changing world: What teachers should learn and be able to do*. Jossey-Bass.

De La Paz, S. (2005). Effects of historical reasoning instruction and writing strategy mastery in culturally and academically diverse middle school classrooms. *Journal of Educational Psychology*, *97*(2), 139–156. https://doi.org/10.1037/0022-0663.97.2.139

DeLuca, C., Chapman-Chin, A. E., LaPointe-McEwan, D., & Klinger, D. A. (2018). Student perspectives on assessment for learning. *The Curriculum Journal*, *29*(1), 77–94. https://doi.org/10.1080/09585176.2017.1401550

Education Services Australia. (2022). *Nationally consistent collection of data on school students with disability (NCCD)*. https://www.nccd.edu.au/

Flavell, J. (1977). *Cognitive development*. Prentice Hall.

Florian, L., & Beaton, M. (2018). Inclusive pedagogy in action: Getting it right for every child. *International Journal of Inclusive Education*, *22*(8), 870–884. https://doi.org/10.1080/13603116.2017.1412513

Gardner, H. (1991). *The unschooled mind: How children think and how schools should teach*. Basic Books.

Kennedy, K., & Henderson, D. (2024). *Curriculum, pedagogy and assessment*. Pearson.

Klenowski, V. (2009). Assessment for Learning revisited: An Asia-Pacific perspective. *Assessment in Education: Principles, Policy, and Practice*, *16*(3), 263–268. https://doi.org/10.1080/09695940903319646

Lee, H., Chung, H. Q., Zhang, Y., Abedi, J., & Warschauer, M. (2020). The effectiveness and features of formative assessment in US K–12 education: A systematic review. *Applied Measurement in Education*, *33*(2), 124–140. https://doi.org/10.1080/08957347.2020.1732383

Lee, P. (2004). Understanding history. In P. Seixas (Ed.), *Theorizing historical consciousness* (pp. 129–164). University of Toronto Press.

Lee, P. (2005). Putting principles into practice: Understanding history. In S. Donovan & J. Bransford (Eds.), *How students learn: History in the classroom* (pp. 29–78). The National Academies Press.

Lee, P. (2011). History education and historical literacy. In I. Davies (Ed.), *Debates in history teaching* (pp. 63–72). Routledge.

Lee, P., & Shemilt, D. (2003). A scaffold, not a cage: Progression and progression models in history. *Teaching History*, (113), 13–23. https://www.history.org.uk/publications/resource/83/a-scaffold-not-a-cage-progression-and-progressio

Monte-Sano, C., & De La Paz, S. (2012). Using writing tasks to elicit adolescents' historical reasoning. *Journal of Literacy Research*, *44*(3), 273–299. https://doi.org/10.1177/1086296X12450445

Moorhouse, D. (2018). *Differentiation in the history classroom*. https://schoolshistory.org.uk/topics/differentiation/

Nokes, J. D. (2011). Recognising and addressing barriers to adolescents' "Reading like historians". *The History Teacher, 44*(3), 379–404.

Seixas, P. (2006). What is historical consciousness? In R. W. Sandwell (Ed.), *To the past: History education, public memory, and citizenship in Canada* (pp. 11–22). University of Toronto.

Seixas, P. (2017). A model of historical thinking. *Educational Philosophy and Theory, 49*(6), 593–605.

Seixas, P., Gibson, L., & Ercikan, K. (2015). A design process for assessing historical thinking: The case of a one-hour test. In K. Ercikan & P. Seixas (Eds.), *New directions in assessing historical thinking* (pp. 102–116). Routledge.

Sheehan, M. (2013). History as something to do, not just something to learn: Historical thinking, internal assessment and critical citizenship. *New Zealand Journal of Educational Studies, 48*(2), 69–83.

Shemilt, D. J. (2018). Assessment of learning in history education: Past, present, and possible futures. In S. A. Metzger, & L. M. Harris (Eds.), *The Wiley international handbook of history teaching and learning* (pp. 449–472). John Wiley and Sons.

Stahl, S. A., Hynd, C. R., Britton, B. K., McNish, M. M., & Bosquet, D. (1996). What happens when students read multiple source documents in history? *Reading Research Quarterly, 31*(4), 430–456. https://doi.org/10.1598/RRQ.31.4.5

Stobart, G. (2008). *Testing times: The uses and abuses of assessment*. Routledge.

Tancredi, H., Graham, L. J., Killingly, C., & Sweller, N. (2023). Investigating the impact of impairment and barriers experienced by students with language and/or attentional difficulties. *Australian Journal of Learning Difficulties, 28*(2), 173–194. https://doi.org/10.1080/19404158.2023.2285270

Taylor, T., & Young, C. (2003). *Making history: A guide to the teaching and learning of history in Australia*. Curriculum Corporation.

Warnich, P., & Lubbe, H. (2019). Taking the sting out of assessment: The experiences of trainee teachers experimenting with innovative alternative performance assessment in the history classroom. *Yesterday and Today, 22*, 88–118. https://doi.org/10.17159/2223-0386/2019/n22a5

Wiggins, G., & McTighe, J. (2005). *Understanding by design* (2nd ed.). Gale Virtual Reference Library.

Wiliam, D. (2011). What is assessment for learning? *Studies in Educational Evaluation, 37*(1), 3–14. https://doi.org/10.1016/j.stueduc.2011.03.001

3 Designing inclusive Assessment for Learning in English Language Arts

Julie Arnold and Michael Holden

Introduction

Assessment for Learning (AfL) is well-established around the world as 'everyday practice by students, teachers and peers that seeks, reflects upon and responds to information from dialogue, demonstration and observation in ways that enhance ongoing learning' (Klenowski, 2009, p. 265). Ideally, AfL invites *all* learners to achieve their best and develop disciplinary expertise. However, its inclusive potential is often confounded by the pedagogic pull of summative and standardised assessment, as well as the intrinsic social and cognitive demands of AfL's suite of interdependent practices (Willis et al., 2023): sharing learning intentions and success criteria; strategic questioning and other activities that elicit evidence of learning; teacher feedback; and peer- and self-assessment.

English Language Arts (ELA) teachers are well-positioned to navigate the challenges and possibilities of inclusive AfL. As a discipline, ELA sits at the crossroads between 'traditional' literature and language skills, broad-based multiliteracies, and students' developing agency and interpersonal skills (McLean Davies et al., 2018; Patterson, 2000). Every day, ELA teachers draw on their professional capacities to make pedagogically complex decisions about teaching, learning, and assessment (Black & Wiliam, 2018; Deane et al., 2015). This chapter highlights how teachers may design inclusive AfL opportunities for their students and navigate the competing pressures of student agency, coherence, individual assessment events, and the fundamental goal of accessible, inclusive teaching, learning, and assessment. These insights were drawn from an international collaboration that took place over several conversations and analytic memos focused on the intersecting complexities of assessment practice. The vignettes presented in this chapter have been edited to serve as illustrative extracts. They do not provide thorough portraits of the two projects or the participants' practice. They were selected on the basis that they reveal something about assessment tension (Chan & Tan, 2022) and how teachers negotiated these tensions to make their AfL practices more accessible.

Conceptual framework

We suggest that assessment can be understood through the tripartite framework of *event*, *occasion*, and *invitation* (see Figure 3.1). Each of these terms has been described separately in the literature. Brought together, they allow for a conceptualisation

DOI: 10.4324/9781003463184-5

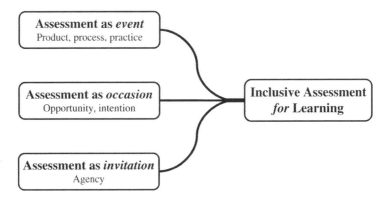

Figure 3.1 Conceptualising inclusive Assessment for Learning as an event, occasion, and invitation.

of AfL as more than a series of discrete assessment events (Pellegrino & Chudowsky, 2003), instead attending to the various processes and products of assessment (event), the learning opportunities those events open up (occasion), and how opportunities for agency are extended to all students (invitation). The purpose of this framing is deliberately inclusive. As Graham (2020) contends, inclusive AfL requires planning for teaching and learning by first considering the barriers that surround students and then reducing those barriers in advance, with the goal of benefiting all students and reducing the number of specific adjustments individual students may need. For example, a teacher may share success criteria at the beginning of a unit (event). They may also create opportunities for students to self-assess in relation to these criteria (occasion). These activities may or may not be accessible opportunities for all learners to regulate their own learning in meaningful ways (invitation). Just as a focus on assessment *events* prioritises the things that happen – assignments, conferencing, peer assessment, and the like – attending to *occasion* and *invitation* may support teachers' ability to intentionally create occasions where all students are included as active agents in assessment and learning.

Assessment as an event is the frame best represented by classroom assessment research and lay perspectives. Etymologically, an event is 'that which happens' (Harper, 2023a, para. 1). Assessment events encompass both the products of assessment (tests, quizzes, essays, performance tasks, etc.) as well as AfL processes. For example, an activity such as engaging in peer feedback is an event. Events clarify, elicit, and analyse evidence; they provide feedback; and they use that feedback to achieve their goals and move learning forward. There is more to AfL, however, than just the selection and ordering of events.

Assessment as occasion stems from Davis and Sumara's (2006) work in complexity thinking, a conceptual arena largely interested in understanding how complex systems like classrooms function. As Davis and Sumara (2006) assert, 'teaching cannot cause learning' (p. 13). Indeed, the entire reason teachers assess is to gather evidence of the unseen: what students understand, what skills they are developing, and what gaps remain (Popham, 2009). Although occasion is often synonymised with event (e.g., Fenwick et al., 2011), it has a broader meaning, that of 'opportunity; grounds for action or feeling; [a] state of affairs that makes something else possible' (Harper, 2023c, para. 1). This is the frame that Davis and Sumara (2006) use. Since teachers cannot cause learning – I may teach *Hamlet* without guaranteeing students learn about death and the human condition – they may instead focus on occasioning opportunities for learning to occur.

This sense of assessment as occasion is implicit in most conceptions of AfL. Teachers engage students in assessment processes because they hope to develop students' ability to assess and regulate their own learning (Andrade, 2013; Baird et al., 2017). Often, an assessment event is visible – the things teachers and students picture when thinking about assessment – while assessment as occasion may include less visible opportunities to interact and connect current assessment events to past and future learning. To offer one example, sharing success criteria is an event and it is also an occasion because the teacher attempts to set the stage for students to understand and invest in their own learning.

Graham et al. (2018) extend this line of thinking with their framing of assessment as invitation. Invitation is an 'act of inviting, solicitation', though the connotation may be 'to go after something, pursue with vigour' (Harper, 2023b, para. 1). Both conceptions are important because assessment is done in the pursuit of learning. AfL is also an invitation because an explicit goal is to foster student agency – students' capacity to directly influence the learning process (Vaughan, 2020) – in interpreting, responding to, and enacting particular assessment events and occasions. As Graham and colleagues (2018) observed, 'these invitations must be evaluated in terms of the affordances they provide for different learners and whether learners can transform those affordances into action' (p. 119). That is, where occasioning explicitly recognises that teaching cannot directly cause learning, and that any one assessment event might give rise to many possible outcomes, invitation attempts to design AfL so that assessment events and their attendant occasions do extend opportunities for agency to all learners (Assessment Reform Group, 2002). Bearman and Ajjawi (2021) synthesise this concept by asking teachers to consider: *What does the assessment invite?*

Illustrative examples from English Language Arts

To illustrate the event–occasion–invitation framework, in this section we present vignettes from ongoing assessment research with three ELA teachers: Morgan, Hannah, and Melody (pseudonyms). Morgan teaches ELA in Queensland, Australia, with students in Grade 10 (ages 14.5–16.5). Morgan's vignette reflects on two related assessment events where she attempts to occasion and invite certain assessment moments. The two remaining teachers, Hannah and Melody, teach ELA in Alberta, Canada, with students in kindergarten (ages 4–5) and Grade 10–12 (ages 15–18), respectively. Hannah's and Melody's vignettes draw on a series of events, occasions, and invitations from multiple assessment reflections. Together, these vignettes illustrate how teachers in different contexts approach assessment as event, occasion, and invitation across their practice.

Morgan: South-East Queensland, Australia

Morgan participated in a 10-week professional learning inquiry to enhance AfL practice, with a particular focus on the practice of sharing success criteria as a way to centre inclusive practice in teachers' AfL work (Arnold & Willis, 2023; Willis et al., 2023). Morgan described two AfL events across a unit of study on narrative writing. What she tried in the professional learning inquiry illuminates how teachers might decide on an AfL event, then occasion learning that is accessible to students, and invite them to be agentic participants.

Co-constructed success criteria

For her first AfL *event*, Morgan selected a common AfL process: co-constructing success criteria. The poster students created with her was a visible representation of 'evergreen' success criteria because it was referred to and adapted throughout the unit. To produce it, students synthesised the qualities of successful task performance they noticed when they reflected on what they already knew about the target genre and by referring to some expert task performances (published short stories). Morgan's AfL design deliberately set the stage for students to understand and invest in their learning by co-creating a visible reference point for ongoing learning. The process of activating prior knowledge and clarifying what quality looks like provided an opportunity to *occasion* learning to be accessible and make connections to future learning.

Co-constructing an assessment event is an *invitation* to agency and Morgan regarded the timing of the invitation as crucial. A co-construction event at the beginning of a unit sent a clear signal to students that Morgan was offering them agency. She reflected:

> In the past, we've thought we've made it clear, but by front loading our assessment, by talking about it, by having it on the wall as our evergreen success criteria, I realise how much more helpful that is, for the kids to see why everything we're doing fits with something … So I feel like they feel more empowered.

Morgan's deliberate occasioning created the conditions for agency and for securing continuity in the learning. She saw it as particularly important for the students in her class with language and attentional difficulties because 'they need to know what it needs to look like at the end, because they don't deal with abstract concepts well'. Morgan understood the invitation needed to be clear and intentional in allowing her students to hold on to the assessment purposes.

Another effect of the timing of Morgan's invitation was the possibility of occasioning more authentic learning. Morgan realised that bringing summative expectations forward could create space, perhaps counterintuitively, to focus on building expansive disciplinary knowledge and skills:

> Normally we talk about what the task is at the start, but we don't really ever look at the criteria early on. [But] that's what they're being assessed on, so why wouldn't you teach to that? ... They are learning creative writing skills in general, but it needs to be through this lens, because that's what they're being assessed on ... whereas in the past, what we might have just done is 'Let's learn a bunch of things and now let's learn what the assessment is and focus on that'. So I think now it's sort of, tighter, and then it's wider knowledge, and then it comes back down again. So it's almost like a Christmas cracker that way (laughs).

Morgan's 'Christmas cracker' metaphor is illuminating. She acknowledged assessment tension – the primacy of the summative assessment task as a narrower lens for teaching and its synthetic purpose for learning – and she used AfL to negotiate through it. She suggested here that, by moving success criteria forward, the shape of the unit was 'like a Christmas cracker' – a cylindrical tube that narrows at both ends. Morgan's assessment was tightened at first by the early focus on quality in the summative assessment. However, the occasion as she constructed it allowed then for authentic disciplinary learning that she described as 'wider knowledge' before returning to the narrower focus of the summative task. In this way, Morgan created opportunities for expansive disciplinary learning, knowing that she and her students could readily return to their visible and agreed success criteria. Her AfL event was also inclusive. The occasion involved all learners in developing a feel for quality, invited participation from the outset, and set the scene for future opportunities where students could develop disciplinary expertise together.

Peer assessment

Later in the unit, Morgan selected another common AfL *event*: peer assessment. After students submitted their short story drafts, Morgan reviewed her students' work and identified the success criteria that emerged as common pressure points. The students then engaged in a collaborative peer review process following a peer feedback protocol (Andrade et al., 2012). By supporting students' foundational assessment literacy in their knowledge of the success criteria in Week One, Morgan created an opportunity to *occasion* learning that was accessible, because students shared an understanding of quality that they then used to assess different aspects of quality task performance across multiple rounds of review. Students were thus *invited* as developing disciplinary experts who could be trusted by their peers to provide useful feedback on work in progress. Their reports about the process were overwhelmingly positive and acknowledged their role as agentic participants. One student identified as having a likely language and/or attentional difficulty said:

> The point was to get a better understanding of how others write. Marking somebody else's work can also help the student … When I was marking somebody else's, I realised that maybe with my merging in and merging out phrases, maybe I needed to add more detail on why I chose the quote and … what word or section represents something else.

The occasioning in this instance was in creating a tangible connection between assessment events, helping students to learn about their own writing by evaluating a peer's work. Morgan created the conditions for learning when she invited students to interact again around their shared (and developing) understanding of quality and in doing so opened access to self-regulation. She also noticed the difference between this AfL event and others she experienced with students in the past: 'They usually hate peer feedback, because they're like, "Oh, I don't really know, or I don't want people to judge me". So it's good that they saw the purpose of that'.

Hannah and Melody: Alberta, Canada

Like Morgan, Hannah and Melody participated in a study examining teachers' approaches to classroom assessment and emergent learning (Bolden & DeLuca, 2016; Holden, 2024). We include Hannah and Melody's vignettes here because of their diverse ELA contexts and their mutual interest in inclusive AfL.

Hannah: Kindergarten

Hannah is a kindergarten teacher in a faith-based programme in a mid-sized urban community in southern Alberta. In her role as her school's literacy coach, Hannah was especially concerned about assessment *events* that did not occasion meaningful learning for students at different literacy levels. She reflected:

> The English kindergarten teacher will just give everybody [the same activity]. But meaningfully, only 6 kids on that class, that's a good thing for them to do. The rest of them either already know it, or they have no idea. So it becomes a case of cutting and pasting rather than actual literacy learning. Two of my students are already reading. So why would I make them take home and practice a poem about 'Mom makes muffins' when they're already reading chapter books?

As Hannah observed, while an assessment event might align with a particular curriculum standard, what learning that event *occasioned* would depend on the diversity of students' actual learning levels. Indeed, if a curriculum standard did not match students' contextual needs, then the kind of learning that was occasioned

Designing inclusive Assessment for Learning 33

may be wildly inconsistent, particularly for students with disabilities or language learning needs (Graham et al., 2018). As a result, Hannah was interested in both the assessment events and how she could better understand where students were in their learning, adjusting her teaching and assessment practices accordingly:

> [I'm] trying to push everybody forward. Trying to find that proximal zone of development. Trying to challenge all the kids without losing your ones that need that extra support. I find often it's our highest kids that get lost. And then we see consequences of that later. ... [For example,] there's a couple of kids in the grade 2/3 class who are reading at a high school level. Well, awesome. That's great. So let's challenge them in writing, then.

Here, Hannah applied Davis and Sumara's (2006) notion of occasioning by attempting to create the conditions for students to learn according to their various needs. Rather than accepting that these two students were reading above grade level, and so required no further assessment events to meet the provincial standard, Hannah instead attempted to occasion new assessment opportunities that would challenge her students in areas where they were not as proficient, in this case writing.

Hannah emphasised that her students – kindergarteners as young as 4–5 years old – could exercise agency in the assessment process (Brookhart, 2013; Graham et al., 2018). In conversations with her students, Hannah regularly asked:

> What do you need? What do you want to learn about reading? Do you want to learn to read faster? Do you want to learn to read bigger words? Do you want to read better in French or in English? Do you want to be able to read a specific book?

As she later explained,

> I'm really curious to hear what their own goals are for their own literacy learning, and then work with them, even if I may be pulling out letter sounds and digraph sounds, helping them to see how this contributes to their goals.

These questions were explicitly *invitational*. Hannah wanted to understand what students' goals were so that they became active agents in the learning process. This directly implied the event–occasion–invitation framework. By inviting students into assessment processes, Hannah was attempting to ensure that the assessment events they encountered (e.g., the books they read, the literacy activities they did) included occasions that were relevant to students' interests, goals, and current literacy levels. This did not mean that assessment invitations absolved Hannah of the difficult pedagogical decisions that assessment involves (Black & Wiliam, 2018). Instead, Hannah worked with students to develop challenging goals that she hoped would lead to more meaningful assessment events and learning occasions.

Melody: Grade 10–12

Hannah's examples are from an early elementary level. In Melody's vignette, we see the same role for inclusive AfL at secondary school. Like Hannah, Melody was concerned with the (un)intentional consequences of assessment *events*. She explained:

> We block kids with our assessment, especially in English, because we are the gatekeeper for everything. It's really harmful for society as a whole. We have to make sure that we're opening the doors to the possibilities, not shutting them down.

English is foundational to students' learning across the curriculum. As Melody described, this 'gatekeeper' status (Hamid et al., 2018; McBee Orzulak, 2013) comes with real risk. How English Language Arts teachers approach assessment can have serious consequences for the ways that students engage in learning (Graham et al., 2018). Hannah therefore advocated for a deliberately *invitational* approach:

> Find another way. Find another way to express [their learning] – which of course, brings us back to that UDL model and multiple means of engagement, representation, and expression. Which of course leads us to multiple means of assessment.

Broadly, Melody was concerned about assessment practices that *lacked* invitation – what she called 'shutting them down'. She was instead much more interested in inclusive models that attempted to invite students into the assessment process by *occasioning* inclusive learning through the UDL (Universal Design for Learning) framework (CAST, 2018). Melody expressed particular concern for widespread grade obsession (Holden et al., 2022) and increased expectations for secondary school students. She explained:

> We're seeing higher levels of stress and anxiety about going to postsecondary. About making the grade, about doing well. ... High schools are not joyful right now. They're actually quite intense pressure cookers for the kids who are in the academic track. The ones who have chosen to not be academic, they are quite a bit happier and quite a bit more well-rounded.

This negative assessment environment arises out of specific assessment events and the kinds of learning they occasion. Facing what they perceive as high-stakes assessment events (e.g., Alberta's diploma exams, which until recently were worth 50% of students' grades in several courses), it is unsurprising that students would experience ELA as a 'pressure cooker' that invited certain behaviours such as grade obsession (Baird et al., 2017).

When asked to describe her approach to assessment and how she invited students through a more inclusive approach, Melody said:

> Over the last 5 to 10 years, I've really moved away from formalized testing to project-based learning, inquiry-based learning tasks. [Those include] multiple points where you can observe the assessment, looking at

the learning outcomes from a broad perspective in terms of skill. [In our programme of study], there's 5 general outcomes. The first one is 'express thoughts, feelings, and ideas'. So what is my task? Design my assessment in line with recognizing their ability to express thoughts, feelings, and ideas. And of course, that's multiple modalities: reading, writing, speaking, listening, and viewing.

Melody's response included changes to both the assessment events she used, and the kinds of learning she tried to occasion. Her assessment events – which used to emphasise 'formalized testing' – now focused on performance tasks that offered her (and her students) multiple opportunities to gather evidence of student learning. Similarly, Melody focused her attention on occasioning opportunities for students to express thoughts, feelings, and ideas in diverse formats. The invitations Melody made were explicitly framed to invite students to actively engage in assessment events:

I don't even use the word tasks. It's a celebration of learning. So when my Grade 12s wrote their diploma exam, they were like, 'Oh my god, that was so easy'. [I said,] 'I told you, it's a celebration of how smart you are'. So, [It's] a totally different frame of reference. ... As we refer to now, [we're] gathering a body of evidence, a balanced body of evidence that represents the different ways of learning and being.

Here, Melody invited her students to engage in assessment events – even provincially mandated standardised tests – as celebrations, rather than adversarial trials. If taken up by her students, and aligned with how she occasions those learning opportunities, there was a real possibility for her students to take ownership over their own learning with a focus on the broad skills that Melody (and the Alberta programme of study) were most interested in fostering.

Paths forward for inclusive Assessment for Learning in English Language Arts

At the beginning of this chapter, we problematised AfL as common and effective pedagogy. We recognised tensions experienced by students and teachers who must deliver on summative assessment purposes alongside more elevated or expansive disciplinary learning purposes. We also recalled that teachers employ AfL practices not only to secure outcomes for the 'majority'; a guiding principle of AfL is to enhance learning opportunities for *all* students and so its generic practices will need to be modified for inclusive classrooms (Tay & Kee, 2019). Our analysis of three teachers' AfL vignettes highlights that participating teachers did indeed recognise these competing tensions and planned for learning experiences to generate opportunities for their students to be agentic participants able to take responsibility for their learning. By conceptualising inclusive AfL through the lenses of event, occasion, and invitation, we were able to consider our selected data in new ways that may be helpful to educators and researchers.

Assessment as event, occasion, and invitation does not require some radical reinvention of assessment practice or a new lexical debate in how teachers parse their practice in academic terms (Black & Wiliam, 2018; Popham, 2009). Instead, as we saw with Morgan's use of co-constructed success criteria, teachers may consider their existing AfL practices and how these events may occasion new learning or invite students to take active, agentic roles in the assessment process (Andrade, 2013). Our analysis illuminated how attending to timing and cohesion amongst AfL practices enhanced accessibility for students.

Importantly, the three teachers featured here – working in different countries and ELA contexts – attempted to make their assessment practices more accessible for all their learners, as with Hannah's 'trying to push everybody forward' and Melody's use of the 'UDL model and multiple means of engagement, representation, and expression'. From an assessment literacy perspective, while there is value in teachers' ability to notice and name the assessment events, occasions, and invitations in their practice, such nomenclature is not itself a prerequisite for inclusive AfL. What these terms do afford is a purposeful selection of practices deployed in principled ways so that the processes and purposes are clear and opportunities for learning are characterised by developing disciplinary expertise and the associated benefits of student agency.

While this chapter has focused on teachers' AfL practices, we concur with Brookhart (2018), Shepard (2019), and others in their calls for assessment coherence; that is, alignment between the formative practices teachers engage in on a daily basis and the summative events these activities often lead to. Morgan's Christmas cracker analogy illustrates that inclusive AfL practice can indeed cohere with summative assessment events while also occasioning meaningful disciplinary learning and student agency. This was equally apparent in Melody's invitation to view provincially mandated standardised tests as an opportunity to celebrate the knowledge and skills students have developed. Given the challenges of vertical coherence (Shepard, 2019), finding ways to foster student agency in the often low-agency space of standardised and summative testing may be quite valuable.

As teachers and teacher educators, we may sometimes encounter colleagues who lament that, in effect, inclusive AfL is an ideal they cannot implement. While AfL must necessarily be responsive to teachers' contexts (DeLuca et al., 2012; Heitink et al., 2016), we contend that these three vignettes drawn from across ELA grades, school boards, nations, and studies support the value of striving for inclusive AfL in all classrooms.

Acknowledgement

This chapter draws on research supported by Canada's Social Sciences and Humanities Research Council and was partially supported by the Australian Government through the Australian Research Council's Linkage Projects funding scheme (LP180100830) and our industry partners. The authors acknowledge that this manuscript draws on these wider projects and thank all team members, partners, and participants for their contributions to this research.

References

Andrade, H. L. (2013). Classroom assessment in the context of learning theory and research. In J. H. McMillan (Ed.), *SAGE handbook of research on classroom assessment* (pp. 17–34). SAGE Publications.

Andrade, H., Huff, K., & Brooke, G. (2012). Assessing learning. *Education Digest, 78*(3), 46–53.

Arnold, J., & Willis, J. (2023). *From fragmentation to coherence: Student experience of assessment for learning.* Australian Educational Researcher. https://doi.org/10.1007/s13384-023-00668-y

Assessment Reform Group. (2002). *Assessment for Learning: 10 principles. Research-based principles to guide classroom practice.* https://www.nuffieldfoundation.org/project/the-assessment-reform-group

Baird, J. A., Andrich, D., Hopfenbeck, T. N., & Stobart, G. (2017). Assessment and learning: Fields apart? *Assessment in Education: Principles, Policy and Practice, 24*(3), 317–350. https://doi.org/10.1080/0969594X.2017.1319337

Bearman, M., & Ajjawi, R. (2021). Can a rubric do more than be transparent? Invitation as a new metaphor for assessment criteria. *Studies in Higher Education, 46*(2), 359–368. https://doi.org/10.1080/03075079.2019.1637842

Black, P., & Wiliam, D. (2018). Classroom assessment and pedagogy. *Assessment in Education: Principles, Policy and Practice, 25*(6), 551–575. https://doi.org/10.1080/0969594X.2018.1441807

Bolden, B., & DeLuca, C. (2016). Measuring the magical: Leveraging assessment for emergent learning. *Assessment Matters, 10*, 52–73. https://doi.org/10.18296/am.0017

Brookhart, S. M. (2013). Classroom assessment in the context of motivation theory and research. In J. H. McMillan (Ed.), *SAGE handbook of research on classroom assessment* (pp. 35–54). SAGE Publications.

Brookhart, S. M. (2018). Learning is the primary source of coherence in assessment. *Educational Measurement: Issues and Practice, 37*(1), 35–38.

CAST. (2018). *Universal design for learning guidelines Version 2.2.* https://udlguidelines.cast.org/

Chan, K. T., & Tan, K. (2022). How teachers experience assessment tension and its effect on formative assessment practices. *Educational Research for Policy and Practice, 21*, 447–464. https://doi.org/10.1007/s10671-022-09316-1

Davis, B., & Sumara, D. J. (2006). *Complexity and education: Inquiries into learning, teaching, and research.* Routledge.

Deane, P., Sabatini, J., Feng, G., Sparks, J., Song, Y., Fowles, M., O'Reilly, T., Jueds, K., Krovetz, R., & Foley, C. (2015). Key practices in English language arts (ELA): Linking learning theory, assessment, and instruction. *ETS Research Report Series, 2015*(2), 1–29. https://doi.org/10.1002/ets2.12063

DeLuca, C., Luu, K., Sun, Y., & Klinger, D. A. (2012). Assessment for learning in the classroom: Barriers to implementation and possibilities for teacher professional learning. *Assessment Matters, 4*, 5–29.

Fenwick, T., Edwards, R., & Sawchuk, P. (2011). *Emerging approaches to educational research.* Routledge. https://doi.org/10.4324/9780203817582

Graham, L. J. (Ed.). (2020). *Inclusive education for the 21st century: Theory, policy and practice.* Allen & Unwin.

Graham, L. J., Tancredi, H., Willis, J., & McGraw, K. (2018). Designing out barriers to student access and participation in secondary school assessment. *The Australian Educational Researcher, 45*, 103–124. https://doi.org/10.1007/s13384-018-0266-y

Hamid, M. O., Hoang, N. T. H., & Kirkpatrick, A. (2018). Language tests, linguistic gatekeeping and global mobility. *Current Issues in Language Planning, 20*(3), 226–244. https://doi.org/10.1080/14664208.2018.1495371

Harper, D. (2023a). *Event.* EtymOnline: Online Etymology Dictionary. https://www.etymonline.com/word/event

Harper, D. (2023b). *Invitation*. EtymOnline: Online Etymology Dictionary. https://www.etymonline.com/word/invitation

Harper, D. (2023c). *Occasion*. EtymOnline: Online Etymology Dictionary. https://www.etymonline.com/word/occasion

Heitink, M. C., Van der Kleij, F. M., Veldkamp, B. P., Schildkamp, K., & Kippers, W. B. (2016). A systematic review of prerequisites for implementing assessment for learning in classroom practice. *Educational Research Review*, *17*, 50–62.

Holden, M. (2024, April 11–14). *Formative classroom assessment as a complex systems process: K–12 teachers' perspectives* [Poster presentation]. American Educational Research Association Conference (AERA).

Holden, M., Rickey, N., & DeLuca, C. (2022, April 22–25). *Assessment innovations: Understanding the "fundamental driver" of teachers' classroom practice* [Paper presentation]. AERA Conference.

Klenowski, V. (2009). Assessment for learning revisited: An Asia-Pacific perspective. *Assessment in Education: Principles, Policy & Practice*, *16*(3), 263–268. https://doi.org/10.1080/09695940903319646

McBee Orzulak, M. J. (2013). Gatekeepers and guides: Preparing future writing teachers to negotiate standard language ideology. *Teaching/Writing: The Journal of Writing Teacher Education*, *2*(1), 12–20. https://scholarworks.wmich.edu/wte/vol2/iss1/5

McLean Davies, L., Buzacott, L., & Martin, S. K. (2018). Growing the nation: The influence of Dartmouth on the teaching of literature in subject English in Australia. In A. Goodwyn, C. Durrant, W. Sawyer, L. Scherff, & D. Zancanella (Eds.), *The future of English teaching worldwide: Celebrating 50 years from the Dartmouth Conference* (pp. 146–158). Routledge.

Patterson, A. (2000). English in Australia: Its emergence and transformations. In R. Peel, A. Patterson, & J. Gerlach (Eds.), *Questions of English: Ethics, aesthetics, rhetoric, and the formation of the subject in England, Australia and the United States* (pp. 235–253). Routledge Falmer.

Pellegrino, J. W., & Chudowsky, N. (2003). The foundations of assessment. *Measurement: Interdisciplinary Research and Perspectives*, *1*(2), 103–148. https://doi.org/10.1207/s15366359mea0102_01

Popham, W. J. (2009). Assessment literacy for teachers: Faddish or fundamental? *Theory into Practice*, *48*(1), 4–11. https://doi.org/10.1080/00405840802577536

Shepard, L. A. (2019). Classroom assessment to support teaching and learning. *The Annals of the American Academy of Political and Social Science*, *683*(1), 183–200. https://doi.org/10.1177/0002716219843818

Tay, H. Y., & Kee, K. N. N. (2019). Effective questioning and feedback for learners with autism in an inclusive classroom. *Cogent Education*, *6*(1). https://doi.org/10.1080/2331186X.2019.1634920

Vaughan, M. (2020). What is student agency and why is it needed now more than ever? *Theory into Practice*, *59*(2), 109–118. https://doi.org/10.1080/00405841.2019.1702393

Willis, J., Arnold, J., & DeLuca, C. (2023). Accessibility in assessment for learning: Sharing criteria for success. *Frontiers in Education*, *8*, 1–15. https://doi.org/10.3389/feduc.2023.1170454

4 Daily Discourse

Empowering every student in mathematics through Assessment for Learning

Catherine Challen and Sarah Strong

Classroom vignette:

> *Twenty Grade 9 students were preparing to have their mathematics class in front of an audience of over 40 teachers, administrators, instructional coaches, parents, researchers from local universities, and other community members in a public lesson. To start the lesson, the teacher invites students to write down everything they notice and wonder about a scatterplot showing the relationship between distance travelled to school and the time taken to get to school for students in their class. After a few minutes of individual think-time, the students are invited to share their ideas with the person next to them. Two minutes later, the teacher asks students to share ideas out loud with the whole class. After a few minutes of eliciting student ideas, the following interaction occurred:*

Student 1: I noticed the line of best fit passes through zero on the y-axis, so that means that zero would be the y-intercept.
Teacher: The y-intercept is zero – is that what you said?
Student 1: Yes.
Teacher: [Addressing the whole class] Wait, now I'm worried because I'm pretty sure last week you convinced me that a line of best fit does not need to pass through (0,0), so now I'm worried that this shouldn't go through (0,0). Can you turn to the person next to you and state whether you think this line of best fit should go through (0,0)?

Students spend time talking with the person next to them – they use hand gestures to describe how they are making sense of the y-intercept.

Teacher: What do we think team – should this line of best fit go through (0,0)?
Student 2: It should because if you travel zero miles it should take zero minutes to travel zero miles.
Teacher: Sorry, can you please say that one more time, loudly?
Student 2: If you travel zero miles it's going to take zero minutes. It's not going to take you any time if you're not travelling.

DOI: 10.4324/9781003463184-6

Teacher: Can anyone please restate what [Student 2] is saying?

The teacher waits for most students to raise their hands before selecting a volunteer.

Student 3: For me to stay where I am it's going to take me zero minutes.
Teacher: So, you're feeling like this line should go through (0,0).
Student 3: Yes.
Teacher: Do we agree? [Addressing the whole class]

Students in the room nod their heads in agreement.

Teacher: It might make sense for this one.

Over the course of the entire lesson[1], every single student spoke at least once, and twelve of the twenty students presented ideas to the whole class (and the public audience). Some of the ideas were incorrect, but they were interrogated until consensus was reached around an accurate solution. After the lesson, in response to a prompt from the Equity Commentator, a parent in the audience stated, 'it is very hard to distinguish between smarter kids in this class ... because every one of them is sharing their ideas ... I was surprised by the critique from one student to the other'.

Introduction

Mathematics curricula around the world expect students to reason mathematically, to justify their thinking, and to develop robust problem-solving skills. The Common Core State Standards for Mathematical Practice in the United States, for example, require students to make sense of problems; reason abstractly and quantitatively; and construct viable arguments and critique the reasoning of others (Common Core State Standards Initiative, 2021). In the Australian Curriculum, mathematics includes proficiencies that develop students' understanding, fluency, reasoning, and problem-solving skills (Australian Curriculum, Assessment and Reporting Authority [ACARA], n.d.). Mathematical discussions involving explanations, justification, and argumentation are now essential features of a quality classroom learning experience. Teachers must, therefore, provide opportunities for all students to practise these skills, assess their progress, and provide feedback. However, many mathematics classrooms remain primarily didactic, leading students to believe that mathematics is all about getting the correct answer when in fact our aim is for them to learn mathematics.

Positioning students as constructors and creators of mathematics, as opposed to simple consumers, leverages students' strengths and funds of knowledge to create mathematical understanding that is inherently connected to their lives and more equitable. Classrooms that provide space for students to reason, make sense of a problem, and justify their thinking are necessary and might require some shifts in the way we currently do things. In this chapter, we describe an Assessment for Learning (AfL) approach in mathematics that connects our goals for students with classroom practices that promote equity and inclusion.

Mathematical discussions as Assessment for Learning

Formative assessment has been shown to improve student learning outcomes and narrow achievement gaps between low-achieving students and others (Black & Wiliam, 1998). While formative assessment can be defined in many ways, at its core it helps teachers learn more about what students understand, so that they can respond in class effectively (Duckor et al., 2017). Through discussions, students construct their mathematical ideas and the language of mathematics, while providing valuable information to a teacher about where students are in their learning journey. Classroom conversations about mathematics, therefore, are a central tenet of teaching formatively, and studies suggest that giving students opportunities to discuss their mathematical ideas and make meaning together results in them having a better mathematical understanding (Ball & Bass, 2000; Michaels et al., 2008; Yackel & Cobb, 1996).

When students explain ideas to themselves out loud, they learn more than when they work in silence, and when students explain ideas to another student, they learn even more (Rittle-Johnson et al., 2008). As one study indicates, time spent articulating a mathematical strategy may lead to better understanding and retention than the equivalent amount of time spent practising a procedure (McEldoon et al., 2013). When students start to articulate an idea in words, they are likely to find gaps in their own understanding. Effective classroom discussions, therefore, should give students a chance to both share and revise their thinking (Chi, 2000). When students have opportunities to explain their thinking, compare ideas, and evaluate the ideas of others in mathematics, their depth of understanding increases. A recent study showed that a discourse-based approach to learning mathematics improved students' conceptual and procedural understanding, dispelling myths that procedural learning is sacrificed in a discussion-based classroom (Yimam & Kelkay, 2022).

Hodgen and Marshall (2005) compared Assessment for Learning in English and mathematics classes and identified the criticality of effective discourse. The authors provided useful comparisons of two disciplines that are seemingly opposite: in English, generating and discussing a wide variety of student responses is paramount, whereas mathematics is often focused on generating agreement around a small number of valid responses, for example (Hodgen & Marshall, 2005). It is not immediately obvious that mathematics teachers would want, or need, to elicit multiple student perspectives. Surely it is easier just to tell students what is correct? However, this approach violates a critical principle of learning – that students must be active in the process (Hodgen & Wiliam, 2006). The learning must be done *by* them, not *for* them. The study emphasised the need for mathematics teachers to elicit a wide range of responses and the value of uncovering correct and incorrect ideas to determine where students are in their understanding and guide them toward improvement.

To develop a classroom community where all students feel like capable contributors to a mathematics discussion, students need to feel safe and supported to share their incorrect and incomplete ideas. This can be challenging, particularly given the increasing diversity in our classrooms and the greater rate at which students experience mathematics anxiety.

Mathematics anxiety

It has become increasingly common to find both adults (including many teachers) and students with an aversion to mathematics. Mathematics anxiety may be defined as an irrational dread of mathematics that inhibits number manipulation and problem-solving in everyday and academic situations (Battista, 1990; Gresham, 2009; Tobias, 1998). This is learned behaviour that is perpetuated by societal messages and cultural stereotypes. For people with mathematics anxiety, learning mathematics can be difficult. Negative attitudes toward mathematics stemming from anxiety have been linked to poor academic performance and feelings of frustration (Battista, 1990; Gresham, 2009; Tobias, 1998). The commencement of students' mathematics anxiety often coincides with timed tests in school (Boaler, 2014). This is a possible consequence of the narrow focus on speed and calculations as the primary metric of what it means to be 'good at maths' in schools. Students lose their sense of belonging when we don't value the range of ways they are mathematical. Ultimately, this impacts identity and can result in students disengaging from mathematics.

It may seem counter-intuitive that more open discussion in mathematics is a potential remedy to mathematics anxiety. However, when teachers are primarily focused on understanding the way students understand a concept, there is less emphasis on getting the correct answer, reducing student anxiety about having the correct response. Importantly, discourse in mathematics has been shown to support the growth of a diverse range of students, including those historically marginalised in mathematics classrooms.

Inclusion in mathematics

Mathematics achievement continues to be predictable based on students' socioeconomic backgrounds (Chudgar & Luschei, 2009). Rather than reflecting student abilities, the discrepancy in student achievement may be a consequence of fewer opportunities to learn. In the United States, for example, students from low socioeconomic backgrounds are more likely than their counterparts to be funnelled into classes with weaker instruction and less cognitively demanding tasks that provide opportunities for reasoning and justification, exacerbating SES inequality (American Educational Research Association [AERA], 2006; Oakes, 1985). However, when we broaden our definition of what it means to be mathematical to more than just memorising and applying formulas, we create opportunities for all students to see themselves as active mathematical thinkers. A five-year longitudinal study of approximately 700 high school students showed that a discourse-based approach to teaching mathematics was highly effective for culturally and linguistically diverse students at a financially under-resourced school in the United States (Boaler & Staples, 2008). The mere act of honouring contributions from all students is an inclusive pedagogical strategy in mathematics (Walshaw & Anthony,

2008). However, it is important to note that the equity outcomes of mathematical discourse rely on a shared understanding of the expectations for participation in discourse – teachers must establish and reinforce the need for all students to participate, listen to each other, accept different viewpoints, and engage in an exchange of ideas (Yackel & Cobb, 1996).

Educators and researchers have advocated for discussion as a means of learning mathematics, yet it remains rare in many classrooms in the United States. Curriculum and policy documents promote reasoning and justification skills, but assessments still predominantly focus on procedural fluency. There are many possible explanations for this reluctance to change classroom practices. Conversations with teachers reveal that they feel pressure to prepare students for exams that primarily assess procedural fluency. Teachers also cite hesitancy to relinquish control as a reason for maintaining a didactic approach. It's not just about teachers either. Students can also find mathematical discussions challenging, particularly when most of their prior mathematics learning experiences have involved mimicking a teacher rather than defending or justifying their thinking. The fear of being wrong can prevent students who lack confidence in mathematics from participating at all. When Sarah Strong invited her students to write letters to mathematics, she discovered that many students found the subject intimidating (Strong & Butterfield, 2022). When students enter a mathematics classroom full of fear, the amount of learning that can happen is already limited. Teachers must acknowledge this power dynamic and actively dismantle it.

Strong proposed a pedagogical routine to support teachers in developing students' reasoning skills and overcoming the intimidation that prevents students from actively learning mathematics – she named it Daily Discourse (DD) to describe the frequency and the central goal which is to have mathematical discourse. It is an Assessment for Learning routine that requires little preparation and minimal changes to the setup of a classroom, while promoting inclusivity and reducing anxiety.

DD – A starting point for fostering mathematical discussions

DD is an opening routine that provides a clear and brief structure for students to discuss mathematics safely. It draws on thinking routines like Notice and Wonder (National Council of Teachers of Mathematics [NCTM], n.d.), requires minimal preparation, and can take just ten to fifteen minutes at the beginning of class. It is an effective first step for any teachers looking to foster more reasoning and justification through discussion in their mathematics classes.

Why do we think DD is useful?

DD addresses many of the challenges teachers and students face when making the shift to a more discussion-based classroom. Although it follows a clear, time-bound structure, it does not require lengthy preparation – teachers simply select a stimulus for the mathematical discussion. Presented alongside the prompt 'write down everything you know, think you know or wonder', appropriate stimuli can range from images to equations, to graphs or even headlines: anything that will prompt a mathematical discussion.

Importantly, the stimulus for discussion does not require students to solve a problem or answer a question but is sufficiently open-ended to generate a variety of ideas. This both increases the challenge of the task but also creates access for all students. An open prompt reduces the anxiety associated with being wrong in front of peers and can foster a greater sense of belonging for students. The low-stakes nature of the prompt supports the expectation that everyone participates. To that end, the teacher pays close attention to which students are voluntarily joining in the discourse and encourages those who are not.

DD can also be a great way to activate retrieval of previously learned content, build on something from the prior day, or even help students see that mathematics has relevance to real life. By connecting the stimulus to the content being studied, DD becomes an effective formative assessment tool and helps teachers see what students know and understand, and misconceptions they might have, to inform instruction.

Ultimately, DD helps students and teachers get more comfortable talking about mathematics. Effective facilitation can prompt students to reason, justify, and participate in ways they might have otherwise been reluctant to do.

DD in action

The authors have both used DD extensively in their middle and high school mathematics classes. Here we describe how DD might typically be implemented, recognising that adjustments will be made to suit the needs of teachers, students, and the school context. We have separated the routine into three stages: (1) The Launch; (2) The Discussion; and (3) The Debrief and Evaluation.

The Launch

For the first few weeks of school, the teacher begins each lesson by projecting a prompt and inviting students to write silently and individually everything they notice or wonder about the prompt. During a statistics unit, the teacher might select graphs to analyse, and in a quadratics unit, she might show the parabolic trajectory of a projectile. The prompts are always different, but the routine remains the same: three minutes of individual think time, followed by two minutes to share ideas with a partner.

If students are trying this routine for the first time, they might not know how to respond to the prompt. They might get stuck, in which case, it can be helpful to advertise some guidance for students:

- I always start by looking for something I DO know.
- I am never 'done' because I always ask the next question.
- I may be asked to share my work on the board.

- I work collaboratively with people around me and value their strengths.
- I will often make mistakes but recognise that they are where my brain grows the most.

As students share their ideas with a partner or at their tables, the teacher actively monitors what students have written down and listens to what they are saying. Depending on her primary goal for the discourse, the teacher uses this monitoring time to select students to share a specific mathematical idea or a common misconception that might be arising.

Goals for the discourse will vary and may include:

- Effective retrieval of a previously taught concept.
- Participation by students whose ideas are not typically valued.
- Revealing a common misconception.
- Identifying multiple representations of the same mathematical concept.

Since this routine is conducted at the beginning of a class, it must establish academic safety such that all students have access to the task. Common 'warm-ups' in traditional mathematics classrooms require students to solve a problem, usually something that they worked on the day before. If a student is unable to solve the problem, it can create the kind of anxiety that leads to rapid and irreparable disconnection right from the beginning of class. For DD, therefore, we encourage the use of open questions or prompts, rather than ones that converge on a single answer.

In our opening vignette, the teacher prompts student ideas and discussion by sharing a scatterplot of data from the class. There is nothing to be solved; however, the teacher has an opportunity to assess what students understand about bivariate data, which they have been studying for approximately four weeks before this lesson.

The Discussion

After students have shared in small groups, the whole-class discussion commences. At the very beginning of the school year, this discussion is facilitated by the teacher, but eventually, student facilitators and scribes are nominated. The discussion is a critical moment in establishing classroom culture, where the teacher reinforces norms that students will listen to the ideas of others, be sceptical, disagree politely, and connect related ideas.

White (2003) showed that teachers who facilitate mathematical discussions illustrate four themes: valuing students' ideas; exploring students' answers; incorporating students' background knowledge; and encouraging student-to-student conversation. When a student shares an idea, it is not evaluated by the teacher to be correct or incorrect. However, the teacher might explore student answers by asking a follow-up question like, 'What makes you think that?' This helps the teacher, and the students, better understand how a student is thinking about the prompt. Similarly, the teacher might ask, 'Does anyone disagree/agree with this idea and why?' to promote student-to-student conversation. In younger grades, or with less experienced students or to support English learners, teachers might post a series of sentence frames to encourage respectful argumentation. Possible sentence frames include:

- I agree with [name] because …
- I disagree with [name] because …
- I want to build on [name's] idea by …
- I don't understand why [name] thinks … can someone else please restate the idea?

Consider the vignette from a high school class at the beginning of this chapter. Students were not asked to calculate or even evaluate anything – they were simply prompted to notice and wonder. By the end of the 10-minute DD described in that class, ten of the 20 students had shared something they noticed or wondered, or restated someone else's idea for clarity. The teacher was setting students up to interpret and contextualise the slope of a line of best fit and introduce the idea of residuals. To do this, she needed to be sure that students understood some fundamental things about scatterplots and the data being presented. By the end of the DD, the class had established the axes labels, the relationship between the two variables, the presence of a possible outlier, and discussed the y-intercept in the context of the data.

Although the discussion is primarily amongst students, teachers use their authority creatively to elevate certain ideas that might be critical for future understanding. One method is through revoicing, which O'Connor and Michaels (1993) defined as repeating, rephrasing, or expanding student talk to clarify or highlight content, extend reasoning, or move a discussion in a new direction. Once teachers have developed some confidence in facilitating mathematics discussions, they might even deliberately argue for an *incorrect* solution to encourage more students to present evidence for why that outcome is incorrect. In our vignette, the teacher poses a question to the class in response to a student who noticed that the y-intercept was zero. The teacher strategically used this observation to address a misconception she identified the week before – students thought that a line of best fit always needed to pass through the origin. The teacher then shifted the mathematical authority to students by asking them to decide if the y-intercept made sense based on the data, honouring their contributions as mathematicians. When a student provided a correct explanation, the teacher used revoicing to emphasise the importance of that student's response.

Aligned with White's (2003) research, DD creates safety for students whose voices are not normally heard in mathematics to speak up and be valued. During the class discussion stage, being valued means accepting all ideas as valid – even mathematically incorrect ones. Often incorrect ideas result in rich conversations. Being valued also means that every idea is recorded with the student's name next to it. A simple strategy for encouraging more voices is to extend the time between asking a question and students responding. In our vignette, the teacher pauses after posing a question to the whole class and waits for more students to raise their hands. Because she is keeping track of who has participated, she deliberately selects a student who has not shared with the class yet, promoting equity and the expectation that everyone participates.

The Debrief and Evaluation

The final step in a DD is an evaluation of the process. Students list specific ways in which the facilitator and the scribe supported the discussion, leading to a list that might look like this:

The facilitator supported the discussion by…

- Asking someone from every table to share.
- Asking follow-up questions.
- Posing a question to the class.
- Calling on volunteers and people who haven't said anything yet.

The scribe supported the discussion by…

- Writing everyone's names next to their ideas.
- Drawing arrows between ideas to show connections.
- Clarifying what students said to make sure she was writing it down accurately.

This step is an important way to establish the expectations for students as they start to take on the roles of scribe and facilitator.

One of the remarkable things about DD is the gradual relinquishing of control to students. As students become familiar with the routine and adopt the facilitation roles, the more capacity the teacher has to monitor participation and assess for learning. The teacher can gather data on what students know, misconceptions that are emerging, which students are contributing, and whose ideas are being valued. Teachers have used a simple system of q, i, and b to denote whether a student shared a question (q), idea (i), or built on someone else's idea (b) during DD. These data are critical for making instructional decisions, attending to status and equity issues, and creating an inclusive classroom culture.

Like most new practices, teachers find that DD can feel uncomfortable for both teachers and students when it is first implemented in classrooms. It takes time for students to understand the expectations and for teachers to get comfortable accepting every response, including the incorrect ones. We encourage teachers to persist and find collaborators with whom they might develop their own improvements and adjustments. Many teachers we have worked with said they would continue to include the routine in their classrooms because they learned so much about their students' ways of thinking and they were starting to hear from students who never spoke up in mathematics.

Conclusion

Discussion in mathematics classrooms has been proposed to enhance students' mathematics learning. Many curriculum documents have promoted the development of students' problem-solving, justification, and reasoning skills, which discussion can also help develop. However, most mathematics classrooms remain primarily didactic, which could be the result of educator scepticism and/or lack of knowledge and skills to effectively implement productive discussions in classrooms (Walshaw & Anthony, 2008). The latter is understandable since orchestrating productive discussions can require changes to teacher preparation and often a fundamental shift in the way a classroom is set up and run.

DD is a student-centred, Assessment for Learning strategy that removes barriers to access for historically marginalised students and promotes engagement in mathematics by broadening how students can demonstrate understanding and contribute to a mathematics learning community. When students discuss mathematics, they deepen their conceptual understanding and develop reasoning and justification skills. Even when students think they understand a mathematical concept, the act of verbalising it to another person can help identify misconceptions or gaps in their knowledge. Moreover, by gradually encouraging student responsibility for the discussion, teachers gain the capacity to assess for learning and actively attend to equity and access in mathematics.

Note

1 The full lesson was conducted as a research lesson study and you can find footage of it here: https://www.mathagency.org/post/hth-maic-public-lesson-study-4-9th-grade-lines-of-best-fit

References

American Educational Research Association (AERA). (2006). Do the math: Cognitive demand makes a difference. *Research Points: Essential Information for Education Policy, 4*(2). https://eric.ed.gov/?id=ED497645

Australian Curriculum, Assessment and Reporting Authority (ACARA). (n.d.). *Australian Curriculum.* https://www.australiancurriculum.edu.au

Ball, D. L., & Bass, H. (2000). Making believe: The collective construction of public mathematical knowledge in the elementary classroom. In D. Phillips (Ed.), *Yearbook of the National Society for the Study of Education, constructivism in education* (pp. 193–224). University of Chicago Press.

Battista, M. (1990). The relationship of mathematics anxiety and mathematical knowledge to the learning of mathematical pedagogy by preservice elementary teachers. *School Science and Mathematics, 86*(1), 10–19. https://doi.org/10.1111/j.1949-8594.1986.tb11580.x

Black, P., & Wiliam, D. (1998). Assessment and classroom learning. *Assessment in Education: Principles, Policy & Practice, 5*(1), 7–74. https://doi.org/10.1080/0969595980050102

Boaler, J. (2014). *Fluency without fear: Research evidence on the best ways to learn math facts.* YouCubed at Stanford University. www.youcubed.org/wp-content/uploads/2015/03/FluencyWithoutFear-2015.pdf

Boaler, J., & Staples, M. (2008). Creating mathematical futures through an equitable teaching approach: The case of Railside School. *Teachers College Record, 110*(3), 608–645. https://doi.org/10.1177/016146810811000302

Chi, M. T. (2000). Self-explaining expository texts: The dual processes of generating inferences and repairing mental models. In R. Glaser (Ed.), *Advances in instructional psychology* (Vol. 5, pp. 161–238). Lawrence Erlbaum Associates.

Chudgar, A., & Luschei, T. F. (2009). National income, income inequality, and the importance of schools: A hierarchical cross-national comparison. *American Educational Research Journal, 46*(3), 626–658. https://doi.org/10.3102/0002831209340043

Common Core State Standards Initiative. (2021). *Common core state standards for mathematics*. https://corestandards.org/wp-content/uploads/2023/09/Math_Standards1.pdf

Duckor, B., Holmberg, C., & Becker, J. R. (2017). Making moves: Formative assessment in mathematics. *Mathematics Teaching in the Middle School, 22*(6), 334–342. https://doi.org/10.5951/mathteacmiddscho.22.6.0334

Gresham, G. (2009). An examination of mathematics teacher efficacy and mathematics anxiety in elementary pre-service teachers. *Journal of Classroom Interaction, 44*(2), 22–38.

Hodgen, J., & Marshall, B. (2005). Assessment for learning in English and mathematics: A comparison. *The Curriculum Journal, 16*(2), 153–176. https://doi.org/10.1080/09585170500135954

Hodgen, J., & Wiliam, D. (2006). *Mathematics inside the black box*. GL Assessment.

McEldoon, K. L., Durkin, K. L., & Rittle-Johnson, B. (2013). Is self-explanation worth the time? A comparison to additional practice. *British Journal of Educational Psychology, 83*(4), 615–632. https://doi.org/10.1111/j.2044-8279.2012.02083.x

Michaels, S., O'Connor, C., & Resnick, L. B. (2008). Deliberative discourse idealized and realized: Accountable talk in the classroom and in civic life. *Studies in Philosophy and Education, 27*, 283–297. https://doi.org/10.1007/s11217-007-9071-1

National Council of Teachers of Mathematics (NCTM). (n.d.). *What is Notice and Wonder?* https://www.nctm.org/Classroom-Resources/Features/Notice-and-Wonder/Notice-and-Wonder/

Oakes, J. (1985). *Keeping track: How schools structure inequality*. Yale University Press.

O'Connor, M. C., & Michaels, S. (1993). Aligning academic task and participation status through revoicing: Analysis of a classroom discourse strategy. *Anthropology & Education Quarterly, 24*(4), 318–335. https://doi.org/10.1525/aeq.1993.24.4.04x0063k

Rittle-Johnson, B., Saylor, M., & Swygert, K. E. (2008). Learning from explaining: Does it matter if mom is listening? *Journal of Experimental Child Psychology, 100*(3), 215–224. https://doi.org/10.1016/j.jecp.2007.10.002

Strong, S., & Butterfield, G. (2022). *Dear Math: Why kids hate math and what teachers can do about it*. Times Ten Publications.

Tobias, S. (1998). Anxiety and mathematics. *Harvard Education Review, 50*, 63–70.

Walshaw, M., & Anthony, G. (2008). The teacher's role in classroom discourse: A review of recent research into mathematics classrooms. *Review of Educational Research, 78*(3), 516–551. https://doi.org/10.3102/0034654308320292

White, D. Y. (2003). Promoting productive mathematical classroom discourse with diverse students. *Journal of Mathematical Behavior, 22*(1), 37–53. https://doi.org/10.1016/S0732-3123(03)00003-8

Yackel, E., & Cobb, P. (1996). Sociomathematical norms, argumentation, and autonomy in mathematics. *Journal for Research in Mathematics Education, 27*(4), 458–477. https://doi.org/10.2307/749877

Yimam, M., & Kelkay, A. D. (2022). Evaluation of the effects of discourse-based mathematics instruction on eleventh grade students' conceptual and procedural understanding of probability and statistics. *Cogent Education, 9*(1), 2007742. https://doi.org/10.1080/2331186X.2021.2007742

5 Supporting children's spatial understanding through technology

The importance of dialogical exchange analysed through inclusive research

Francesca Granone and Glenn Knudsen

Introduction

The importance of supporting children's mathematical learning has been clearly demonstrated in the literature (Clements & Sarama, 2009; Clements et al., 2013; Sarama & Clements, 2008, 2009). It has also been described that early identification can help reduce the long-term effects of low mathematical skills (Davidsen et al., 2008). The purpose of observing is to investigate children's needs and consequently design individual adapted measures that can support children's learning (Buli-Holmberg & Jeyaprathaban, 2016). Mathematics can be described following Bishop's classification (Bishop, 1988; Sando, 2017) as divided into six activities: counting, locating, measuring, designing, playing, and explaining. Young children use all the mathematical activities in their everyday lives (Solem & Reikerås, 2017) as well as when they play with coding toys (Granone & Reikerås, 2021). Literature has described digital play as a preferential channel for stimulating children's skills and competencies (Pramling et al., 2019) such as, for example, reasoning and problem-solving skills (Çiftci & Bildiren, 2020; Granone & Reikerås, 2021) or other mathematical aspects (Vogt et al., 2020).

From an inclusive perspective, research shows that people with neurodiversity (Armstrong, 2012) often have problems learning mathematics. The term 'neurodiversity' has been adopted in this context, selected over other descriptors such as 'intellectual disability' or 'learning difficulties', which may not encompass the full spectrum of diversity (Chapman, 2020; Kapp et al., 2013; Walmsley et al., 2018). The introduction of the term 'neurodiversity' aims to instigate a paradigm shift in conceptualising individuals in inclusive education. Rather than framing these individuals in terms of deficits, diseases, or dysfunctions, neurodiversity encourages a focus on their strengths (Armstrong, 2012, pp. 9–10). This paradigm is gaining traction within the autistic community and extends to encompass diverse disability categories such as learning disabilities, intellectual disabilities, ADD/ADHD, and mood disorders (Armstrong, 2012). The term 'neurodiversity' is increasingly prevalent in scholarly literature, as evidenced by its utilisation in various studies (Armstrong, 2015; Clouder et al., 2020; Den Houting, 2019; Masataka, 2017; Rosqvist et al., 2020). Embracing neurodiversity in research nomenclature reflects a broader and more inclusive perspective that goes beyond traditional labels and fosters a holistic understanding of cognitive diversity.

Focusing on the difficulties that people with neurodiversity can have with mathematics is quite relevant because it has been proven that reducing people's difficulty in learning mathematics can have an impact not only on their learning development, but also in their everyday life (Soares et al., 2018), for example, in the abilities of spatial orientation, reading tables, and reading a watch.

In the Norwegian context, inclusion is a concept that involves all children, grounded on the understanding that each child is different and that children can learn and behave differently because of their different types of intelligence (Gardner, 2011). Norwegian policy guidelines present an inclusive learning environment as a value for all and make an effort to remove barriers to learning and enhance participation for all (Booth et al., 2021). In education, the term *inclusion* is used to describe a situation in which the school guarantees a teaching approach that can give each child or student a satisfactory educational offer (Lundh et al., 2014), independent of their neurodiversity. In order to develop an inclusive approach in line with 21st-century learning (Bolstad, 2012), it is important to realise that all learners have unique learning needs and that those needs have to be considered and addressed both in the teaching methods and in the assessing methods (Howie, 2019). It is important to specify that the term 'assessment' is correct if used in a school environment, while 'observation' is more correct in early childhood education and care (ECEC) institutions. For this reason, we use the term observation in this book chapter. Although the relevance of an inclusive approach is clearly presented in educational frameworks (Kunnskapsdepartementet, 2017; Regjeringen, 2017), the Norwegian Inclusive Community Report (Nordahl et al., 2018) emphasises that current inclusive education provisions in schools are exclusionary and not functional, especially in subjects such as mathematics and technology. Moreover, a discussion should be had about assessment (which, as we have stated, will be identified with the term 'observation' in this chapter). In accordance with Howie (2019), during observations, the focus should not be on the needs but on the possible methods that teachers should use to address those needs (Feuerstein et al., 1991; Howie, 2019). Consequently, the focus is not just on the learner's outcome, but on the learner's process (Howie, 2019). In fact, Feuerstein suggested that 'good assessment of process can lead to a diagnosis of difficulties that will be more available in suggesting intervention or remedial strategies than an outcome measure on its own' (Howie, 2019, p. 118).

Inclusive research

In accordance with research, we believe that a key for reaching a better inclusive practice can be to apply an inclusive research method (Nind, 2014; Seale et al., 2014). Inclusive research has been defined as a method that can increase the participation of people with neurodiversity in order to reach a better understanding of the difficulties that they can encounter (Østby & Haugenes, 2019). While inclusive research is well established in England and Australia, its introduction in Norway is relatively recent (Østby & Haugenes, 2019). Notably, this approach is particularly novel in the context of research projects focusing on early childhood education (ECE) (Granone, Johansen, et al., 2023).

The concept of inclusive research denotes a research methodology wherein individuals with neurodiversity actively engage beyond the traditional roles of research subjects or respondents (Johnson & Walmsley, 2003). Inclusive research emphasises the active involvement and contribution of individuals with neurodiversity throughout the research process (Johnson & Walmsley, 2003; Walmsley et al., 2018). Within the terminology associated with participants in inclusive research, alternatives such as 'participant researcher' or 'co-researcher' exist, with the latter being selected herein to convey the notion that each individual involved can contribute collaboratively, drawing upon their unique perspectives and conditions (Walmsley & The Central England People First History Project Team, 2014).

The aim of the present study is to raise interest and attention about the importance of considering neurodiversity, not only in planning the pedagogical activities important for supporting children's learning but also in designing the assessment/observation tools that should be used in schools or in ECEC. The case study presented in this chapter highlights the different points of view that a researcher and a co-researcher with autism spectrum disorder (ASD) can have while preparing a play activity with a coding toy for a group of children 3–5 years old, and how this can affect the observations/assessments.

How to realise inclusive research

Before proceeding with the description of the study, we think that it is important to describe how an inclusive research method can be realised, or more precisely, how it has been realised in Norway. We have followed the description presented by Johnson and Walmsley (2003), as reported by Østby and Haugenes, that explains five fundamental characteristics that have to be in place to establish a real inclusive research approach: ownership, interests, collaboration, control, and availability (Østby & Haugenes, 2019).

Ownership within the research context denotes the attribution of the research question to the co-researcher, signifying an active involvement in its formulation and direction. The term interest in this context implies that the research topic holds significance specifically for individuals with neurodiversity, emphasising the importance of relevance and applicability to this demographic.

Collaboration is a fundamental aspect characterised by the joint efforts of researchers and co-researchers working in tandem to contribute to the research endeavour. This collaborative approach underscores the shared responsibility and mutual participation of both parties throughout the research process.

The concept of control within the framework of neurodiversity research accentuates the delineation of responsibilities, highlighting that certain facets of the project should primarily be developed by co-researchers. This principle ensures a balanced and equitable distribution of tasks, acknowledging the expertise and perspectives of individuals with neurodiversity.

Furthermore, the principle of availability underscores the imperative that the entire research project must be comprehensible to all participants, regardless of their neurodiversity. This emphasis on accessibility promotes inclusivity, ensuring that the research findings and processes are transparent and understandable to individuals with diverse cognitive profiles.

In summary, the dynamics of ownership, interest, collaboration, control, and availability collectively contribute to the framework of neurodiversity research, fostering a participatory and inclusive approach that recognises the unique contributions and needs of individuals with diverse neurological experiences.

In accordance with Johnson and Walmsley's (2003) perspective, the added value of inclusive research is identified as co-researchers contributing different and unique views to data definition and analysis. This is precisely what the co-researcher offered in the present study.

A case study: Dialogical assessment of mathematics and technology in ECEC

Participants, ethics, data collection, and analysis

Eight groups of four children, each with their teacher, participated in these activities from two different ECEC institutions. Both ECEC institutions were already involved with the University of Stavanger in a research project where inclusive research was already in place, investigating how coding toys could support children's mathematical learning.[1]

In the present study, each teacher supported children's play by using a coding toy (a robotic car) that they could programme collaboratively by giving logical messages to the robot intuitively through direct interaction. The robot, which is called 'Rugged Robot', can be programmed by pressing directly on buttons on the robot, where arrows are represented (Figure 5.1). The activity was prepared by the co-researcher, and observations were conducted by the researcher and the co-researcher together. A chessboard with nine squares was drawn on the ground (Figure 5.1).

The children had the task of rolling the dice. The number they got on the dice showed the square to which the children had to lead the robot. Each square corresponded exactly to the distance travelled by the robot after pressing one arrow 'move forward'. This meant that the children had to identify how many times they had to press the button on the car to get to the square corresponding to the number that they got rolling the dice. The plan was for the children to find out for themselves how many times and which buttons they had to press to get to the square, which they thought was corresponding to the number on the dice. After three attempts, the researcher suggested to both ECEC institutions that they write numbers on the squares to better identify the starting position (the robot should begin at square number one and finish at square number nine). This can be seen in Figure 5.1.

54 *Francesca Granone and Glenn Knudsen*

Figure 5.1 The drawing after the introduction of the number sequence.

This chapter presents only short extracts of the transcriptions, chosen because they are representative of the whole dataset and specifically relevant to the aim of the present study. Out of all the varied transcriptions, we chose to present here similar situations conducted at each institution. Both the researcher and the co-researcher were present during all activities. However, the co-researcher suggested intervening by establishing a dialogue (dialogical exchange) with the children only during the activity which took place in the second ECEC institution. These examples clearly show how the dialogical exchange suggested by the co-researcher changed the understanding of the results obtained from the observation session.

Field notes and pictures were used for collecting data, and information was anonymised immediately. Written consent from the parents of the children involved in the research was received, and the project received confirmation from the Norwegian Agency for Shared Services in Education and Research (Sikt) that no ethical issues were involved.

The data were analysed through a multimodal approach (because notes reported both verbal exchanges and gestures) using the observation tool MIO, which was used to map preschool children's mathematical skills (Davidsen et al., 2008). This observation tool is designed as a circle that is divided into the age

Supporting children's spatial understanding through technology 55

stages 2–3 years, 3–4 years, and 4–5 years, where the fields must be filled in according to the skill level of the child within the categories 'not mastering', 'partial mastering', and 'mastering' (Davidsen et al., 2008, p. 42). The form is categorised in the areas of numbers and counting, geometry, and problem-solving (Davidsen et al., 2008).

Results

Transcription from the first ECEC institution

[T = Teacher; C1–4 = Children 1–4]

- *T:* 'Do you want to try?'
- *C1:* 'Of course! I push the buttons' (pointing to the buttons with the arrow symbol on the robot).
- *T:* 'Who rolls the dice?'
- *C3:* 'I'll roll it!'
- *C1:* 'You made three! I press the button three times ....'
- *T:* 'The idea was for you to understand how many times you have to press the button, and which ones, to get to square number three' (the teacher indicates the third square, or the last one on the same line as the starting one).
- *C2:* 'I know! Press three times!'

The children try, and the robot reaches the desired square. Big cheers.

- *T:* 'Ok, let's see if it gets more difficult. Who rolls the dice now?'
- *C1:* 'Me!'

C1 rolls the dice and gets the number six. To have the possibility of reaching a number higher than six, C1 rolls the dice another time.

- *C1:* 'I got nine!'
- *C2.* 'Now I push the forward arrow ... nine times?'
- *T:* 'Let's think together. Who can show me box number nine?'

Children point in different directions.

- *T:* 'Shall we choose the one on the opposite side?' (The teacher indicates the space furthest from the starting point).
- *T:* 'Who presses arrows now?'
- *C4:* 'It's my turn!'

C4 puts himself in the robot's place and travels the necessary distance: three steps forward, a 90° rotation, two steps forward. The children push the forward arrow three times, one command each, the arrow twice, which makes the robot

rotate 45°, and then the forward arrow twice more. The robot proceeds correctly. The children rejoice.
[...]
C1 rolls the dice and gets the number three. The children indicate different squares, which they think could indicate the square corresponding to the number three. To simplify understanding and eliminate ambiguities, the researcher draws numbers in each square, in ascending order.

T: 'Who programs the robot now?'
C4: 'Can I do it? Can I? Can I? Can I?'

Before others do it, C4 walks the path from number one to number three. The children then work in groups and then C1 presses the forward arrow twice. The robot takes the right path, and the children jump cheering.

C2: 'Now me!!!' (C2 speaks in an angry tone).

C3 rolls the dice and gets the number six.
C2 follows the path, but instead of rotating the robot 90° and moving directly from square one to square six, he decides to follow what he did before to get to square three and then continues with a series of correct but rather complex commands (two steps forward, two 90° rotations, and two more steps forward). Because of the difficulty of the programming part, C2 looks around and searches for confirmation.

Transcription from the second ECEC institution

T: 'C3, it is your turn now. Do you want to roll the dice?'
C3: 'Yes ...'
C4: 'I press the buttons.'

C3 rolls the dice and two comes out.

T: 'Great! C3, where should you go? And how many times do you have to press the button? What button?'
C3: 'Forward ...' (C3 points out with his finger the direction that he thinks the robot should go).
C1: 'Two times!'
C3: 'Yes, I know!' (C3 presses the button 'forward' two times).

The robot moves forward two times and stops in the second square. The children are satisfied.

T: 'What can you do to give the robot the instruction to go to the centre of the grid?'

C2: 'Turn 90° and move one step forward.'
T: 'I think that you are right.'

[...]

To make things easier, the researcher writes numbers in each square. C1 rolls the dice and receives five. This means that the robot must move in exactly the same position as just before. C4 stands in the starting position; then he moves step after step through the squares where numbers two, three, and four are written, and stops in the square where number five is represented.

T: 'Can you show us what you did again?'

C4 does the same.

T: 'Why did you do this? Wasn't it easier to move two steps forward, then turn 90°, and then move forward one step, like we did just before you rolled the dice?'
C3: 'It's not allowed!'
T: 'What do you mean? There are no walls; it's just a drawing to visualise the boxes.'

The teacher seems uncertain.

C1: 'But I can't count one, three, five .... We know how to count!'

Discussion: Teachers' competence and the importance of a dialogical exchange

The examples reported show that children can be supported in learning how to play with a coding toy and how to programme it. The play situation described can support children in learning different skills, such as computational thinking (Wing, 2006) and space orientation (Granone & Reikerås, 2023). Children show that they prefer to create an unplugged activity ('C4 puts himself in the robot's place and travels the necessary distance') and then to start a plugged activity ('The children push the forward arrow three times ... the arrow twice, which makes the robot rotate 45°, and then the forward arrow twice more. The robot proceeds correctly.'). This is in accordance with the literature, in which the bodily perspective is described as important in children's learning to follow (Hermans & Aivaloglou, 2017). The importance of considering children's bodily perspective is understandable from the transcription presented because children show their thoughts through gestures ('Children point in different directions'). Using the observation tool MIO, it was possible for the researcher to understand that children were able to use their mathematical understanding of space, managing to 'go to a specific place in the room' (Davidsen et al., 2008, p. 42). They also show that they understand how to programme the robot ('The children push the forward arrow three times, one command each, the arrow twice, which makes the robot rotate 45°, and then the forward arrow twice more. The robot proceeds correctly.'), indicating that they are developing their computational thinking skills (Wing, 2006). The example, in fact, allows observation of children's ability to decompose, think recursively, and generalise (Granone, Reikerås, et al., 2023; Wing, 2006).

A similar example is reported in the first part of the transcription from the second ECEC institution. In this case, too, children show their ability to understand space ('C3 points out with his finger the direction that he thinks the robot should go') (Davidsen et al., 2008) and in programming ('C3 presses the button "forward" two times') (Wing, 2006).

At a certain time, in both examples, the teacher introduces, as suggested by the researcher, a new element for supporting children's agreement about how to identify the different squares: the number sequence (Figure 5.1). The play continues in the same way, but both transcriptions report situations in which the numbers indicated by the dice were higher, and the children seemed more uncertain. This happened in both examples, but what was different between the two transcriptions was that in the second one, the teacher received a suggestion from the co-researcher for starting a dialogical exchange with the children.

The evaluation of children's uncertainty could suggest a condition of partial comprehension of space (Davidsen et al., 2008, p. 42). In reality, the comparison between the two examples leaves open the possibility that the uncertainty could be unrelated to an under-developed spatial understanding, but to a stronger interest in respecting numerical sequences: 'But I can't count one, three, five … We know how to count!' This could then suggest that the observation tool should have also included observation of children's competence about numbers (Davidsen et al., 2008, p. 50).

The instances presented accentuate the pivotal role of teachers' competencies. Although the teacher's primary intent was to observe the children's spatial orientation, equal importance should be accorded to assessing their understanding of numerical order. The fact that children gave more relevance to the necessity of following the number sequence was expressed by a child during the dialogical exchange: 'But I can't count one, three, five … We know how to count!' This was expected by the co-researcher, but not by the researcher. This implies that it is imperative for educators to recognise that children may exhibit a heightened focus on numerical aspects, potentially diverting attention from spatial orientation. This underscores the necessity for teachers to possess the competence for observation/assessments that integrate a dynamic approach (Aastrup, 2010; Aastrup & Johnsen, 2014).

The methodology of observation and dialogical exchange, as underscored by Howie (2019), resonates with her steadfast assertions regarding the pivotal role of educators and the critical imperative to enhance their professional competencies (Howie, 2019). Howie's scholarly contributions elucidate a profound recognition of the multifaceted responsibilities shouldered by teachers within the educational milieu. In particular, she accentuates the nuanced significance of fostering a dynamic and engaging pedagogical environment through the judicious application of observational techniques and sustained dialogical exchanges.

Howie's perspective draws attention to the centrality of teachers in shaping the learning experiences of students. Within the broader context of educational discourse, her emphasis on observation implies a deliberate and reflective process in which educators keenly scrutinise group dynamics, student interactions, and instructional strategies. This meticulous observation, when coupled with dialogical exchange, underscores the interactive and communicative dimensions that characterise effective pedagogy.

The literature offers guidance on mediating the learning process, as suggested by Haywood (1993), through the use of 'how questions' and a technique known as 'bridging'. The implementation of 'how questions' involves teachers supporting students in reflecting upon the motivations that underlie their choices. Examples of such queries include prompting students to contemplate, 'How did you choose the solution?' or 'Could you have chosen differently?' This approach facilitates a deeper exploration of the decision-making process, encouraging metacognitive engagement.

Alternatively, 'bridging', as described by Howie (2019), constitutes a process that prompts children to consider diverse applications of their thinking processes and strategies. This technique involves establishing connections between the intellectual endeavours within the learning environment and their potential relevance to everyday life. By encouraging students to relate their cognitive processes to real-world scenarios, the bridging technique aims to enhance the transferability of acquired knowledge and skills beyond the immediate educational context. This approach aligns with the broader pedagogical objective of fostering a more holistic understanding of concepts and their practical implications.

Note

1 https://www.uis.no/en/research/dicote-increasing-professional-digital-competence-in-ecte-with-focus-on-enriching-and

References

Aastrup, S. (2010). Dynamic assessment by overall evaluation in connection with difficulties in mathematics. In H. Guðjónsdóttir, J. Vala Kristinsdóttir, & E. Óskarsdóttir (Eds.), *Conference proceedings from the fifth Nordic research conference on special needs education in mathematics: Challenges in teaching mathematics: Becoming special for all* (pp. 27–37). University of Iceland.

Aastrup, S., & Johnsen, K. (2014). Kartlegging og undervisning i dynamisk perspektiv. In T. S. Gustavsen, K. R. C. Hinna, I. C. Borge, & P. S. Andersen (Eds.), *QED 1–7* (pp. 757–814). Cappelen Damm Akademisk.

Armstrong, T. (2012). *Neurodiversity in the classroom: Strength-based strategies to help students with special needs succeed in school and life.* ASCD.

Armstrong, T. (2015). The myth of the normal brain: Embracing neurodiversity. *AMA Journal of Ethics, 17*(4), 348–352.

Bishop, A. J. (1988). Mathematics education in its cultural context. *Educational Studies in Mathematics, 19*(2), 179–191. https://doi.org/10.1007/BF00751231

Bolstad, R. (2012). Principles for a future-oriented education system. *New Zealand Annual Review of Education, 21,* 77–95. https://doi.org/10.26686/nzaroe.v21i0.4043

Booth, A., Sutton, A., Clowes, M., & Martyn-St James, M. (2021). *Systematic approaches to a successful literature review*. SAGE.
Buli-Holmberg, J., & Jeyaprathaban, S. (2016). Effective practice in inclusive and special needs education. *International Journal of Special Education, 31*(1), 119–134.
Chapman, R. (2020). Neurodiversity, disability, wellbeing. In H. B. Rosqvist, N. Chown, & A. Stenning (Eds.), *Neurodiversity studies: A new critical paradigm* (pp. 57–72). Routledge.
Çiftci, S., & Bildiren, A. (2020). The effect of coding courses on the cognitive abilities and problem-solving skills of preschool children. *Computer Science Education, 30*(1), 3–21.
Clements, D. H., Baroody, A. J., & Sarama, J. (2013). *Background research on early mathematics*. National Governor's Association, Center Project on Early Mathematics.
Clements, D. H., & Sarama, J. (2009). Learning trajectories in early mathematics – Sequences of acquisition and teaching. *Encyclopedia of Language and Literacy Development, 7*, 1–6.
Clouder, L., Karakus, M., Cinotti, A., Ferreyra, M. V., Fierros, G. A., & Rojo, P. (2020). Neurodiversity in higher education: A narrative synthesis. *Higher Education, 80*(4), 757–778.
Davidsen, H., Løge, I., Lunde, O., Reikerås, E., & Dalvang, T. (2008). *MIO-matematikken-individet-omgivelsene. Observasjonsark [MIO—The mathematics, the individual and the environment.* Registration form]. Aschehoug.
Den Houting, J. (2019). Neurodiversity: An insider's perspective. *Autism, 23*(2), 271–273. https://doi.org/10.1177/1362361318820762
Feuerstein, R., Klein, P. S., & Tannenbaum, A. J. (1991). *Mediated learning experience (MLE): Theoretical, psychosocial and learning implications*. Freund Publishing House Ltd.
Gardner, H. E. (2011). *Frames of mind: The theory of multiple intelligences*. Hachette UK.
Granone, F., Johansen, M., Reikerås, E. K. L., & Kvalø, T. M. (2023). 'Nothing about us without us': The first example of inclusive research in early childhood education in Norway. *Consultori Familiari Oggi, 31*(1), 69–82.
Granone, F., & Reikerås, E. K. L. (2021). Preschoolers learning by playing with technology. *Education in childhood*. IntechOpen. https://doi.org/10.5772/intechopen.97791
Granone, F., & Reikerås, E. K. L. (2023). Teachers' support for children's mathematical learning through interactions while playing with a coding toy. *Nordic Studies in Mathematics Education, 28*(3–4), 55–76.
Granone, F., Reikerås, E. K. L., Pollarolo, E., & Kamola, M. (2023). Critical thinking, problem-solving and computational thinking: Related but distinct? An analysis of similarities and differences based on an example of a play situation in an early childhood education setting. In F. Gomez Paloma (Ed.), *Teacher training and practice*. IntechOpen. https://doi.org/10.5772/intechopen.110795
Haywood, H. C. (1993). A mediational teaching style. *International Journal of Cognitive Education and Mediated Learning, 3*(1), 27–38.
Hermans, F., & Aivaloglou, E. (2017). To scratch or not to scratch? A controlled experiment comparing plugged first and unplugged first programming lessons. In *Proceedings of the 12th workshop on primary and secondary computing education* (pp. 49–56). https://doi.org/10.1145/3137065.3137072
Howie, D. R. (2019). *Thinking about the teaching of thinking: The Feuerstein approach*. Routledge.
Johnson, K., & Walmsley, J. (2003). *Inclusive research with people with learning disabilities: Past, present and futures*. Jessica Kingsley Publishers.
Kapp, S. K., Gillespie-Lynch, K., Sherman, L. E., & Hutman, T. (2013). Deficit, difference, or both? Autism and neurodiversity. *Developmental Psychology, 49*(1), 59–71.
Kunnskapsdepartementet (2017). *Rammeplan for barnehagen: Forskrift om rammeplan for barnehagens innhold og oppgaver*. Udir.

Lundh, L., Hjelmbrekke, H., & Skogdal, S. (2014). *Inkluderende praksis: gode Erfaringer fra barnehage, Skole og fritid.* Universitetsforlaget.
Masataka, N. (2017). Implications of the idea of neurodiversity for understanding the origins of developmental disorders. *Physics of Life Reviews, 20,* 85–108.
Nind, M. (2014). Inclusive research and inclusive education: Why connecting them makes sense for teachers' and learners' democratic development of education. *Cambridge Journal of Education, 44*(4), 525–540. https://doi.org/10.1080/0305764X.2014.936825
Nordahl, T., Nordahl, S., Sunnevåg, A.-K., Berg, B., & Martinsen, M. (2018). *Det gode er det fremragende sin fiende: Resultater fra kartleggningsundersøkelser i kristiansand kommune 2013–2017.* Aalborg Universitetsforlag.
Østby, M., & Haugenes, M. (2019). *Inkluderende forskning sammen med personer med utviklingshemming: En metodebok* [*Including research with people with learning disabilities: A method book*]. Universitetsforlaget.
Pramling, N., Wallerstedt, C., Lagerlöf, P., Björklund, C., Kultti, A., Palmér, H., Magnusson, M., Thulin, S., Jonsson, A., & Pramling Samuelsson, I. (2019). *Play-responsive teaching in early childhood education.* Springer Nature.
Regjeringen. (2017). *Overordnet del–verdier og prinsipper for grunnopplæringen.* Utdanningsdirektoratet Oslo.
Rosqvist, H. B., Chown, N., & Stenning, A. (2020). *Neurodiversity studies: A new critical paradigm.* Routledge.
Sando, S. (2017). Fundamentale matematikkaktiviteter. *Tangenten, 4,* 38–45. https://tangenten.no/wp-content/uploads/2021/12/tangenten-4-2017-nettet.pdf
Sarama, J., & Clements, D. H. (2008). Mathematics in early childhood. In O. N. Saracho & B. Spodek (Eds.), *Contemporary Perspectives on Mathematics in Early Childhood Education* (pp. 67–94). Information Age Publishing.
Sarama, J., & Clements, D. H. (2009). *Early childhood mathematics education research: Learning trajectories for young children.* Routledge.
Seale, J., Nind, M., & Parsons, S. (2014). Inclusive research in education: Contributions to method and debate. *International Journal of Research & Method in Education, 37*(4), 347–356. https://doi.org/10.1080/1743727X.2014.935272
Soares, N., Evans, T., & Patel, D. R. (2018). Specific learning disability in mathematics: A comprehensive review. *Translational Pediatrics, 7*(1), 48–62. https://doi.org/10.21037/tp.2017.08.03
Solem, I., & Reikerås, E. (2017). *Det matematiske barnet* [*The mathematical child*] (3rd ed.). Caspar.
Vogt, F., Hauser, B., Stebler, R., Rechsteiner, K., & Urech, C. (2020). Learning through play–pedagogy and learning outcomes in early childhood mathematics. In O. Thiel & B. Perry (Eds.), *Innovative approaches in early childhood mathematics* (pp. 127–141). Routledge.
Walmsley, J., Strnadová, I., & Johnson, K. (2018). The added value of inclusive research. *Journal of Applied Research in Intellectual Disabilities, 31*(5), 751–759. https://doi.org/10.1111/jar.12431
Walmsley, J., & The Central England People First History Project Team (2014). Telling the history of self-advocacy: A challenge for inclusive research. *Journal of Applied Research in Intellectual Disabilities, 27*(1), 34–43. https://doi.org/10.1111/jar.12086
Wing, J. M. (2006). Computational thinking. *Communications of the ACM, 49*(3), 33–35.

6 A place for all

Inclusive practices in Arts assessment

Tricia Clark-Fookes

Introduction

Evidence of art and the impulse to create art exists from the earliest human endeavour, it spans culture and disregards concepts of age and individual ability. Uniquely, art making and its processes of thinking and acting like an artist are repeated from our earliest impulses in infancy to the most advanced artistry by professional artists. The developmental difference in artistry is marked only by the advancement of artistic skill and intention, the essence of art making and its capacity to communicate remain constant. Art communicates in a language that is more akin to feeling than words. The human capacity to feel and receive feelings in their various modes (sensory, emotional, imaginative) allows the broadest range of people an understanding of its form and utterances. Each artform offers a unique symbol system not bound by the limits of words. Their symbolic languages offer new ways of being and knowing that transcend culture, age, and ability. For this reason, the Arts are recognised for their inclusive qualities, a claim evidenced by a substantial body of research offering arts as a strategy for creating more inclusive classrooms (Allan, 2014).

In spite of suggestions of arts' inclusive capacities, they have equally been charged with exclusivity. These claims reside principally in notions of conservative replication of codified and rigid traditions of practice, and social and cultural bias, particularly Eurocentricity (Bond, 2017; Davis, 2022). These claims cannot be diminished or ignored. Arts educators need to face up to these claims and reflect on the biases in our practice – biases which prevent our classrooms from reflecting the fullest range of abilities, cultures, languages, bodies, and minds.

This chapter seeks to supplement gaps in current literature examining inclusivity in arts assessment by providing guidance on practical strategies for creating more inclusive arts assessment.

Tensions in Arts assessment

Assessment in the Arts is a contentious notion (Andrade et al., 2019) as fundamental understandings of artistic ways of working and thinking sit at odds with the current goals of education, namely, education's performative focus and data-driven accountability measures (Sahlberg, 2016). The goals of artists are personal and involve choice, but artistry in the context of education can cause conflict when predetermined learning goals (outcomes and achievement standards in an arts curriculum) must be met (Andrade et al., 2019). Arts educators resist the notion that artistry can be neatly captured in rubrics/marking guides, or that quality artistic outcomes can be achieved in restrictive assessment timelines and other imposed restrictions. Opposition to rubrics and marking guides resides in the belief that words cannot fully capture the aesthetic qualities or tacit knowledge at the heart of arts practice. It is believed that attempts to capture the unity of the symbolic language of art including its aesthetic or felt qualities by measuring these in a rubric are reductionist and incapable of capturing the wholeness of the work. This is in part due to the inadequacy of language in this context and in part to the construction of marking schemes which tend to compartmentalise elements of the artwork rather than examine its elements working to create 'a unity of experience' (Langer, 1953, p. 126).

Yet, if arts education was to disengage from assessment processes that lie at the heart of current schooling, the Arts may forfeit their well-earned place in the curriculum and risk relegation from the formal curriculum, operating only as an extra-curricular pursuit. The inclusion of arts education in the formal curriculum allows access to the broadest population, helping to meet UNESCO's belief that arts education is a fundamental right of every individual (UNESCO, 2023). In lieu of foreseeable education reform or disengaging from mainstream education which provides access to the greatest proportion of students, arts educators must examine ways of navigating systemic processes and ensuring the best quality outcomes in the given parameters. The tension described here is unlikely to be resolved in this chapter, but it is hoped that key considerations will be laid out and practices suggested that may assist arts educators in balancing the competing agendas.

Formative assessment in the Arts

Formative assessment is a key strategy in navigating the tension between the desire for students to authentically engage in artistic ways of thinking and doing while attempting to meet the pre-determined standards set out in curriculum. To ensure that formative assessment is inclusive of the greatest range of learners, two practices are suggested: resisting criteria compliance and assisting all students to access and apply feedback productively.

Resisting criteria compliance

Formative assessment when working at its best does not funnel students into criteria compliance (Torrance, 2007) or conform to strict scaffolds that prioritise achievement of the standard over artistic development. Formative assessment needs to challenge students' artistry and prioritise the processes of thinking and acting like an artist. Teachers' prompts need to extend beyond meeting standards and scaffold the fundamental processes of artmaking and creative production: play, ideation and experimentation, criticality, curation, refinement, and reflection. By framing formative feedback through arts processes in connection with standards, the duality of artistry and standards can be met while including the greatest range of responses and thus learners.

Accessing and applying feedback

Providing feedback is no guarantee of students being able to access or implement the information required to improve their artwork. Learning how to give and receive feedback is not a skill that all students possess. Hogan (2019) suggests that students receive feedback through 'filters' which can impact how students respond to feedback. It is also known that students on winning streaks perceive feedback differently to students on losing streaks (Goetz et al., 2018; Stiggins, 2007). Further, feedback can be impeded by language barriers (use of jargon, slang, and other culturally biased or opaque language) and the relationship of the learner to the person providing the feedback. Filtering feedback is directly related to social and relational factors. Specifically, the need for a positive, safe, respectful, democratic, and supportive classroom. By creating a positive and productive arts rich environment, students are better able to receive feedback and in turn productively apply this feedback. At a basic level, through the creation of safe supportive relationships in the Arts classroom, students are more likely to trust the feedback provided and feel safe enough to respond with agency.

To effectively engage with feedback, students also require feedback literacy skills: appreciating feedback, making judgements, managing affect, and taking action (Carless & Boud, 2018). Teachers are responsible for explicitly scaffolding these literacy skills by demonstrating and scaffolding feedback skills, modelling these in their own practice, and normalising feedback skills in students' daily classroom activities. Regularly practising and attending to feedback literacy is a potent way of improving students' responsiveness to feedback and the resultant development that occurs from enacting feedback.

Summative assessment in the Arts

Summative assessment design is considered by many as the most important (and high pressure) part of educational practice. For arts educators, as previously discussed, negotiating the tensions between the intrinsic goals of artistry and systemic summative assessment requirements requires negotiation and, at times, calculated compromise. The following discussion of summative arts assessment will highlight practices to promote inclusion in arts summative assessment.

Measure what we value

A key consideration in assessment design is validity, which is concerned with fitness for purpose (Stobart, 2009) or assessment measuring what has been determined as valuable to the subject area and what has been taught. To ensure validity, assessment needs to reflect both the process and the substantive content domain (Boud, 2002).

In the case of the Arts, assessment must attend to the ways of working and thinking that are unique to the artform being assessed. The Arts are concerned with students being creators and critical audience members using the symbol systems of the artform. Students working as artists and audiences are the essential ways we work and assess in arts education. For this reason, summative assessment needs to align to these ways of working. That is, assessment items need to engage students as artist or audience demonstrating the applied understandings they have gained. If the artform's values and processes are at the heart of the assessment then students have the scope to respond in divergent ways, as creativity is central. This diversity of response is inclusion at its best. By way of example, an exam where we ask students to recall definitions of art terms does not allow students to demonstrate the valued features of arts subjects, working as artist or audience. Understanding would be better demonstrated by the application of art terminology by working as artist or audience to reveal praxical understandings. By ensuring that the valued features of arts practice and arts knowledge are prioritised in arts assessment, then arts educators can be assured that assessment is measuring what we value most in arts practice.

Criteria construction

Assessment criteria are a codification of the valued features of the subject and articulate standards. Arts education prioritises aesthetic engagement and the felt qualities of art (Abbs, 1987; Dewey, 2005), qualities that may be seen as subjective in the current paradigm of quantitative accountability. Yet these qualities lie at the heart of art making and reception. Arts curriculum and assessment should attend to aesthetic aspects of arts education, yet in the pursuit of quantitative accountability and increased reliability, there is a temptation to underplay or remove aesthetic considerations from assessment criteria. Abstraction of students' capabilities as criteria has the potential to distance teachers from the values and nature of their practice (Lewis & Hardy, 2017). It is argued that codifications of standards cannot fully represent the richness and complexity of students' ability, understanding, or skill (Balan & Jönsson, 2018).

Assessment criteria construction can involve over-articulating and compartmentalising aspects of the knowledge and skills to be demonstrated and evaluated in the assessment task. The danger here is that an overly detailed description of what is required can assist students to achieve the articulated standards, but equally inhibit the range of ways students can respond to an assessment prompt, diminishing the inclusivity of the task. Further, compartmentalisation of assessment criteria can negatively impact the creative capacities arts educators seek to foster in arts learning. Compartmentalising aspects of the task into separate criteria can lead to inadequate evaluation of the aesthetic value of artwork. As explained by Langer (1953), quality artwork creates the 'illusion' of a unified indivisible whole, bringing together form and feeling. Thus, evaluating artwork needs to account for this unity; the aesthetic quality. To account for the aesthetic qualities of artwork, criteria need to capture the unity of the work not just its parts. The truism, 'the whole is greater than the sum of the parts' applies here. To address this, when arts assessment criteria are being constructed, we must attempt to evaluate the unity of the work and its aesthetic qualities. One way of achieving this may be through the use of qualifiers.

Qualifiers are adjectival words that describe various levels of quality (Alberta Assessment Consortium, 2009) (e.g., cohesive, incisive, excellent, thorough, etc.). Arguments against qualifiers highlight their fuzziness (Sadler, 2014) and slippage in their interpretation that can require experiential understanding from the marker (Wyatt-Smith et al., 2010) which may impact reliability. In the case of the Arts, it may be argued that fuzziness is actually what we need to make space for evaluation of the aesthetic qualities of artwork. Qualifiers have the potential to articulate the qualitative aspects of art such as unity, aesthetic value, and artistry while avoiding explicit description. Qualifiers allow for multiple ways of achieving the standard ensuring creativity is not penalised, thus fostering inclusion.

Developing optimism

For many, assessment has negative connotations, raising anxieties and placing students into a threat state before the task has even commenced. In an attempt to promote assessment confidence and optimism, teachers need to ensure that students feel ready for the assessment task before its distribution. This means that, before they attempt the task, students will be familiar with the subject matter and arts processes being assessed as they will have practised and received feedback. Too often, assessment tasks are distributed to students before they have experienced the range of learning required to complete the task. It is only natural that students presented with tasks they are unprepared for have anxious feelings. When tasks are distributed without adequate preparation, students with prior arts training or greater confidence achieving assessment success have an unfair advantage. To avoid this, educators can give notice of the task and its outcomes early in the unit or course, but refrain from distributing the task until the learners are adequately prepared to engage with the task in an informed and practised way.

Differentiation

Differentiation is intimately connected to inclusion and the right to education for all students (United Nations, n.d.). Differentiation is a means of responding to student diversity in order to provide education for all students (Eikeland & Ohna, 2022). Teachers can differentiate both learning and assessment to include the broadest range of learners.

In the Arts, differentiation can look different to other disciplines. The physical, cognitive, behavioural, and cultural aspects of arts processes need to be examined when differentiating for learners. Four strategies for differentiating arts assessment are presented: choice of texts, adjusting physical processes, understanding and adjusting to meet limits of assistive technology, and the use of generative artificial intelligence (Gen AI).

Choice of texts

Providing students with a choice of texts is a useful differentiation strategy. In the Arts, it must be noted that a 'text' can take many forms: script, musical score, performance, artwork, film, etc. Text is taken here in its broadest sense: 'a configuration of signs that is coherently interpretable' (Hanks, 1989, p. 95). Choice of text can either be student nominated or from a teacher-selected list. Choice offers students agency, which has been proven as an effective strategy to engage student interest in tasks, which has flow-on effects to motivation and achievement (Marzano et al., 2011; Phung et al., 2021). Student-involved text selection can open up important discussions about student needs, interests, where students are at in their learning, where they're aiming to be, and most importantly, how to get there. Teachers can guide students' text selection to meet their specific learning needs, language barriers, emotional maturity, and capitalise on student interest.

Adjusting physical processes

A core tenet of arts education is learning in and through the arts. That is, arts subjects are characterised by experiential learning involving embodied engagement with arts practices. This can present a barrier to learning for some students. Addressing this barrier through adjustments to physical processes is critical.

To address individual limitations, adjustments and translation may be required. Adjustment in the context of arts may include changes to the processes, media, and materials used in the task. For example, adjustment in a film classroom where media and tactile resources are substituted to include students with visual disabilities (Sickler-Voigt, 2023). Translation involves students 'responding to and translating tasks and information to suit their own individual physicality, in order to achieve an equal outcome' (Whatley & Marsh, 2017, p. 6). Critically, students are not asked to replicate or match other students. Instead, by translating the task to meet their individual abilities, they are developing aligned mechanical, creative, or interpretive skills. For example, dance students with individual limitations are invited to engage in movement as it aligns to their body and its abilities. The focus is the concept of a movement rather than matching the movement exactly (Morris, 2015). To promote inclusivity, movement-based assessment should be designed without a focus on technique (Whatley & Marsh, 2017), highlighting that focusing on technique impedes inclusivity as it excludes students with no prior learning, particularly those with individual physical limitations.

Understanding and adjusting to meet limits of assistive technology

Assistive technology is a generic term used to describe any item, piece of equipment, software program, or product system that is aimed at assisting or expanding human function or capabilities (Maor et al., 2011). These technologies can be useful in both teaching and assessment to make assessment tasks more accessible and equitable for students with a range of individual needs. Some students will bring existing assistive technologies with them to class (e.g., wheelchairs, magnifiers, speech-to-text software, iPads, audio description, etc.). Teachers will often assume that the student or a teacher-aide will take full responsibility for the device use in your classroom and this may be the case, but the Arts classroom and ways of working are not the same as 'traditional' classrooms where students are seated behind desks and activities predominantly feature reading, listening, and writing. It is the arts teachers' responsibility to find the most effective combinations of adaptations and teaching strategies for students requiring support to effectively participate in learning and assessment (Coleman & Cramer, 2015). Arts teachers must seek to understand the limitations and capacities of assistive technologies (Morris, 2015). It is only through this understanding that pedagogy and assessment can be designed to ensure that students are afforded the greatest opportunity for inclusion. For example, wheelchairs have different affordances, some have been designed for general mobility while others have been designed for speed and manoeuvrability as in the case of sporting wheelchairs. To ensure that teachers are designing inclusive learning and assessment, these capacities must be fully understood through discussion with the student, learning support staff, and parents.

The Arts classrooms differ from generalist classrooms. The greatest proportion of research into assistive technologies in education caters to general classroom settings not arts classrooms. Resultantly, arts teachers need to work with learning support staff to understand what assistive technologies may be available. Once teachers understand what is available then devices can be adapted or employed perhaps in ways they were not initially designed (Creed, 2018).

Finally, when designing assessment involving assistive technology it is critical that teachers take into account the fatigue students may feel when using assistive technologies, especially when the device is newly introduced. This needs to be accounted for by ensuring task conditions such as time allowance and the scale of task are reflective of the cognitive and/or physical demands on the student.

Use of Gen AI

Gen AI is not a new technology, but recent advances and increased access through lower cost apps means Gen AI has seen an upsurge in use. Views on its use in assessment are wide-ranging, but it is here to stay.

In the context of arts assessment, before Gen AI can be implemented, there must be a clear understanding of the purpose of the assessment task and what the key artistic practices and subject matter are. Once there is an understanding of what is valued and important to the task, then it is possible to consider Gen AI as a tool to assist in making assessment more inclusive and using it to personalise and support individual learners. Research tells us that one of the greatest strengths of Gen AI is its capacity to personalise learning and adapt content to the needs of learners (Kadaruddin, 2023).

Arts educators should be encouraged to explore the range of Gen AI tools available and consider how these might be leveraged to improve accessibility and inclusivity in assessment tasks and processes. To achieve this, a clear understanding of the purpose of the assessment task and what the key artistic practices and subject matter are is critical. From this knowledge, arts teachers can examine where assessment tasks may be modified or extra scaffolding provided to assist students to overcome barriers that are not relevant to the task. For example, for students with English as an Additional Language or Dialect (EAL/D), if the task does not assess students' English proficiency but focuses on art-making skills, there is no reason that the task sheet could not be translated into their first language via Gen AI (Wang et al., 2023).

Examples of Gen AI's use in the assessment context include re-writing task sheets to cater for specific reading levels, creating step-by-step guides to completing a task, providing an organising structure, offering suggestions for starting the work, audio description of images, image generation when drawing skills are not the focus, and chatbots to answer questions out of school hours.

This is just a handful of ways that teachers can harness Gen AI to improve assessment accessibility. As the field of Gen AI burgeons, increasing opportunities emerge for educators to harness the power of Gen AI to lower or remove barriers to inclusion in arts assessment.

Enabling constraints in assessment design

The Arts are synonymous with creativity and creative thinking (Snepvangers et al., 2018). Creativity celebrates novelty and a range of responses which is synergistic with inclusion. Earlier in this chapter, the tension between assessment and artistry was discussed. A concern expressed by arts teachers is that conformity to rubrics and achievement standards endangers, or at the least impedes, creativity and inclusion. The tension arises between providing openness and structure (Cremin & Chappell, 2021). So how can arts educators promote creativity while meeting the demands of standards?

There is a persistent belief that creativity is associated with openness and freedom of choice. Yet research tells us that quality creative outcomes occur when operating within constraints (Clark-Fookes, 2023; Cremin & Chappell, 2021). It is suggested that constraints are effective because they reduce the solution set for a problem or inquiry (Bix & Witt, 2020). In short, too much choice can impede students' ability to know what is required. Embedding enabling constraints (Clark-Fookes, 2023; Haught-Tromp, 2017) allows arts teachers to navigate openness and structure in assessment tasks. Enabling constraints are productive because they reduce the scope of the 'problem' and provide students scaffolding to navigate their way through art making and creative tasks. For example, the use of inquiry or limiting resources. Artistic inquiry provides a constraint within which students respond to an artistic problem or question, exploring and responding to the inquiry through creative process using artistic methods (Clark-Fookes, 2023). Importantly, artistry is privileged while students are still afforded agency and the capacity for creative responses. Limiting the materials used in an artwork, such as defining a specific number of shot types used in a film, limiting students to a particular scale in musical composition, or requiring choreography to be created for a specific site, can reduce the problem set and engender greater creativity. The purpose of these examples is to provide students with parameters in which they can exercise creativity while maintaining the capacity for diverse artistic responses and inclusion.

Conclusion

Arts education, unlike other fields of knowledge, is premised on individual taste and judgement. Art is a tool through which individuals' unique ways of perceiving and engaging with the world are celebrated. For this reason, arts education offers an enormous capacity for inclusion.

This chapter has examined the tensions operating in arts assessment, particularly concerning alignment to standards. The Arts resist conformity and standardisation, and this value sits in tension with the aims of formal schooling. Although this tension will remain, there are strategies to assist arts educators to navigate both formative and summative arts assessment.

In conclusion, arts assessment provides opportunities to transform young people's lives through inclusion and valuing their unique capacities and experiences of the world. To ensure that arts teachers harness these possibilities while creating equitable learning opportunities, it is critical that arts assessment attend to the ways of working and thinking that are unique to the artform being assessed and teachers have clarity about the purpose of every assessment item. Assessment should reflect the intended purpose even when differentiated. Returning to the touchstones of purpose and artform values will ensure that arts teachers can provide equity while engaging in inclusive assessment practices.

References

Abbs, P. (1987). *Living powers: The arts in education*. Falmer Press.
Alberta Assessment Consortium. (2009). *The AAC rubric wordsmith*. https://www.aac.ab.ca/wp-content/uploads/Rubrics/BBRp18-23.pdf
Allan, J. (2014). Inclusive education and the arts. *Cambridge Journal of Education, 44*(4), 511–523. https://doi.org/10.1080/0305764X.2014.921282
Andrade, H. L., Bennett, R. E., & Cizek, G. J. (Eds.). (2019). *Handbook of formative assessment in the disciplines*. Routledge.
Balan, A., & Jönsson, A. (2018). Increased explicitness of assessment criteria: Effects on student motivation and performance. *Frontiers in Education, 3*, 81. https://doi.org/10.3389/feduc.2018.00081
Bix, S., & Witt, P. (2020). Introducing constraints to improve new product development performance. *Research–Technology Management, 63*(5), 29–37. https://doi.org/10.1080/08956308.2020.1790238
Bond, V. L. (2017). Culturally responsive education in music education: A literature review. *Contributions to Music Education, 42*, 153–180.
Boud, D. (2002). *The unexamined life is not the life for learning: Rethinking assessment for lifelong learning* [Professorial Lecture]. Trent Park.
Carless, D., & Boud, D. (2018). The development of student feedback literacy: Enabling uptake of feedback. *Assessment & Evaluation in Higher Education, 43*(8), 1315–1325. https://doi.org/10.1080/02602938.2018.1463354
Clark-Fookes, T. (2023). Navigating the tension between openness and quality artistic encounters in intermedial experience: A teaching artist's account. *Research in Drama*

Education: The Journal of Applied Theatre and Performance, 28(4), 563–577. https://doi.org/10.1080/13569783.2023.2176215

Coleman, M. B., & Cramer, E. S. (2015). Creating meaningful art experiences with assistive technology for students with physical, visual, severe, and multiple disabilities. *Art Education*, 68(2), 6–13. https://doi.org/10.1080/00043125.2015.11519308

Creed, C. (2018). Assistive technology for disabled visual artists: Exploring the impact of digital technologies on artistic practice. *Disability & Society*, 33(7), 1103–1119. https://doi.org/10.1080/09687599.2018.1469400

Cremin, T., & Chappell, K. (2021). Creative pedagogies: A systematic review. *Research Papers in Education*, 36(3), 299–331. https://doi.org/10.1080/02671522.2019.1677757

Davis, C. U. (2022). *Dance and belonging: Implicit bias and inclusion in dance education*. McFarland & Company.

Dewey, J. (2005). *Art as experience*. Perigee Books.

Eikeland, I., & Ohna, S. E. (2022). Differentiation in education: A configurative review. *Nordic Journal of Studies in Educational Policy*, 8(3), 157–170. https://doi.org/10.1080/20020317.2022.2039351

Goetz, T., Lipnevich, A., Krannich, M., & Gogol, K. (2018). Performance feedback and emotions. In A. Lipnevich & J. Smith (Eds.), *The Cambridge handbook of instructional feedback* (pp. 554–574). Cambridge University Press. https://doi.org/10.1017/9781316832134.027

Hanks, W. F. (1989). Text and textuality. *Annual Review of Anthropology*, 18(1), 95–127. https://doi.org/10.1146/annurev.an.18.100189.000523

Haught-Tromp, C. (2017). The *Green Eggs and Ham* hypothesis: How constraints facilitate creativity. *Psychology of Aesthetics, Creativity, and the Arts*, 11(1), 10–17. https://doi.org/10.1037/aca0000061

Hogan, S. L. (2019). Social filters shaping student responses to teacher feedback in the secondary drama classroom. *NJ: Drama Australia Journal*, 43(1), 4–19. https://doi.org/10.1080/14452294.2018.1509368

Kadaruddin, K. (2023). Empowering education through generative AI: Innovative instructional strategies for tomorrow's learners. *International Journal of Business, Law, and Education*, 4(2), 618–625. https://doi.org/10.56442/ijble.v4i2.215

Langer, S. K. (1953). *Feeling and form: A theory of art*. Charles Scribner's Sons.

Lewis, S., & Hardy, I. (2017). Tracking the topological: The effects of standardised data upon teachers' practice. *British Journal of Educational Studies*, 65(2), 219–238. https://doi.org/10.1080/00071005.2016.1254157

Maor, D., Currie, J., & Drewry, R. (2011). The effectiveness of assistive technologies for children with special needs: A review of research-based studies. *European Journal of Special Needs Education*, 26(3), 283–298. https://doi.org/10.1080/08856257.2011.593821

Marzano, R. J., Pickering, D., & Heflebower, T. (2011). *The highly engaged classroom*. Marzano Research.

Morris, M. L. (2015). Pushing the limits: Making dance accessible to different bodies through assistive technology. *Journal of Dance Education*, 15(4), 142–151. https://doi.org/10.1080/15290824.2015.1031901

Phung, L., Nakamura, S., & Reinders, H. (2021). The effect of choice on affective engagement: Implications for task design. In P. Hiver, A. H. Al-Hoorie, & S. Mercer (Eds.), *Student engagement in the language classroom* (pp. 163–181). Multilingual Matters.

Sadler, D. R. (2014). The futility of attempting to codify academic achievement standards. *Higher Education*, 67, 273–288. https://doi.org/10.1007/s10734-013-9649-1

Sahlberg, P. (2016). The global educational reform impact on schooling. In K. E. Mundy, A. Green, B. Lingard, & A. Verger (Eds.), *The handbook of global education policy* (pp. 128–144). Wiley Blackwell.

Sickler-Voigt, D. C. (2023). Media arts and assistive technologies as empowering global communication tools for students with visual impairments. In A. D. Knochel & O. Sahara (Eds.), *Global media arts education* (pp. 251–266). Palgrave Macmillan. https://doi.org/10.1007/978-3-031-05476-1_15

Snepvangers, K., Thomson, P., & Harris, A. (Eds.). (2018). *Creativity policy, partnerships and practice in education*. Springer. https://doi.org/10.1007/978-3-319-96725-7

Stiggins, R. (2007). Assessment through the student's eyes. *Educational Leadership, 64*(8), 22–26.

Stobart, G. (2009). Determining validity in national curriculum assessments. *Educational Research, 51*(2), 161–179. https://doi.org/10.1080/00131880902891305

Torrance, H. (2007). Assessment *as* learning? How the use of explicit learning objectives, assessment criteria and feedback in post-secondary education and training can come to dominate learning. *Assessment in Education: Principles, Policy & Practice, 14*(3), 281–294. https://doi.org/10.1080/09695940701591867

UNESCO. (2023). *The future of culture and arts education: Highlights from the UNESCO multistakeholder dialogue (25–26 May 2023)*. https://www.unesco.org/en/articles/future-culture-and-arts-education-highlights-unesco-multistakeholder-dialogue-25-26-may-2023

United Nations. (n.d.). *Education for all*. https://www.un.org/en/academic-impact/education-all

Wang, T., Lund, B. D., Marengo, A., Pagano, A., Mannuru, N. R., Teel, Z. A., & Pange, J. (2023). Exploring the potential impact of artificial intelligence (AI) on international students in higher education: Generative AI, chatbots, analytics, and international student success. *Applied Sciences, 13*(11). https://doi.org/10.3390/app13116716

Whatley, S., & Marsh, K. (2017). Making no difference: Inclusive dance pedagogy. In S. Burridge & C. Svendler Nielsen (Eds.), *Dance, access and inclusion: Perspectives on dance, young people and change* (pp. 3–11). Routledge.

Wyatt-Smith, C., Klenowski, V., & Gunn, S. (2010). The centrality of teachers' judgement practice in assessment: A study of standards in moderation. *Assessment in Education: Principles, Policy & Practice, 17*(1), 59–75. https://doi.org/10.1080/09695940903565610

7 Learning and assessment in school science

Assistive technologies for diverse learners

Nicholas K. Teh and James P. Davis

Teaching and assessment in school science education often simulate the ways scientific knowledge is typically derived from empiricism, which means learning through experiences of real phenomena using bodily senses or technologies. The generation and dissemination of scientific knowledge is a human endeavour that is understood from sociological and philosophical perspectives known as the nature of science (NOS; Schwartz & Lederman, 2008). In science education, science ways of knowing are often replicated and embedded in Assessment for Learning (AfL) through techniques such as project work with science inquiry, performing explanations using analogies and metaphors, analysing or presenting data, evaluating and justifying methods, and argumentation related to socio-scientific issues (Dawson & Venville, 2019). Some school science curricula also assess the nature of science as a human endeavour (Australian Curriculum, Assessment and Reporting Authority [ACARA], 2023).

To ensure fair and equitable access to educational opportunities, science teachers should be aiming to develop learning contexts that target support for learners with different needs. This chapter adopts the term *diverse learners* to describe people with different learning needs. This is an expansive term aimed at contributing to social justice through equity, access, and empowerment of individuals. Diverse learners include people with disabilities but also broader categories of learners such as: Indigenous or ethnic minorities; gifted and talented; culturally and linguistically diverse (CALD); or LGBTQI+ people. The needs of diverse learners may be achieved by implementing equitable adjustments in teaching and assessment methods, catering to learners who may face disadvantages or possess diverse capabilities (Fincke et al., 2021). Equitable adjustments aim to level the playing field via actions such as providing specialised equipment, modifying teaching pedagogies and assessments, and offering additional in-class support (Norwich, 2022). Some of these adjustments include assistive technologies, which are any form of equipment and/or technique for using equipment that improves accessibility to learning opportunities (Bright, 2022).

Our aim in this chapter is to stimulate practical thinking about the needs of diverse learners in science education and we illustrate an important strategy using assistive technologies. Our ideas are grounded in our practitioner experiences as we explore how science educators may implement assistive technologies for diverse learners, with a focus on people with disabilities.

DOI: 10.4324/9781003463184-9

Accessibility of science knowledge for diverse learners

Science education, like science itself, is inherently complex. It combines elements of scientific inquiry, epistemic values such as objectivity, validity, and reliability, the use of specific techniques and technologies, diverse methods of analysing and presenting data and ideas, and the employment of language that can be technical and/or metaphorical. This complexity presents a significant barrier for many diverse learners as teaching may not accommodate differences in learning or how learners express their understanding (cf. Israel et al., 2016). Consequently, learners who might excel in more adaptive and inclusive educational environments often underperform in traditional summative assessments. There are various frameworks to assess learner capabilities, such as integrating assessment approaches (Bourke & Mentis, 2014). Such pedagogical frameworks are often informed by systems-level frameworks that may be a useful starting point for schools to develop inclusive teaching practices (International Institute for Educational Planning [IIEP-UNESCO], 2023). In the Australian context, diverse learners with a disability are supported by the Nationally Consistent Collection of Data on School Students with Disability (NCCD) framework. NCCD categorises school students into four main groups of disabilities: cognitive, social-emotional, physical, and sensory impairments (NCCD, 2023a). Following, each category is described with examples from science education contexts.

Cognitive disabilities primarily affect an individual's cognitive processes and abilities. This category includes intellectual disabilities, speech and language impairments, autism spectrum disorder (ASD), dyslexia, and attention deficit hyperactivity disorder (ADHD). Learners with these disabilities might struggle with processing complex information, maintaining attention, understanding abstract concepts, or communicating effectively. For example, science teachers often use analogies that start with a familiar concept to connect with unfamiliar more abstract concepts. For diverse learners, a range of analogies may be needed, including intermediate or bridging analogies (Harrison & Coll, 2008).

Social-emotional disabilities refer to conditions that affect an individual's social and emotional functioning. This category includes ASD, anxiety disorders, and other mental health conditions. These disabilities can influence how individuals perceive, interpret, and interact with others and their environment, as well as their ability to manage and regulate their emotional and mental well-being. Social-emotional conditions can impact participation in group activities or discussions in science education. Assessment for Learning in school science often involves science inquiry and working in groups adaptively, where uncertainty about science data and knowledge are commonly created by the teacher as a vehicle for learning. A learner with ASD might find group assessments challenging due to difficulties in social interaction and collaboration, leading to feelings of isolation. Such students need to be understood by the teacher and additional scaffolding and support provided.

Physical disabilities include conditions that affect physical functioning. This category encompasses disabilities that may limit mobility, coordination, strength, or other aspects of physical activity, as well as learners with constant or prevalent medical conditions significantly impacting physical health and capabilities. Physical disabilities may hinder the ability to conduct experiments or manipulate laboratory equipment and tools. For example, limited mobility might restrict access to specific lab setups, and prevalent medical conditions could impact attendance and energy levels, affecting consistent participation in science learning. A learner with a physical disability might find it challenging to participate in hands-on laboratory experiments, especially if the lab is not accessible or the experiment requires fine motor skills, such as dissecting onion cells or conducting acid-base titration experiments. Chronic medical conditions could lead to absenteeism, resulting in missed lessons or assessments. Fortunately, digital technologies are playing a significant role in science education that can improve equity for diverse learners with physical disabilities.

Sensory disabilities affect how individuals perceive and process sensory information, impacting their ability to communicate and learn. Sensory impairment can significantly affect access to visual or auditory information. In science, this could limit participation in observing rapid events during demonstrations or using a particular sense in some areas of scientific inquiry. For example, a learner with a hearing disability might struggle to follow verbal instructions in a science laboratory with echoing acoustics or with noise from adjacent groups. In contrast, a learner with a vision disability may struggle with assessments involving graph, diagram, or visual data interpretation, especially if these are overly small or cluttered.

These barriers result in an uneven playing field for learners with disabilities, affecting both their access to scientific knowledge and their performance in summative assessments. Not all learners are equally equipped to tackle these challenges, leading to disparities in their learning experiences and outcomes. In the following section, we discuss planning support for diverse learners.

Planning support for diverse learners

Before implementing adjustments to summative assessments, educators should thoroughly understand the specific needs of each learner. This understanding can be developed by reviewing data from previous educators or through detailed assessments conducted by specialists such as paediatricians, psychologists, special education teachers, or therapists. Additionally, consulting with the learner's case manager at school about appropriate adjustments can be beneficial. Once their needs are identified, adjustments can be made based on the NCCD classification (NCCD, 2023b), or equivalent frameworks in international contexts. In the following sections, we focus on diverse learners with disabilities, and we explore the role of assistive technologies for different contexts and learners in science education.

What are assistive technologies?

Assistive technologies are commonly defined as tools, techniques, or software designed to support diverse learners, enabling them to perform tasks that would otherwise be difficult or impossible. These technologies vary in complexity, ranging from simple, low-tech tools like pencil grips and digital rulers to advanced equipment such as speech-to-text software and C-Pens, which can read text aloud. Additionally, adaptive educational software, such as Smart Sparrow™[1] or DreamBox Learning™,[2] supports learners with dyslexia by facilitating learning through repetition and tracking their progress. Meanwhile, distance education learners may use software like Stile Education™[3] and Education Perfect™[4] to access school curricula. These technologies aim to provide accessibility in science education, making adjustments as needed to enhance the learner's ability to effectively perform and complete tasks within an educational context.

Application of assistive technologies in summative science assessments

Assistive technologies are essential for adapting summative science assessments. For example, screen readers vocalise text and describe images for visually impaired learners, while speech-to-text software enables learners with motor disabilities to write responses verbally. Adaptive testing platforms adjust question difficulty based on a learner's answers, providing a personalised assessment experience. Assistive technology encompasses simulation software and virtual laboratories such as ChemCollective Virtual Labs™,[5] PhET Interactive Simulations™,[6] Labster™,[7] and ExploreLearning Gizmos™.[8] These tools offer learners with disabilities the opportunity to participate in hands-on experiments within a safe, virtual environment, thereby eliminating the need for a physical laboratory. These types of software enable learners to simulate a wide range of scientific activities.

Applied to science classrooms specifically, we may consider a Grade 7 chemistry course on the topic of *Separating Mixtures and Renewable Resources* (ACARA, 2023), where learners are required to write a report as part of their summative assessment. This report is based on their investigation into mixture separation techniques used in mining. They need to select appropriate techniques to extract identified resources from a mining sample, aiming to collect as much of each resource as possible using the correct separation methods. In this context, the virtual lab enables interactive simulations that closely replicate real-life experiments involving the separation of substances in both solvents and solutions. Learners with disabilities can interact with virtual lab equipment, such as beakers, filters, and heating devices, enabling them to make decisions and take action by conducting processes like filtration, evaporation, and distillation. This allows them to participate in the assessment and gather the necessary data fully without the need for a physical lab to complete their summative assessment. Such flexibility enables learners with diverse abilities to engage in experiential learning and summative assessment within a lab or from any location.

Guide to implementing assistive technologies for classroom adjustments

In this section, we document a guide to implementing assistive technologies drawn from teaching practices. This guide incorporates the four NCCD categories mentioned previously, with a three-phase adjustment process including initial implementation, mid-term adjustments, and summative adjustments. These adjustments are based on how learners perform in classroom settings, their previous adjustments, conversations with their case managers, and understanding the changes they may face in a new class environment. We continuously evaluate the effectiveness of these

Table 7.1 Guided checklist to making appropriate adjustments

Identifying	Categorising	Accessibility	Implementing	Review
Gathering information and identifying needs	*Understanding needs and categorising adjustments*	*Gaining accessibility by overcoming barriers*	*Implementing and assessing the process*	*Reflective questions to consider*
• Identify learners who may require adjustments • Collect relevant data from the school database to determine learners' accessibility needs, such as previous adjustments, paediatrician diagnoses, or discussions with learners' case managers or parents	• Determine the category of adjustment required, whether it be cognitive, social-emotional, physical, or sensory • Identify the specific difficulties learners face in accessing science content at school • Analyse and list each individual barrier they encounter, being as specific as possible	• State each barrier and how it impedes the learner's learning • Identify which assistive technologies could help learners overcome these barriers • Predict the potential benefits of these technologies and explain how they will positively impact the learners	• Describe the method of implementing the assistive technology • Check the availability of the required technology • Conduct reassessments after a few weeks to ensure the success of the implementation • Keep a record of all implementations for each learner	• Does the strategy address functionality or accessibility? • What are the positive and negative aspects of the strategies? • Did the adjustments overcome any barriers? • What are the following steps to make adjustments?

adjustments throughout the term and make necessary changes to the assessment tasks to better align them with the learners' abilities. The three-phase adjustment process is typically carried out during a 10-week term using the adjustment guide checklist for each phase, as outlined in Table 7.1. This checklist is a guide and is structured as a set of reflective questions to prompt planning and actions. The primary goal of this process is to increase accessibility in science learning and make appropriate adjustments for formative and summative assessments in each term.

Vignette case study of Lachlan

The following is a brief case study of a fictitious learner named Lachlan, who is 12 years old and in Grade 7 of junior secondary school in Australia. Across the three phases, we applied the checklist guide from Table 7.1. This vignette is learner-focused and could be applied in science or other subject areas.

Phase 1: Initial implementation

At the start of each term, we identify learners who need adjustments. We begin by familiarising ourselves with the learners, aided by a list of verified diverse learners from the Head of Student Services (HoSS). We then gather further information through observation and the school's database. From this data, we determine the necessary adjustments for each learner, focusing on how to facilitate their access to science content knowledge. Once we identify these barriers, we employ customised assistive technology to meet their needs.

For instance, the HoSS's list identified Lachlan as having a cognitive disability under the NCCD categorisation, coming from a low socio-economic background, appearing to be disengaged, and disruptive at times. Records in the school database indicated that Lachlan was diagnosed with dyslexia by a paediatrician and received support in primary school. Lachlan required a checklist to complete his work and had shown difficulty distinguishing certain letters and numbers, such as mistaking the number 4 for the letter *h* and the number 9 for the letter *P*. Additionally, Lachlan often uses a laptop, particularly when a teacher aide was unavailable.

In response, the class was adjusted to incorporate laptops as a standard learning tool, allowing Lachlan to use assistive technology discreetly. Our school's 'Bring Your Own Device' (BYOD) policy ensured most learners had laptops. However, we secured an equity device for Lachlan, who couldn't afford a laptop, to provide equal access. After ensuring that all learners had laptops and internet access, we uploaded class notes, work documents, and lesson plans to the school database. We used a projector for most lessons, enabling the use of dyslexia-friendly fonts,[9] modified text colours and sizes, and incorporated images to support Lachlan's learning. Additionally, we employed seating plan software to optimise classroom arrangements, projecting the plan for learners at the start of each lesson to orient Lachlan.

We provided all learners with a digital checklist of learning objectives and success criteria, helping them track their progress throughout the term. Interactive software like Padlet™[10] was used for anonymous feedback during certain lessons, offering various digital response options. This approach promoted independence for Lachlan and enabled his seamless participation in science lessons without feeling conspicuous among his peers.

Phase 2: Mid-term adjustments

Phase 2 of the teaching term, typically between weeks 5 and 6, is critical for gathering comprehensive data and feedback from learners, parents, and educators. This phase is dedicated to analysing this information to identify any necessary adjustments for the mid-term formative assessment. The aim is to refine our initial strategies and inform the adjustments for the summative assessment. Part of this process involves evaluating the effectiveness of prior adjustments, determining which were successful and which require modification.

During this phase, adjustments may involve altering seating arrangements or incorporating assistive technologies in formative assessments. For instance, recognising that Lachlan struggled with wordy short answer questions such as those asking to describe changes in states of matter like solid, liquid, and gas, we transformed the formative assessment into a more interactive, game-based quiz. This quiz involved activities like clicking and dragging pictures to match the different states of matter. This adjustment helped us better understand Lachlan's grasp of the subject and highlighted areas where additional support may be needed. By continuously adapting teaching methods, we ensured they were responsive and tailored to the evolving needs of learners.

Maintaining fairness in these adjustments is crucial, ensuring they do not alter the assessment's core intention and remain aligned with the achievement standards. While assessing learners using varied methods is permissible, it's crucial to ensure that these modifications do not inadvertently alter the difficulty level of the questions themselves.

Final phase: Summative adjustments

As the term progresses towards its conclusion, we make final adjustments to modify summative assessments like exams, lab reports, and practical exams, tailoring them to the learners' diverse needs through assistive technology. For example, learners with social and emotional issues may be provided with noise-cancelling headphones. At the same time, those with low literacy might use a C-Pen in exams for text-to-speech conversion, and speech-to-text software can assist learners with physical disabilities. In some instances, learners have the option to present their written lab reports in alternative formats, such as PowerPoint presentations, to suit their learning styles better.

Take Lachlan, for instance. He was given the choice to present his lab report via PowerPoint. His presentation still needed to cover all the traditional sections of a lab report: introduction, method, safety, results, analysis, and conclusion. The key aim was to allow Lachlan to engage with the task using digital technology, enabling him to convey his understanding through visual aids like pictures, graphic organisers, tables, and flow charts instead of relying solely on text.

Just like in formative assessments, the goal here is not to lower the task's difficulty level but to ensure that all learners have equal opportunities to demonstrate their understanding through means that cater to their individual needs. This approach is part of creating an inclusive environment that respects and addresses the various learning requirements of learners.

Reflecting on this term, we observe how Lachlan transitioned smoothly from primary to secondary school. His engagement with the class content significantly improved due to the use of a laptop, a tool without which he might have struggled. As a result, he has become less disruptive and more comprehending of the concepts taught, and his performance has improved, as evidenced by his achievements in both formative and summative tasks, culminating in a passing grade for his Term 1 results.

Conclusion: Reflection on assistive technologies

Integrating assistive technology in both formative and summative assessments is a highly effective strategy to cater to diverse learner needs. The wide range of resources and digital tools available can revolutionise how we meet each learner's unique circumstances. These tools are essential and play a vital role in helping learners demonstrate their skills and knowledge in science, effectively breaking down barriers and creating a level playing field. This approach moves away from the 'one-size-fits-all' mindset, embracing more flexible, personalised evaluation techniques. Such methods align with Universal Design for Learning principles, which advocate for varied ways of learner expression (Evmenova, 2018).

A significant benefit of using assistive technologies is their ability to remove barriers in education, enabling learners to participate equitably (McNicholl et al., 2021). These solutions enable learners to access work created by educators, acquire scientific knowledge, and participate in assessments that accurately measure their capabilities. An unintended consequence is enhanced learner engagement. For instance, iPads or laptops can provide visual representations of scientific concepts, deepening learners' understanding and aiding retention. Disengagement in the classroom, leading to disruptive behaviour and truancy, often stems from learners' struggles to participate. Assistive technology not only benefits diverse and disabled learners but also fosters engagement under the right conditions. Moreover, it allows for personalised adjustments tailored to individual learners, especially in summative assessments.

However, implementing assistive technology comes with challenges. The technical difficulties associated with these often complex and new technologies are a significant issue. Not understanding how these technologies are programmed or designed can make troubleshooting difficult. Other challenges include obtaining access to the technology, securing permissions for classroom use, and ensuring ongoing support and maintenance (Evmenova, 2020). Both learners and educators may need specialised training to use the technology effectively. Ensuring standardised adjustments in summative assessments can be tricky, as avoiding bias towards learners using assistive technology is essential.

There's also a risk of creating disparities in learners' experiences with the technology, potentially affecting outcomes in formative assessments. For example, learners using speech-to-text software with internet access might unfairly benefit in exams if not appropriately managed. Other concerns may include the initial costs of acquiring assistive technologies, maintaining them, and software subscriptions. There's also a risk of learners becoming overly reliant on assistive technology, which could hinder the development of their independent skills. For instance, over-reliance on speech-to-text software might impede learning to write or spell correctly.

Overall, assistive technologies are essential for making appropriate adjustments for diverse learners and those with disabilities. While there are significant benefits, especially in summative science assessments, all adjustments must be carefully planned and managed to avoid complications. This involves proper training for educators, securing funding for technology, fair and standardised implementation of assistive technology, and balancing the development of learners' skills. With proper implementation, assistive technology can be a transformative tool, creating a more inclusive environment where all learners can access the curriculum, and educators can obtain accurate assessments of their learners' abilities.

Future opportunities in assistive technology

The potential for assistive technology, particularly in science assessment, is immense. This field is constantly evolving, which offers opportunities to design innovative software or equipment that can help learners in the classroom. Such technologies are pivotal in transforming our education system into a more inclusive and accessible environment for all. One of the most exciting prospects is the development of artificial intelligence (AI), which could revolutionise assessments by providing real-time adaptability in both formative and summative evaluations (Minn, 2022). Tasks that are challenging for educators to perform manually could be easily managed with AI integration in assistive technologies. AI's rapid processing ability can tailor the complexity of tasks based on individual learner responses, offering questions suited to their understanding level. This adaptive approach means educators can obtain more accurate results and identify knowledge gaps through statistical reports.

Another significant advantage of AI in assistive technologies is the provision of real-time feedback and support during classes and formative assessments. An intelligent AI system can offer standardised feedback, helping learners identify mistakes or misconceptions in their learning process (Zdravkova et al., 2022). This ensures that learners comprehend lessons as they progress, reducing the need for constant educator intervention and potentially lessening the reliance on teaching aids in the classroom.

The advancement of virtual reality (VR) and augmented reality (AR) has the potential to revolutionise learning and assessment in science. Learners can have an interactive and immersive learning experience by combining VR and AR technologies. This technology can benefit learners with disabilities, including those with physical limitations. For example, learners can use VR glasses like the Meta Quest 3[11] to learn about chemical reactions through the VR Chemistry Lab app[12] without having to enter a lab physically. Additionally, apps such as the Human Anatomy VR[13] for Institutions can present 3D human models, enabling learners to learn through interactive visual and verbal components. This can provide alternative methods of education and enhance the learning experience with greater engagement.

In conclusion, the future of assistive technology is bright, with new advancements emerging daily. As these technologies evolve, they promise a more inclusive future for learners. Personalised and accessible learning and assessment experiences not only level the playing field for diverse learners and those with disabilities but also support them in developing their knowledge to demonstrate their academic potential fully. These advancements represent a significant step towards ensuring a more equitable learning environment for all learners.

Notes

1 https://www.smartsparrow.com/
2 https://www.dreambox.com/
3 https://stileeducation.com/au/
4 https://www.educationperfect.com/
5 http://chemcollective.org/vlabs
6 https://phet.colorado.edu
7 https://www.labster.com/simulations/chemistry
8 https://www.gizmos.explorelearning.com
9 For an example, see https://www.dyslexiefont.com/
10 https://padlet.com/site/product/education
11 https://www.meta.com/au/quest/quest-3/
12 https://www.meta.com/en-gb/experiences/3919613214752680/
13 https://www.meta.com/en-gb/experiences/3662196457238336/

References

Australian Curriculum, Assessment and Reporting Authority (ACARA). (2023). *Science (Version 8.4). The Australian Curriculum.* https://www.australiancurriculum.edu.au/f-10-curriculum/science/

Bourke, R., & Mentis, M. (2014). An assessment framework for inclusive education: Integrating assessment approaches. *Assessment in Education: Principles, Policy & Practice, 21*(4), 384–397. https://doi.org/10.1080/0969594X.2014.888332

Bright, D. (2022). An integrative review of the potential of wireless assistive technologies and internet of things (IoT) to improve accessibility to education for students with disabilities. *Assistive Technology, 34*(6), 653–660. https://doi.org/10.1080/10400435.2021.1956639

Dawson, V., & Venville, G. (2019). *The art of teaching science: A comprehensive guide to the teaching of secondary school science.* Routledge.

Evmenova, A. (2018). Preparing teachers to use universal design for learning to support diverse learners. *Journal of Online Learning Research, 4*(2), 147–171.

Evmenova, A. (2020). Implementation of assistive technology in inclusive classrooms. In D. Chambers (Ed.), *Assistive technology to support inclusive education* (pp. 177–193). Emerald Publishing Limited.

Fincke, K., Morrison, D., Bergsman, K., & Bell, P. (2021). Formative assessment for equitable learning. *The Science Teacher, 89*(2), 32–36.

Harrison, A. G., & Coll, R. K. (2008). *Using analogies in middle and secondary science classrooms: The FAR guide – An interesting way to teach with analogies.* Sage.

International Institute for Educational Planning (IIEP-UNESCO). (2023). *Inclusive student assessment systems.* https://policytoolbox.iiep.unesco.org/policy-option/inclusive-student-assessment-systems/

Israel, M., Wang, S., & Marino, M. T. (2016). A multilevel analysis of diverse learners playing life science video games: Interactions between game content, learning disability status, reading proficiency, and gender. *Journal of Research in Science Teaching, 53*(2), 324–345. https://doi.org.10.1002/tea.21273

McNicholl, A., Casey, H., Desmond, D., & Gallagher, P. (2021). The impact of assistive technology use for students with disabilities in higher education: A systematic review. *Disability and Rehabilitation: Assistive Technology, 16*(2), 130–143. https://doi.org/10.1080/17483107.2019.1642395

Minn, S. (2022). AI-assisted knowledge assessment techniques for adaptive learning environments. *Computers and Education: Artificial Intelligence, 3*, 100050. https://doi.org/10.1016/j.caeai.2022.100050

Nationally Consistent Collection of Data on School Students with Disability (NCCD). (2023a). *Definitions of disability and the NCCD categories.* https://www.nccd.edu.au/wider-support-materials/definitions-disability-and-nccd-categories

Nationally Consistent Collection of Data on School Students with Disability (NCCD). (2023b). *Nationally consistent collection of data on school students with disability* [website]. https://www.nccd.edu.au/

Norwich, B. (2022). Research about inclusive education: Are the scope, reach and limits empirical and methodological and/or conceptual and evaluative? *Frontiers in Education, 7*, 937929. https://doi.org/10.3389/feduc.2022.937929

Schwartz, R., & Lederman, N. (2008). What scientists say: Scientists' views of nature of science and relation to science context. *International Journal of Science Education, 30*(6), 727–771. https://doi.org/10.1080/09500690701225801

Zdravkova, K., Krasniqi, V., Dalipi, F., & Ferati, M. (2022). Cutting-edge communication and learning assistive technologies for disabled children: An artificial intelligence perspective. *Frontiers in Artificial Intelligence, 240*, 970430. https://doi.org/10.3389/frai.2022.970430

8 Inclusive practice and geographical assessment

Practical tips to increase task accessibility

Sarah Adams, Theresa Bourke, Reece Mills, and Ashlee Drew

Introduction

Research around assessment in geography education is limited at best, but when it comes to the nexus of assessment and inclusion, studies, particularly those based in the Australian educational context, are virtually non-existent.

A detailed review of educational literature focusing on 'geography, inclusion, and assessment' revealed that studies rarely encompass all three concepts. Studies of this ilk include Boyle (2017), Kleeman (2012), and Caldis (2019). Boyle's (2017) study, for example, concentrates on geography discipline and inclusion with only a nebulous link to assessment. This writer suggests text adjustment to promote reading accessibility, namely adjusting font size, and simplifying language. Additionally, visual stimuli are recommended to enhance understanding. Another study that focuses on geography and inclusion is Kleeman (2012). This writer highlights the need to meaningfully embed Indigenous perspectives in geography lessons. Once again, there is only an arbitrary link to assessment. Caldis' study (2019), on the other hand, is more focused on assessment and geography. She maintains that by including formative and summative approaches, formalised diagnostic assessment, spatial reasoning, active construction of knowledge, and multiple perspectives, geography assessments are likely to be more effective for *all* students. However, there is not an explicit mention of inclusion. The only hint is that by using diagnostic assessment, teachers can ascertain how complex or simple instructions need to be throughout the learning process. The paucity of research crossing over the three concepts of geography, inclusion, and assessment reveals the importance of the chapter that follows.

In this chapter, we use the definition of inclusive education as outlined in General Comment No. 4 (GC 4), established in 2016 by the UN (United Nations) Convention on the Rights of Persons with Disabilities (CRPD). This document defines *inclusion* as a 'systemic reform embodying changes and modifications in content, teaching methods, approaches, structures and strategies in education' (United Nations, 2016, paragraph 11). This definition asks educators to make the necessary adjustments to teaching and learning to ensure all students have an equitable learning experience. Here, we apply this definition to assessment, defined as the gathering of evidence to make well-informed judgements about a student's knowledge and understanding so that learning can be improved (Brookhart & McMillan, 2020).

This chapter will examine a geography assessment task designed by a pre-service teacher (Ashlee Drew) and comment on task specifics targeted at inclusivity. Additionally, suggestions will be made to make the task more accessible.

Context

This study examines a pre-service teacher's response to an assessment piece in a Master of Teaching (MTeach) university unit, as part of the first year of their two-year course at the Queensland University of Technology (QUT) in Brisbane, Australia. The aim of this unit is to get pre-service teachers to think deeply about assessment task design and how it can be made accessible to the diverse learners they will have in their classrooms. Specifically, pre-service teachers must design a Response to Stimulus summative task (unseen questions responding to graphs, maps, etc., under examination conditions), an associated rubric, a sample 'A' response, and a reflection which includes a rationale justifying their assessment design and what they have learned through the design process. The pre-service teachers are given parameters that they must follow to ensure the task is authentic and relevant to their future students. In this chapter, we outline how one pre-service teacher responded to this assessment piece in relation to the Grade 10 topic from the Australian Curriculum (AC), Geographies of Wellbeing. Recommendations for future practice in inclusive assessment in geography education are made. By designing out these barriers it is hoped that students achieve success in geography.

Method of analysis

Graham et al.'s (2018) model of visual, procedural, and linguistic complexities was used as a heuristic tool to examine the geography task developed by the pre-service teacher. This model proposes a layered analysis approach for ascertaining visual accessibility, procedural accessibility, and linguistic accessibility so that barriers can be 'designed out' to improve access for all students. These layers are defined as:

Layer 1: visual accessibility – reducing information that is not necessary to complete the task.
Layer 2: procedural accessibility – ensuring alignment in the steps needed to complete the task.
Layer 3: linguistic accessibility – ensuring the language used, both vocabulary and syntactic structure (arrangement of words in a sentence), are accessible to the reader.

Breakdown of the assessment piece for the pre-service teacher

The summative assessment piece for this unit had to adhere to the guidelines for Response to Stimulus tasks outlined in curriculum documents for Grade 10. These documents include the Australian Curriculum, Assessment and Reporting Authority

(ACARA) and Queensland Curriculum and Assessment Authority (QCAA) documents, including time for completion (90 minutes), number of sources (six), number of questions that make up the task (three: two short response and one extended response), and word limits (ACARA, 2021; QCAA, n.d.). Additionally, to aid their design, pre-service teachers are provided with a school/classroom context. The context is the school's socio-economic status, technology access, and a class of 28 students and their literacy levels.

Pre-service teachers must also submit a rationale for their design and reflect on what they learned during the assessment design process (750 words). The rationale needs to refer to assessment principles: content validity – did the task relate to the topic taught?; construct validity – how is the task authentic?; and consequential validity – how does the task acknowledge diversity? The reflection (250 words) is framed as a possible discussion with a Head of Department/Faculty whereby pre-service teachers need to consider their understanding of assessment.

In summary, the assessment piece required the pre-service teacher to design three tasks that would give their students a total of 50 possible marks. A summary of the three tasks designed by the pre-service teacher follows.

Summary of the pre-service teachers' assessment design

Task 1 (10 marks): The pre-service teacher selected two sources (Sources 1 and 2) – the first a green choropleth map related to the human development index (HDI). The HDI is a summary measure of key dimensions of human development: a long and healthy life, a good education, and a decent standard of living. The second source was also a choropleth map (blue and red), this time related to global gender equality – the best and worst places in the world to be a girl. Students were asked to synthesise the two sources and explain the general pattern and trend between gender equality and human development. Guidance was given regarding word count (50–100) and what to include in the response such as a justification, using data to support identified patterns as well as pointing out any anomalies (see Figure 8.1).

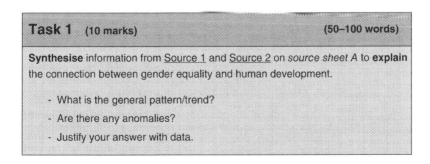

Figure 8.1 Task 1 written by the pre-service teacher.

> **Task 2** (10 marks) (50–100 words)
>
> Use source 3, source 4, and source 5 on *source sheet B* to **identify, analyse,** and **explain** the issues affecting gender equality in Africa.
>
> - Include social, political, and economic factors

Figure 8.2 Task 2 written by the pre-service teacher.

Task 2 (10 marks): In this task, students were asked to look at three sources (Sources 3, 4, and 5) and explain the issues affecting gender equality in Africa. Source 3 was a variety of different types of graphs (pie charts, bar graphs) comparing numbers of women in formal versus informal employment roles, as well as share of women across senior leadership positions. Source 4 was an infographic focusing on African women's land rights and Source 5 was a cartoon about schools not accepting pregnant women. Students were guided with cognitive verbs such as 'identify, analyse, and explain' to assist them with their responses. They were also given a word count (50–100) and what to include in the explanation (social, economic, and political factors) (see Figure 8.2).

Task 3 (30 marks): Students were required to use the information from four sources (combined together to produce Source 6) to evaluate the Microloan Foundation Program (microfinance institution providing loans and training to women in sub-Saharan Africa) (Microloan Foundation, 2021). These sources included a statement from the Microloan Foundation incorporating their vision and mission (approximately 250 words). It also included six relevant statistics (displayed in percentages) relating to women who have been positively impacted by the Microloan Foundation, for example, the number of women who are now able to save because of the program. There was also an infographic showing how the program works, detailing how the cycle starts with an assessment by an officer and concludes with women being able to apply for further loans. Finally, this infographic was further explained in eight dot points (approximately 250 words). The tasks asked students to predict what changes the program would have on development in Africa and explain the consequences of these changes. Students had to justify their explanations and predictions by referring to any of the four sources in Source 6. They were also given an indicative word count (300–400) and were asked to consider social, economic, and political criteria as well as the viability of the program (see Figure 8.3).

Analysis of the tasks constructed by the pre-service teacher

The current authors used the model outlined by Graham et al. (2018) to examine the design of the assessment tasks that the pre-service teacher had developed for their Grade 10 students. The layers (visual, procedural, and linguistic) were used to assess the inclusiveness of the tasks.

Inclusive practice and geographical assessment 87

> **Task 3** (30 marks) (300–400 words)
>
> **Evaluate** the program in <u>Source 6</u> (*source sheet C*) which addresses the challenge of gender equality in Africa. **Predict** the changes this program would have on development in Africa and **explain** the consequences of these changes. **Justify** your response using evidence from <u>sources.</u>
>
> Consider:
>
> - Social, economic, and political criteria
> - Could this program be used in all African countries?
> - How might this change the spatial distribution of development?
> - What are the consequences of these changes?

Figure 8.3 Task 3 written by the pre-service teacher.

Visual

Visually, there were strengths and weaknesses. For example, in terms of strengths, the task layouts were appealing; there was consistency with font type, font size, and justification (left aligned), and visual cues using 'bold', 'italics', and/or 'underline' for emphasis in the question. Additionally, there was ample use of 'white space' to separate sections and add to the appeal of the tasks visually. However, much of the information students needed to answer the tasks (namely the sources) was in another document, creating a visual barrier for students as they had to 'flick' from the task to the sources.

Procedural

Procedurally, the tasks for Grade 10 students had authentic contexts looking at gender inequality in sub-Saharan Africa. This aligned very well with the Geographies of Wellbeing from the Australian Curriculum (AC). There was space offered for students to write their responses which would allow them to meet the demands of the task. However, this could present as a barrier for some students who struggle to write at length. Conversely, some students may require more space. There were no other choices to answer the questions in a different format apart from writing the response. The questions were written using concise language to limit the amount of text students had to read. However, there were too many sources (Source 6 included four separate pieces of information alone) adding to what students had to read, which could create yet another barrier to achieving success in this task.

Linguistic

Linguistically, the language used in the task was free of bias; in other words, direct and free from opinion and emotion. Specialist language was defined in a glossary; for example, micro-finance. Students could refer to this glossary during the test, improving accessibility. However, the topic of gender inequality was included in Source 3 and this could be a barrier to success for students who identify as non-binary or similar. Furthermore, using vocabulary in the tasks which needs to be defined, such as 'synthesise', could create a barrier to students understanding the questions as they again 'flick' from the glossary to the task, trying to decipher what they have been asked to do.

Based on the analysis of the task, the following reflection uses Graham et al.'s layers (visual, procedural, and linguistic) to outline the limitations present in the tasks. Not only does this reflection seek to address these limitations, but it also aims to provide practical strategies to make the tasks more accessible. Each task (1, 2, and 3) will now be examined, and suggestions made.

Overcoming visual, procedural, and linguistic barriers

Task 1: There were two barriers for completing this task – linguistic and procedural. Linguistically, these included the word choices made by the teacher. For example, students were asked to 'synthesise information' from the two sources provided. However, synthesis does not align with 'what is the pattern or trend', which is the stem of the question. Better word choices would have been to 'identify the relationships' or to 'analyse'. If students could look at the two sources and decipher the relationship between the data sets, they would be able to complete the remaining part of the question which asks for anomalies. This also links to procedural accessibility as there is a mismatch between what the cognitive verb used is asking them to do and what they are being marked on. The criteria sheet is assessing the students on their 'analysis and syntheses' of the two sources, yet it is unlikely that the students are able to synthesise because with the information provided, there is little chance that they will be able to develop any new understanding. According to the Queensland Curriculum and Assessment Authority (QCAA, 2018), when students synthesise, they create new understandings. Based on the sources provided and the examination conditions, it is almost impossible for students to be able to achieve this. Cognitive verbs in questions need to be considered carefully and matched closely to the criteria sheet to minimise procedural complexity and reduce the barriers to success. Figure 8.4 shows Task 1 rewritten to overcome the barriers mentioned.

Task 2: In Task 2, all three barriers were present. For this task, there were ten possible marks for students to achieve. This is the same marking allocation as for Task 1. However, the degree of complexity in this question (having three sources and determining the relationships between them) is of a higher thinking level. Therefore, mark allocation should have reflected this. Visually, there is enough space for students to answer the question asked; however, it would have been better

> **Task 1** (10 marks) (50–100 words)
>
> **Analyse** the information from <u>Source 1</u> and <u>Source 2</u> on *source sheet A* to **explain** the connection between gender equality and human development.
>
> - What is the general pattern/trend?
> - Are there any anomalies?
> - Justify your answer with data.

Figure 8.4 Task 1 rewritten to overcome some barriers.

to give students a table to guide their responses (see Figure 8.5). Procedurally, students did not have to answer this task in sentences and a table would accurately align to the criteria sheet as well as reduce the time students spent writing their response. Furthermore, procedurally there should have been more guidelines given to students as to how much of the 50–100 words should be given to social, political, and economic factors. This degree of complexity makes the word limit

> **Task 2** (15 marks) (100–150 words)
>
> Use the table below and <u>source 3</u>, <u>source 4</u> and <u>source 5</u> on *source sheet B* to **identify, analyse*,** and **explain** the issues affecting gender equality in Africa.
>
> - Include social, political, and economic factors
>
> *Analyse: consider in detail for the purpose of finding meaning or relationships, and identifying patterns, similarities, and differences (QCAA, 2019).
>
> | TASK 2 | Issues affecting gender equality | This is evident in source? |
> |---|---|---|
> | Social factors | 1. | |
> | | 2. | |
> | Economic factors | 1. | |
> | | 2. | |
> | Political factors | 1. | |
> | | 2. | |

Figure 8.5 Task 2 rewritten to overcome some barriers.

seem unrealistic. The word limit should be increased to match what has been asked. Linguistically, the task asks students to 'analyse'; this cognitive verb should be defined below the task to make the task accessible. If students do not know what analyse means, they will be unable to answer the task. Figure 8.5 shows Task 2 rewritten to improve inclusivity.

Task 3: Task 3 also had evidence of the three barriers. Here, students had to look at a source sheet and make predictions about the likelihood of changes to development in Africa. This is a complex task where students procedurally must process detailed information as well as look at four sources. For this reason, the text contained in the sources should be reduced, specifically text related to the Loan and Training Officers (LTOs). These sources account for approximately 500 words which is too much for students to read under examination conditions. This information that students need to read could easily be condensed to reduce the visual complexity of the task. Images could have been used to clearly depict the information. Procedurally, there are many elements that students need to address to answer the task. Ideally, the task should be broken into sub-sections to reduce the information students have to process. For example, the first part of the question could ask students to describe the program using the sources as evidence. Then, students could predict development changes, and finally they could be asked to explain the consequences of these changes. Like Task 2, complex vocabulary is used such as 'spatial distribution'. This should be defined below the question to reduce linguistic barriers. Additionally, the task gives students points to 'consider'. Visually, one of the four points (consequence of the change) is a repeat of what students have been asked to do four sentences earlier. This consideration should be deleted to reduce the amount students have to read. Furthermore, the word 'consider' should be changed to 'include' to give students more direction. Points which students should 'consider' have direct alignment to how they are being marked on the criteria sheet, subsequently, if they do not 'consider' these points it is unlikely that they will be able to demonstrate the criteria, thus creating another barrier. Figure 8.6 details these suggested changes which will hopefully reduce the visual, procedural, and linguistic barriers for Grade 10 students.

Overcoming structural barriers

In this study, Graham et al.'s (2018) three layers of visual, procedural, and linguistic accessibility have been used as a heuristic tool to examine a Grade 10 geography task developed by a pre-service teacher for their assessment piece in an MTeach unit. Designing inclusive geography assessment ensures all students can achieve success. The assessment task was analysed, and observations were made around potential barriers and how to overcome them.

It was found that the pre-service teacher constructed a task which had some barriers for students to overcome to achieve success. Visually, Task 3 contained superfluous information, creating a possible barrier due to repetition of information. Procedurally, there was misalignment in Task 1 with what students had been asked and how they were being marked. For Tasks 2 and 3, more guidelines were needed

Inclusive practice and geographical assessment 91

> **Task 3** (35 marks) (350–450 words)
>
> **Question 1:** Using source 6, **describe** the program which addresses gender equality in Africa (5 marks, 50–100 words).
>
> **Question 2: Predict** what changes this program would have on development in Africa using evidence from source 6 (15 marks, 150–200 words). Ensure you include social, economic and political criteria when considering the changes. Also, how might the changes in development impact the spatial distribution* of development?
>
> **Question 3:** Considering the changes you mentioned in Question 2 (above), **explain** what consequences are likely to occur using evidence from source 6 (15 marks, 150–200 words). Ensure you include the criteria in your response (social, economic, and political). Also, could this program be used in all African countries? Why/why not?
>
> *Spatial distribution: the arrangement of a particular phenomena or activities across the surface of the Earth (QCAA, 2019).

Figure 8.6 Task 3 rewritten to overcome some barriers.

to ensure students could answer the task effectively. Linguistically, Tasks 2 and 3 had geographic-specific vocabulary which, if students did not understand, they could not have answered the question; hence, definitions for these terms need to be provided. While these visual, procedural, and linguistic barriers are easy to design out, there are additional barriers when creating inclusive assessments which need to be considered. We refer to these as structural barriers. In what follows is a list of such structures and possible strategies to make the assessment item more accessible.

- Timing: There is an increasing amount of research indicating that secondary students learn better based on their 'chronotype' (Wile & Shouppe, 2011). Essentially, the time of day (morning, afternoon, etc.) should be taken into consideration when scheduling a test in line with student preference for when they function best. For external examinations, this would be harder to achieve.
- Mode of assessment: Differentiating assessment items in geography is straightforward and adjustments should be incorporated so all students can achieve success. This is because there are many teaching sources such as texts, maps, graphs, and images which allow for easy, quality, differentiated instruction (Boyle, 2017). Written response exams can be replaced with annotated visual displays, reducing the amount students have to write (Boyle, 2017). Hence, when designing assessment items, it is important to think about non-traditional assessment modes.

- Use of colour: Sources 1 and 2 were choropleth maps detailing HDI (Source 1 – green colour scheme) and Global Gender Equality (Source 2 – blue and red colour scheme). Students can only answer the question if they are able to see colour. If a student were colour blind or had compromised vision, this question would be difficult to answer. One of the most common types of colour blindness is red–green. This is when people struggle to differentiate between these two colours, hence this question could present as inequitable (National Eye Institute, 2019). While there is no definite way to ensure inclusion for all, these two sources could be accessed digitally and depending on colour deficiency, the student could change the colour base to their preferences (Whomsley, 2023).

Additionally, some of the barriers could relate to gender-based barriers like the following example:

- Gender: In this Response to Stimulus exam women were the focus, specifically in Source 6. At times, this topic could compromise equity for students who identify as non-binary or gender fluid as they may find it difficult to contextualise the question (Herman & Cook, 2020). Moreover, although not in this examination, this is further represented when geography students are presented with population pyramids (data which divides the population based on sex – male or female). When designing assessment items, teachers need to consider gender rather than sex. Equity is important; the ability for all students to be able to access the content without any disadvantage should be at the forefront of assessment design (Herman & Cook, 2020).

Conclusion

This chapter has looked at a pre-service teacher's construction of a task for a Grade 10 geography class in Queensland, Australia. The task was specifically designed to ensure accessibility for students by following Graham et al.'s (2018) model of designing out barriers using visual, procedural, and linguistic accessibility. The task was analysed and additional suggestions were made such as the deletion of superfluous information. Finally, while acknowledging Graham et al.'s (2018) model as a useful tool for ascertaining the inclusivity of assessment task design, we add to the model by recommending an examination of structural barriers that might also need to be overcome when designing geography assessment that is inclusive for *all*.

References

Australian Curriculum, Assessment and Reporting Authority (ACARA). (2021). *Geography*. https://v9.australiancurriculum.edu.au/f-10-curriculum/learning-areas/geography-7-10/year-10

Boyle, M. (2017). Differentiation in geography. *Interaction, 45*(3), 9–11. https://doi/10.3316/informit.228936075884966

Brookhart, S. M., & McMillan, J. H. (Eds.). (2020). *Classroom assessment and educational measurement*. Routledge.

Caldis, S. (2019). What makes a geography assessment geographical? *Geography Bulletin*, *51*(1), 67–70. https://doi.org/10.3316/ielapa.397297917983927

Graham, L., Tancredi, H., Willis, J., & McGraw, K. (2018). Designing out barriers to student access and participation in secondary school assessment. *Australian Educational Researcher*, *45*, 103–124. https://doi.org/10.1007/s13384-018-0266-y

Herman, J., & Cook, L. (2020). Fairness in classroom assessment. In S. M. Brookhart & J. H. McMillan (Eds.), *Classroom assessment and educational measurement* (pp. 243–264). Routledge.

Kleeman, G. (2012). Towards a more inclusive curriculum: The perspectives of Aboriginal and Torres Strait Islander Peoples in geography curriculum documents. *Geographical Education*, *25*, 24–28.

Microloan Foundation. (2021). *About us*. https://www.microloanfoundation.org.uk/

National Eye Institute. (2019). *Types of colour blindness*. https://www.nei.nih.gov/learn-about-eye-health/eyeconditions-and-diseases/color-blindness/types-color-blindness

Queensland Curriculum and Assessment Authority (QCAA). (2018). *Geography 2019 v1.1: General senior syllabus*. Queensland Government. https://www.qcaa.qld.edu.au/senior/senior-subjects/humanities-social-sciences/geography/syllabus

Queensland Curriculum and Assessment Authority (QCAA). (2019). *Year 10 standard elaboration – Australian Curriculum: Geography*. https://www.qcaa.qld.edu

Queensland Curriculum and Assessment Authority (QCAA). (n.d.). *Moderation models and processes*. https://www.qcaa.qld.edu.au/downloads/aciq/generalresources/assessment/ac_moderation_mode

United Nations (UN). (2016). *General comment no. 4. Article 24: Right to inclusive education*. United Nations.

Whomsley, M. (2023). *Enhancement of blended learning materials and methodologies to promote inclusivity*. https://fig.net/resources/proceedings/fig_proceedings/fig2023/papers/ts08e/TS08E_whomsley_12071.pdf

Wile, A. J., & Shouppe, G. A. (2011). Does time-of-day of instruction impact class achievement? *Perspectives in Learning*, *12*(1). https://csuepress.columbusstate.edu/pil/vol12/iss1/9

Part II
Interdisciplinary practices

9 Indigenous perspectives in assessment

Applying a place-based approach

Danielle Armour, Antoinette Cole, Amy Thomson, Daniel Kiwa McKinnon, Ren Perkins, and Marnee Shay

In defining place-based education (PBE) in the Australian education context, it is essential to explore the current framing and its implications on education. There's an opportunity through PBE to harness the collective benefit of Indigenous ways of knowing, being, and doing framed through Indigenous worldviews to better prepare young people and future generations to sustain the land. This can be achieved through a shift from Western place-based models. Currently, in education, assessment fails to prepare all young people as future custodians and stewards of the land.

PBE is an umbrella term for pedagogical practices prioritising experiential, community-based, and contextual/ecological learning to cultivate greater connectivity to local contexts, cultures, and environments (Smith, 2002). From a Western viewpoint, Bartholomaeus (2013) argues that place-based approaches use 'the local community and environment as a starting point or a focus for teaching and can be used in any learning area or combination of learning areas' (p. 18). This is often done through a non-Indigenous lens of what it means to be part of the local community, often excluding Indigenous perspectives, particularly that of the local community. Understanding the value of Indigenous ways of being, knowing, and doing within PBE is critical as this provides an opportunity to understand place from different ways of knowing.

Indigenous PBE approaches provide a more connected and relational way of understanding place. Being a 'knower' when confined by Eurocentrism means that disembodied ways of knowing and the individualistic pursuit of knowledges are privileged (Moreton-Robinson, 2013, p. 341). Western place-based models continue to de-contextualise fragments of Indigenous knowledges into a Eurocentric framework, such as the Australian Curriculum, Assessment and Reporting Authority (ACARA) Cross-Curricular Priorities: Aboriginal and Torres Strait Islander Histories and Cultures (Spillman et al., 2023a). The benefits of collective knowing and knowledge (from Indigenous ways of being, knowing, and doing) are yet to be fully realised in Australian education. We pose that through an Indigenous framing of PBE and assessment, all students can share in the rich knowledge, communication, and lessons learnt from human-Earthkin relationships that have been 'accepted for millennia by Indigenous peoples across the globe as "real" and

DOI: 10.4324/9781003463184-12

true' (Spillman et al., 2023a, p. 104). There is a need for a wider understanding of the potential of Indigenous pedagogies as models for PBE in Australian education, and learning can foster a connection to Country (Spillman et al., 2023b). The research also affirms meaningful engagement for young people to engage with Country through a Country as Teacher approach collectively. Such models allow teachers and students to cultivate a practice of relating with Country, where teachers increase their understanding of Country. It can also increase motivation and courage to engage students and use Country as a teacher (Spillman et al., 2023a) in curriculum and pedagogy.

Positioning ourselves in Indigenous education

It is important that we name our positionality because of the focus of this chapter. We are all Indigenous peoples from differing cultures and experienced educators. Four authors are Aboriginal scholars (Armour, Shay, Thomson, and Perkins), one Torres Strait Islander scholar (Cole), and one Māori scholar (McKinnon). We pay our respects to Elders past and present and thank them for caring for Country. We all have a common interest in supporting educators to embed Indigenous perspectives and knowledges into curriculum and assessment so Indigenous students can see their identity in schools and non-Indigenous students can benefit from Indigenous knowledges and perspectives.

Assessment and policy

Australian states and territories are responsible for assessing student learning under the Australian Curriculum (Australasian Curriculum, Assessment and Certification Authorities [ACACA], 2018). While embedding Indigenous perspectives has been highlighted as a national priority (ACARA, 2023b), many teachers still need to learn how to do this effectively. Hogarth (2022) suggests several factors cause this, including the fear of tokenism and making mistakes. Therefore, it is critical to understand how policy and programme approaches have impacted Indigenous place-based approaches to assessment. Assessment refers to the process of evaluating or measuring someone or something. It is a systematic and organised method to gather information and make judgements or decisions. In education, assessment measures students' knowledge, skills, and abilities. Assessment can be formative, providing feedback to improve learning during the instructional process, or summative, evaluating learning outcomes at the end of a period (Kulasegaram & Rangachari, 2018).

Under certain conditions, assessment has considerable potential to enhance learning. When embedding Indigenous perspectives within assessment practices, Assessment for Learning could benefit student learning. Assessment for Learning differentiates from standard assessment practices incorporated by teachers as it aims to promote student learning and not rank their ability to certify competence (Black & Wiliam, 2004). It should be adaptive, responsive, and student-centred, as well as support the professional needs of the teacher (Wiliam, 2011). This chapter advocates the potential of Assessment for Learning in embedding PBE perspectives.

Currently, numerous policies directly relate to Indigenous students and embedding Indigenous perspectives (Gillan et al., 2017). Of note, the Australian Professional Standards for Teachers require teachers to effectively address two focus areas related to this: 1.4 – Strategies for teaching Aboriginal and Torres Strait Islander students; and 2.4 – Understanding and respecting Aboriginal and Torres Strait Islander people to promote reconciliation between Indigenous and non-Indigenous Australians (Australian Institute for Teaching and School Leadership [AITSL], 2017). Another educational policy relating to the Indigenous perspectives in teaching and learning includes the Australian Curriculum's Aboriginal and Torres Strait Islander Histories and Cultures cross-curriculum priority. This aspect of the curriculum has three sets of organising ideas to explain each aspect of Country/Place, Culture, and People (ACARA, 2023b). Together, they identify what many First Nations Australians believe is essential cultural knowledge that all Australians should know. The rationale for PBE and assessment practices that incorporate Indigenous perspectives has considerable potential to impact these broader policy imperatives.

Set against the backdrop of rising geopolitical conflict, cascading climate emergencies, and growing wealth disparity, we argue that educators can surmount these paradoxes by drawing on our model to help them to build capacity for and with Country-centred knowledges and assessment practices. Indigenous place-based approaches call for a different orientation to consuming educational resources. Further, the rationale for Indigenous place-based approaches in assessment practices supports building a more coherent curriculum with Indigenous peoples that articulates a more cogent sense of identity, place, and belonging for all teachers and their students.

Indigenous ways of being, knowing, and doing

Our ways of being (ontology) cannot be separated from Country. Before colonisation, over 500 language groups maintained sovereign lands (Moreton-Robinson, 2013) in ways that sustained Country. Despite the impacts of colonisation, our ways of being in the world are continually informed by how we live, are taught to know, and belong to different tracts of Country through our bloodlines (Moreton-Robinson, 2013, p. 340). Our sense of belonging stems from the Dreaming and informs our understanding of how we are connected as Indigenous peoples (Moreton-Robinson, 2013, p. 340). Country also informs our ways of knowing (epistemology). How we have come to know is influenced by how we understand relationality (Moreton-Robinson, 2013, p. 341). As Indigenous peoples, we learn through cooperation, co-existence, shared experiences, obligation, and reciprocity (Moreton-Robinson, 2000). This learning is only possible due to how we are connected by descent, place, and Country as we experience ourselves as part of a collective, and the collective is part of us (Moreton-Robinson, 2013, p. 341). Our ways of doing (axiology) are an extension of our connections to Country as the way we operate within the world is an 'extension of our communal responsibilities and sovereignties' (Moreton-Robinson, 2013, p. 342).

Learning from and with Country to assess for, of, and as learning

Indigenous place-based approaches consider not just our location, but Country and its relationship with other entities. Providing opportunities to learn from and with Country enables other ways to see the world (Coff, 2021) using a strengths-based learning approach (Shay & Oliver, 2021). Using a place-based approach supports the inclusion of culture-fair assessment, the use of language, cultural content, developmental sequences, framing, content, interpretation, and reporting enabling different groups opportunities to demonstrate their knowledge application.

Spillman et al. (2023a) propose that relating with Country is preparing teachers to engage with using Country as Teacher and to enact the use of Country with students for learning. They suggest Country as Teacher experiences draw on Indigenous practices that teach students about creating a more sustainable, ecologically just society (Spillman et al., 2023a). Spillman et al. (2023a, 2023b) offer insight into how assessment might be considered through the lens of learning from Country as educators by relating *with* Country. Spillman et al. (2023a) suggested that teachers' experiences relating to Country are essential to the motivation and courage for enacting Country as Teacher curriculum and pedagogy.

In considering models of PBE evidenced by Spillman et al. (2023a), assessment could also be posed through the lens of learning from and with Country that uses Assessment *for*, *of*, and *as* Learning for both teacher and student. If building understanding of Country is essential to motivation and courage, then Assessment *for*, *of*, and *as* Learning could be considered as the three-pronged approach for students and teachers in their own professional growth and development that promotes Country as teacher with students.

Teachers' perceptions and motivations in relating with Country:

- Assessment *for* Learning: Planning based on what teachers know in relating with Country to inform their professional learning based on what they need to know to build capability and how to get there *(to understand themselves as teachers – Country – better what do they know? What do they need to know?)*.
- Assessment *as* Learning: Teachers reflecting on their own professional growth and progress – identifying their goals (e.g., to teach cross-curriculum priorities (CCPs), place-based).
- Assessment *of* Learning: Evidence to assess their practice and achievement.

Student engagement with Country as Teacher pedagogy:

- Assessment *for* Learning: Planning based on what students know to inform their learning based on what they need to know and how to get there.
- Assessment *as* Learning: Students reflecting on their progress – identifying their goals.
- Assessment *of Learning*: Teachers use the student's evidence to assess their achievement.

Indigenous perspectives in assessment 101

The next section visually outlines how the work of Spillman et al. (2023a) and our discussion of Assessment *for*, *of*, and *as* Learning informed our Indigenous place-based approach to assessment; this approach prioritises Country.

Conceptual framework

As depicted in Figure 9.1, Country should always be at the centre of Indigenous approaches to place-based assessment. Considering what we know about Western constructions of assessment, we depicted the 'for', 'as', and 'of' of assessment as surrounding Country. However, in this depiction, these constructions are influenced by the curved lines that connect the two, which suggests that learning from and with Country should occur constantly and in a less hierarchal way than in Western conceptions. At the top and bottom of the diagram, we relate with Country and Country as teacher (Spillman et al., 2023a); the curved connecting line suggests that these are equally important, and this process is cyclical.

Considering how this conceptualised framework could work in action, in line with our discussion about how current assessment approaches fail to prepare students to be effective custodians of Country, we contemplated the Sustainability cross-curriculum priority (CCP henceforth). In doing so, we agreed that Sustainability is intertwined and inseparable from Indigenous worldviews due to our relationship with Country. As seen in Figure 9.1, adding 'Custodianship and Stewardship' and 'Sustainable Practices' as an outer ring to our conceptual framework suggests that learning *from* and *with* Country – both as a teacher and through engaging relationally – promotes climate consciousness in all students.

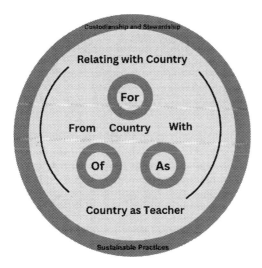

Figure 9.1 Indigenous place-based assessment conceptual framework informed by custodianship and sustainability.

This approach fosters students' sense of citizenship and environmental responsibility within their local community.

Applying Indigenous place-based assessment

Country/Place

As Country is a core element it will be based on content knowledge. However, many different learning areas can be included in the content learned from and with Country. As earlier explained, Country is a living, relational ecology of place that underpins Indigenous knowledges and spirituality (Morgan, 2019). Indigenous knowledges relate to cultural knowledge and values, language, and the interrelatedness of all living things particularly relating to where we are from (place). Incorporating Country or Indigenous knowledges and perspectives into assessment allows all students to have a more informed understanding of Indigenous peoples and the rich connection to Country. Educators should outline the content they would like to assess students on from Country/place and Indigenous perspectives and/or knowledges.

Culture

Refining curricula to incorporate Aboriginal voice and identity, student learning and assessment techniques need to be parallel to Aboriginal worldviews and ways of doing, ways of being, and ways of knowing (Cardinal et al., 2023; Martin, 2003). The way that students learn about Indigenous culture and how it is related will support all students to communicate and understand different cultural practices to their own (Rigney, 2023). Further, it also allows Indigenous students to feel proud of who they are and provides a culturally appropriate assessment that connects to their worldviews. This also allows all students to value the diverse cultural practices of Indigenous peoples in Australia.

Peoples

Indigenous peoples have made major contributions to Australia's landscape over the years. Using a strengths-based approach, teachers can focus on success stories of Indigenous peoples from the local area and the impact they have had on the community, and to extend on this can look at the impact from a national and global level (Shay & Oliver, 2021). As a core element interrelating with Country and culture, kinship can be explored as how it links to Country and how stories are linked through Country and family. Key aspects of quality assessment include collaborating and participating in collegial dialogue and work focusing on assessment practices. When planning a place-based curriculum with content involving Country/Indigenous knowledge and cultural practices, Indigenous community members should be involved to ensure protocols are being followed and the knowledge being shared is correct. Indigenous community members can provide collegial and community advice for educators (Armour, 2016).

Student interest/design

Student-centred assessment is a design element based on pedagogy and strategies that supports students to 'take responsibility for their own learning' (Klenowski, 1995, p. 153). It is a critical intersection between the educator and student where educators learn what students do or do not know, and students receive the feedback if they need to further their learning. Western pedagogies can be quite different to Indigenous ways of knowing, and using a student-centred approach allows Indigenous students to provide ideas for assessment that suit their learning and feedback to their peers. Assessment in student-centred learning allows the student to practice skills and review concepts as they move through the unit of work, ensuring that it reflects students' progress, learning needs, and individual strengths.

Ethical

Ethical assessment is transparent, so students can be meta-aware of the assessment implications, even if it is only an implicit awareness. It should demonstrate learning in its genuine context as much as possible and not cause harm to teachers or students (well-being). Both students and teachers should feel comfortable when assessing or being assessed. Ethical assessment should also frame Indigenous perspectives, knowledges, peoples, histories, and culture from a strengths-based approach (Shay & Oliver, 2021). In alignment with the core element of Peoples, assessment that reflects the priorities that community expresses are ethical and connects with Indigenous ways of knowing, being, and doing. Prioritising classroom assessments, particularly those that support culturally responsive and sustaining mindsets, is critical.

Authentic

Authentic assessment comes from a holistic approach so that students can develop deeper knowledge and critical reflection. It should be beneficial for all involved and involve real-life applications, for example, mitigating sea walls and mitigating fire. These examples align with how assessment can return something to the community and students should see value beyond the assessment. From an Indigenous lens, the elements in the assessment tool are designed so that Indigenous and Western perspectives are not in opposition. Students should be able to see that assessment is not only about the scale of achievement but also the content they are learning about.

Example of applying Indigenous place-based approaches to assessment – Climate change in the Torres Strait Islands

Following is an example of how you can apply Indigenous place-based approaches to assessment to a unit of work. This example is based on climate change in the Torres Strait Islands. The local Torres Strait Islander community has been concerned about climate change for years and has made multiple attempts to get government support for their concerns. These concerns included king tides, erosion, inundation of water, and coral bleaching of reefs and how these events affected the culture and homes of Torres Strait Islander peoples. However, the issues presented to the government were heard on deaf ears, so the community decided to band together, and in 2019, a group of eight Torres Strait Islander people took legal action and went to the United Nations Human Rights Committee (UNHCR). From this legal action, the UNHCR found that the Australian government violated human rights law through inadequate climate policy, were responsible for their emissions under international human rights law, and peoples' right to culture is at risk from climate impacts.

Torres Strait Islander peoples have a deep connection to their Country, and knowing the relatedness to Country for Indigenous peoples, you can understand that there is great concern in the community for Country and cultural practices that relate to Country. The CCPs used to teach this content are Aboriginal and Torres Strait Islander histories, culture, and sustainability, and the curriculum descriptors and elaborations can be chosen according to the key learning areas you are teaching and the grade level. The climate change content used in this example can be taught across any grade level and demonstrates how teachers can teach with Country and use Country as teacher.

In Table 9.1, the key concepts from the CCPs can be used to guide the assessment criteria.

The elements from applying Indigenous place-based approaches align with the CCPs. Some examples of how the assessment can be framed from a multi-grade level approach include understanding what climate change is and what the effect of

Table 9.1 Cross-curriculum priorities for assessment

Country	Sustainability
Country/Place	*SS3*
Recognises the special connection to Country/Place and celebrates the unique belief systems that connect Australian First Nations Peoples physically and spiritually to Country/Place	Social, economic and political systems influence the sustainability of Earth's systems
	SW2
Positions First Nations Australians as the Traditional Owners of Country/Place and highlights how native title law recognises the rights and interests of both the First Peoples of Australia and the First Nations Peoples of the Torres Strait in Country/Place	World views are formed by experiences at personal, local, national and global levels, and are linked to individual, community, business, and political actions for sustainability
	SD3
Acknowledges the impacts of colonisation and the doctrine of terra nullius on First Nations Australians' ownership of, and access to, Country/Place	Sustainable design requires an awareness of place, past practices, research and technological developments, and balanced judgements based on projected environmental, social, and economic impacts

Note: Adapted from ACARA (2023a, 2023c)

rising water levels can have on communities and Country. The Australian Curriculum science content descriptors have been included; however, more content descriptors can be included according to the learning areas that the assessment aligns with.

Grade 4

CURRICULUM DESCRIPTOR

Science – Earth's surface changes over time as a result of natural processes and human activity (ACSSU075).

ASSESSMENT

How does climate change impact Country in the Torres Strait Islands and the people that live there? Students will report on rising sea levels. They will unpack what this means and how Country has changed in the Torres Strait Islands because of the rising sea levels.

ASSESSMENT TOOL ELEMENTS

Country (effects on Country because of sea levels), Ethical (Climate change and developing an understanding of why issues in remote locations need to be reported on), Authentic (Torres Strait Islander peoples' ways of being, doing, and knowing align with Country – when Country hurts, people hurt).

Grade 7

CURRICULUM DESCRIPTOR

Science – Sudden geological changes and extreme weather events can affect Earth's surface (ACSSU096).

ASSESSMENT

Students compare the extreme weather from the Torres Strait Islands to the rest of Australia. Using timelines, they record the frequency of events in the Torres Strait Islands and their impact on Country as well as the extreme weather events in their local community. Once they complete the comparison, students peer assess their work to the criteria sheet and form groups of three and choose how they would like to present their work to the rest of the class (e.g., presentation, poster, speech, essay).

ASSESSMENT TOOL ELEMENTS

Country (impact of climate change on Country), Culture (how does climate change impact ways of knowing, being, and doing and well-being), People (who is telling us about climate change), Ethical (everyone should be aware of climate change in Australia), Authentic (climate change can affect cultural practices and ways of knowing, being, and doing – students are critically thinking), student design/input (students can decide how they present their assessment task).

Grade 9

CURRICULUM DESCRIPTOR

Science – Ecosystems consist of communities of interdependent organisms and abiotic components of the environment; matter and energy flow through these systems (ACSSU176).

ASSESSMENT

Students create a presentation or poster about the Torres Strait 8 (eight Torres Strait Islander community members that campaigned for change on climate change against the government) and define who they are, what they do, and what impact they had on the Torres Strait Islander community. Students can make a proposal on what they can campaign against in the local community in the presentation.

ASSESSMENT TOOL ELEMENTS

Country, People, Culture, Ethical (becoming aware of local community issues), Authentic (making connections between climate change in the Torres Strait Islands and issues in the community), Student input (students can choose something that interests them that they would like to campaign about).

Conclusion

The more students learn about place-based knowledge, the more they can start having real-world experiences and better understand the world around them. Implementing Indigenous knowledge and perspectives using a place-based approach can improve students' critical thinking. Educators can use Country, Culture, and Peoples to grow students' knowledge and skills. Coming from a strengths-based approach, this is not about measuring and ranking students but supporting them in understanding the world around them. Our identity as Indigenous peoples is always grounded in our connection to Country and this is framed by our relationships to Country and to other people (Graham, 2008). Living on Indigenous land means all children born in Australia are inherently connected to Indigenous peoples' stories of connection with Earthkin and Country; we must ensure that all children can benefit from this rich knowledge and that this is part of their birthright, as 'these connections lie within us all' (Spillman et al., 2023a, p. 104; Milroy & Milroy, 2008).

> **Questions for reflection**
>
> The questions can be used before or after a unit of work.
>
> *How does this apply to me as a beginning teacher or an experienced teacher?*
>
> *How will this improve my practice and benefit my students?*
>
> *What are the next steps that I need to take to apply to my next assessment/ unit of learning?*
>
> *What will be my evidence to assess my own practice?*

References

Armour, D. (2016). *Aboriginal education officers working at the cultural interface: Nguli yoo boy ngoo Yulling Ngunya* [Doctoral dissertation, Australian Catholic University]. https://acuresearchbank.acu.edu.au/

Australasian Curriculum, Assessment and Certification Authorities (ACACA). (2018). *Assessment and reporting*. https://www.acaca.edu.au/index.php/schooling/assessment-and-reporting/#:~:text=Assessment%20is%20the%20process%20of,improving%20teaching%20and%20learning%20programs

Australian Curriculum, Assessment and Reporting Authority (ACARA). (2023a) *Aboriginal and Torres Strait Islander histories and cultures.* https://v9.australiancurriculum.edu.au/f-10-curriculum/cross-curriculum-priorities/aboriginal-and-torres-strait-islander-histories-and-cultures?organising-idea=0

Australian Curriculum, Assessment and Reporting Authority (ACARA). (2023b). *Planning, teaching, assessing and reporting*. https://v9.australiancurriculum.edu.au/f-10-curriculum/f-10-curriculum-overview/planning-teaching-assessing

Australian Curriculum, Assessment and Reporting Authority (ACARA). (2023c). *Sustainability*. https://v9.australiancurriculum.edu.au/f-10-curriculum/cross-curriculum-priorities/sustainability?organising-idea=0

Australian Institute for Teaching and School Leadership (AITSL). (2017). *Aboriginal and Torres Strait Islander education*. https://www.aitsl.edu.au/deliver-ite-programs/aboriginal-and-torres-strait-islander-education

Bartholomaeus, P. (2013). Place-based education and the Australian Curriculum. *Literacy Learning: The Middle Years, 21*(3), 17–23. https://search.informit.org/doi/10.3316/aeipt.200572

Black, P., & Wiliam, D. (2004). The formative purpose: Assessment must first promote learning. *Yearbook of the National Society for the Study of Education, 103*(2), 20–50.

Cardinal, T., Murphy, M. S., Huber, J., & Pinnegar, S. (2023). (Re)making assessment in the trans-systemic space shaped in the meeting of personal, Indigenous, and relational ways of knowing and being. *Studying Teacher Education, 19*(2), 186–203. https://doi.org/10.1080/17425964.2022.2137127

Coff, K. (2021). Learning on and from Country – Teaching by incorporating Indigenous Relational worldviews. In M. Shay & R. Oliver (Eds.), *Indigenous education in Australia* (pp. 190–201). Taylor & Francis Group. https://doi.org/10.4324/9780429263453

Gillan, K. P., Mellor, S., & Krakouer, J. (2017). *The case for urgency: Advocating for Indigenous voice in education*. ACER Press.

Graham, M. (2008). Some thoughts about the philosophical underpinnings of Aboriginal worldviews. *Australian Humanities Review, 45*, 181–194.

Hogarth, M. (2022). An analysis of education academics' attitudes and preconceptions about Indigenous Knowledges in initial teacher education. *Australian Journal of Indigenous Education, 51*(2), 1–18. https://doi.org/10.55146/ajie.v51i2.41

Klenowski, V. (1995). Student self-evaluation processes in student-centred teaching and learning contexts of Australia and England. *Assessment in Education: Principles, Policy & Practice, 2*(2), 145–163. https://doi.org/10.1080/0969594950020203

Kulasegaram, K., & Rangachari, P. K. (2018). Beyond 'formative': Assessments to enrich student learning. *Advances in Physiology Education, 42*(1), 5–14. https://doi.org/10.1152/advan.00122.2017

Martin, K. L. (2003). Ways of knowing, being and doing: A theoretical framework and methods for Indigenous and Indigenist re-search. *Journal of Australian Studies, 27*(76), 203–214.

Milroy, G., & Milroy, J. (2008). Different ways of knowing: Trees are our families too. In S. Morgan, T. Mia, & B. Kwaymilla (Eds.), *Heartsick for country: Stories of love, spirit and creation* (pp. 22–42). Fremantle Press.

Moreton-Robinson, A. (2000). Troubling business: Difference and whiteness within feminism. *Australian Feminist Studies, 15*(33), 343–352.

Moreton-Robinson, A. (2013). Towards an Australian Indigenous women's standpoint theory. *Australian Feminist Studies, 28*(78), 331–347. https://doi.org/10.1080/08164649.2013.876664

Morgan, B. (2019). Beyond the guest paradigm: Eurocentric education and Aboriginal peoples in NSW. In E. A. McKinley & L. Tuhiwai Smith (Eds.), *Handbook of Indigenous education* (pp. 111–128). Springer.

Rigney, L. I. (2023). Teachers cultivating Aboriginal child as knowledge producer: Advancing Australian culturally responsive pedagogies. In L. Rigney (Ed.), *Global perspectives and new challenges in culturally responsive pedagogies* (pp. 10–19). Routledge.

Shay, M., & Oliver, R. (Eds.). (2021). *Indigenous education in Australia: Learning and teaching for deadly futures*. Taylor & Francis Group. https://doi.org/10.4324/9780429263453

Smith, G. A. (2002). Place-based education: Learning to be where we are. *Phi Delta Kappan, 83*(8), 584–594. https://doi.org/10.1177/003172170208300806

Spillman, D., Wilson, B., Nixon, M., & McKinnon, K. (2023a). 'New localism' in Australian schools: Country as Teacher as a critical pedagogy of place. *Curriculum Perspectives, 43*(2), 103–114. https://doi.org/10.1007/s41297-023-00201-2

Spillman, D., Wilson, B., Nixon, M., & McKinnon, K. (2023b). Reinvigorating Country as teacher in Australian schooling: Beginning with school teacher's direct experiences, 'relating with Country'. *Curriculum Perspectives, 43*(1), 13–23.

Wiliam, D. (2011). What is assessment for learning? *Studies in Educational Evaluation, 37*(1), 3–14. https://doi.org/10.1016/j.stueduc.2011.03.001

10 Queer(y)ing primary assessment
Bodies, genders, and sexuality diversity

Lisa van Leent and Michelle Jeffries

Diverse bodies, genders, and sexualities in schools

Children with diverse bodies, genders, and sexualities exist in all classrooms and schools (Blaise, 2009; Renold, 2006; Robinson, 2005; van Leent & Walsh, 2020). Statistically, the accuracy of collecting data about human diversity in relation to bodies, genders, and sexualities is difficult due to variations in definitions, questions, and desire to capture such data (Carman et al., 2020). However, the Australian Human Rights Commission (2014) suggests that 11 out of 100 people might have diverse bodies, genders, and/or sexualities. This means in a classroom of 25 children or young people, three might identify as lesbian, gay, bisexual, trans, or queer. Intersex children make up a further 1.7% of the population (Australian Human Rights Commission, 2014). If these statistics are extrapolated to include LGBTIQA+ school staff, parents, and caregivers, the number of people identifying as gender or sexuality diverse (GSD) within schools and schooling communities continues to expand. Moreover, as recent research suggests, higher percentages of young people may identify as GSD (Fisher et al., 2019), and there is no population-level data reflecting statistics about gender diversity in Australia (including those identifying as transgender, non-binary, agender, and so on) (Carman et al., 2020), so the population of GSD young people in schools could indeed be higher than the statistics suggest.

Unfortunately, schools are often not safe places for learning and belonging for LGBTIQA+ children, young people, teachers, and families. Children in schools experience 80% of homophobic bullying at school (Australian Human Rights Commission, 2014), for example. Similarly, teachers who identify as GSD experience ongoing barriers to being themselves in schools, being safe, and even face legal discrimination such as being excluded from being able to work in religious schools (Callaghan & van Leent, 2019; Ferfolja & Stavrou, 2015). LGBTIQA+ parents and their families also experience a range of difficulties related to schools due to processes, policies, and issues with representation and recognition of diverse family forms (Jeffries, 2021). The good news is there are many strategies that schools and teachers can employ to improve student attendance, retention, and academic outcomes, and a sense of belonging for all, including teachers and school leaders.

DOI: 10.4324/9781003463184-13

Queer(y)ing diverse bodies, genders, and sexualities in education

One strategy to promote schools as socially just and safe learning places for children, teachers, and their families is curriculum and assessment practices that recognise that people with diverse bodies, genders, and sexualities exist in schools, and in the real world. Through queer(y)ing the hetero-cis-norms[1] that are represented in resources, language, curriculum, assessment, infrastructure, and everyday interactions, more socially just practices of representation and recognition can be undertaken.

Queer theory encourages 'challenging the multiple oppressions in our lives … [and] requires challenging the many norms that privilege and marginalise different groups or simply different ways of being' (Kumashiro, 2003, pp. 366–367). Kumashiro (2003) nestles queer theory in education as a necessary politics for social justice, arguing for the disruption of norms and celebration of difference. Queer pedagogy has emerged as an effective way to interrupt normative notions of gender and sexuality in education. Britzman (1995, p. 165) describes queer pedagogy as

> one that refuses normal practices and practices of normalcy, one that begins with an ethical concern for one's own reading practices, one that is interested in exploring what one cannot bear to know, one interested in the imagining of a sociality unhinged from the dominant conceptual order.

Here, Britzman talks about the importance of stepping outside of dominant societal norms to think about things in new ways. Research shows that normative notions of gender operate heavily in education contexts and that schools are constructed as non-sexualised spaces while silently reinforcing heterosexuality as the norm (Britzman, 1995; Renold, 2006; van Leent & Spina, 2023). These normative discourses operate alongside notions of childhood-as-innocence to create schooling contexts in which there can be limited to no recognition of gender and sexuality diversity. It can be challenging for teachers to imagine a society outside of these norms or to 'explore what one cannot bear to know', because such thinking moves away from dominant social orders for teachers. For instance, some may not consider that children in the early years or in primary school may be genderqueer or dream of marrying their same-sex friend, yet there are many such stories told by LGBTIQA+ adults about such experiences when reflecting back on their early lives. Robinson (2005) explains how binary genders and heterosexuality are powerfully normalised in early childhood settings thus rendering ways of being beyond such binary constructions as irrelevant, taboo, invisible, and intolerable. Robinson (2005, p. 26) describes queer pedagogy as encouraging 'educators to ask questions that highlight and challenge how particular ways of doing gender and sexuality are normalised to the point that they become unquestionable'. In other words, she challenges teachers to think about dominant ideas circulating in society, for example, there being only two genders, male and female, and the many ways in which ideas about gender and sexuality are presented as unquestionable truths.

Scholars have been calling for the 'queer(y)ing' of primary school practices related to curriculum, pedagogy, and assessment for decades. For instance, various scholars in Letts and Sears' (1999) edited book called for the dismantling of oppressive structures that relate to schooling, fostering an environment that values diversity and then acknowledging the potential fluidity of some identities. By integrating LGBTIQA+ perspectives into the curriculum, educators can provide a more accurate and representative portrayal of the real people who exist in the world, promoting empathy, understanding, and a sense of belonging for all. In doing so, not only do we consider the queer bodies of children who do or may identify with LGBTIQA+ identities, we think about children who know about and already celebrate queer lives and ways of being, such as children who have queer families and friends (Pallotta-Chiarolli, 2000). Further, when gender and sexuality diversity is recognised, represented, and included in education, young people have the opportunity to learn about this diversity and challenge issues such as homophobia and transphobia, creating a potentially more socially just world (Davies & Robinson, 2013). This responsibility of voice and representation cannot belong to children and young people who identify with LGBTIQA+ identities alone and all students should be provided opportunities to be strong allies and engage in leadership related to such matters in schooling contexts.

In this chapter, we think of queer(y)ing assessment as including the objects and subjects of sex, gender, and sexuality, but also moving 'beyond the subjects and objects of sex, gender and sexuality' (Rasmussen & Allen, 2014, p. 442). Queer theory can help deconstruct and challenge rigid categories of identities and social norms. Queer theory also allows us to develop understandings that extend beyond gender and sexuality identities and see that it can support a critical examination of normative structures, social constructions, and subsequent power dynamics (Meyer, 2007). It is important for teachers to understand that people are not entirely defined by their bodies, gender, and sexuality and that queer theory can promote intersectionality of identity and teachers can work to highlight the interconnectedness of different ways of being such as cultures, genders, abilities, and sexualities. This can help teachers to recognise diverse and complex experiences of children and young people, and the systems that work to construct them, in order to create more aware, safe, and celebratory learning environments.

Diverse bodies, genders, and sexualities in assessment policy

In Australia, states and territories are responsible for setting school-based assessment practices. In Queensland, for example, the Queensland Curriculum and Assessment Authority (QCAA) has an assessment policy regarding equitable assessment practices.

The QCAA (2021) defines the principles of equitable practices as:

> All young people in Queensland are entitled to an education that meets their needs, and prepares them for active participation in the creation of a socially just, equitable and democratic global society. Teachers can support students to access a socially just education by:
>
> - Designing teaching, learning and assessment activities that are socially and culturally responsive and inclusive.

- Ensuring access and participation for all learners, on the same basis as their peers.
- Making adjustments, where required, to enhance engagement and equitable outcomes for all students.
- Acknowledging the diverse bodies of knowledge, backgrounds and families of all students.

Assessment is equitable if it provides opportunities for every student to demonstrate what they know and can do.

Each of these points can be queer(ie)d for the purposes of understanding how these principles might be applied to queer bodies, genders, and sexualities and to normalised assessment practices. The point related to assessment activities that are socially just and culturally responsive would recognise, with a queer(y)ing lens, that children with diverse bodies, genders, and sexualities exist in classrooms everywhere and should be included in assessments as visible identities. The second point is related to parity of participation which leads us to consider if 'boy' identities and 'girl' identities are represented in literature, assessment scenarios, and images on worksheets and textbooks, for example, then so should non-binary, trans, and queer identities; parity of participation requires representation of all learners (Hermann-Wilmarth & Ryan, 2015). The third regarding adjustments for children who have been omitted from curricula and assessment practices should expand to queer representations in curriculum resources, assessment tools, and teachers' practices such as their everyday language. The fourth point means that schools and teachers can acknowledge the knowledge that they bring to school already and the reality of their backgrounds and their families. Queerly raised children exist and need a voice (Pallotta-Chiarolli, 2000), and queer families exist too and their knowledge of diversity should be valued in primary schools through curriculum and assessment practices (Jeffries, 2021).

Because assessment should align with curriculum, it is logical to ensure representation in assessment practices following queer curriculum practices. These points laid out by the assessment authority in Queensland align with what theorists have been advocating for decades. As Connell (1992) notes, democratic approaches to curriculum, which we argue extend to assessment practices, mean that if taken seriously, children should have a voice in their assessments including who is represented in the curriculum and assessment material. Social justice is more than an add-on to education; it should underpin and form the foundation for curriculum and assessment practices (Connell, 1992).

Queer(y)ing assessment practices – The literature

Although the body of work relating to queer pedagogy has grown significantly over time, there is limited literature focusing on queer(y)ing assessment. However, what has been written about this topic provides some foundational ideas important to this chapter and our thinking. Two important aspects discussed in the literature include queer(y)ing gender and sexuality normativities in assessment practices and queer(y)ing the ways in which assessment is undertaken more generally.

Queer(y)ing gender and sexuality normativities

One way that assessment can be queered is through deconstructing normative representations and understandings of gender and sexuality in assessment practices and reconstructing them through a queer lens. This approach reflects the importance of ensuring that LGBTIQA+ identities are included and reflected both within assessments and assessment practices. Thomas-Reid (2021, p. 12) states that

> assessment privileges normative bodies, through the heteronormative and cisnormative curation of the content to be assessed, the heteronormative and cis-normative curation of the standards to be assessed, and even in the procedures used, which often require trans* students to deadname themselves (use a name associated with a gender or identity that they do not possess) on a summative examination because this is the name on their permanent record.

What Thomas-Reid is referring to here is that assessment content, standards, and processes tend to draw on dominant normative notions of gender and sexuality (such as the perspective that there are just two genders – male and female – and that one's gender aligns with one's sex recorded at birth) as well as content reflecting hetero-cis-norms, rather than a range of genders and sexualities. Such an approach not only excludes and makes invisible LGBTIQA+ identities, it also advantages students who have normative understandings of gender and sexuality. Supporting this idea, Guerrero et al. (2017, p. 2) share concerns that culturally responsive pedagogy has been theorised as important to improving student outcomes and assisting with disengagement with a notable 'omission of critical conversations addressing gender identity, LGBTQ identities and the ways in which they figure into the lived experiences of students'. Deconstructing and queer(y)ing assessment practices is an important part of creating safe and socially just schooling spaces for a range of identities, rather than just those who identify with dominant social norms.

Queer(y)ing assessment approaches/practices

Queer(y)ing involves critical examination of normative structures, social constructions, and subsequent power dynamics beyond gender and sexuality diversity. Thomas-Reid (2021), for example, suggests one way of queering assessment could be to ask students how they might best be able to demonstrate their learning, rather than using prescribed assessment tasks. It is clear here that this kind of approach shifts the usual power dynamics of assessment, where those in power provide an assessment piece to students through which they need to perform in particular ways to pass or exceed expectations. While this is not a focus of this particular chapter, we encourage teachers and those involved in the creation of assessment to consider ways in which they can queer(y) approaches to assessment.

114 *Lisa van Leent and Michelle Jeffries*

A warning from the literature

The literature warns us that providing specific examples of ways to queer assessment can be counterproductive when thinking through a queer theoretical lens. This is because the premise of queer(y)ing involves thinking about the familiar in new ways, as well as deconstructing, troubling, and resisting norms. This means that in providing examples of how to queer assessment, we risk reifying particular ideas and establishing new regulatory regimes. This is reflected by Thomas-Reid (2021, p. 13) when they state that:

> I suggest ... that trying to give examples of queer assessment would be somewhat counterproductive, as they might well form a blueprint for assessment that would defeat the point of a queer method.

As authors, we take Thomas-Reid's point on board; however, we also think it is important to provide some practical ideas for teachers as to how they might consider queer(y)ing assessment. As such, we do not provide these ideas as a blueprint or a checklist for ways to queer(y) assessment. Rather, we offer these ideas as the beginning point of a conversation, some ideas to perhaps think about the familiar in new ways, and some ways to trouble GSD norms in assessment. We do this with the hope that teachers will continue to interrogate and deconstruct such norms in assessment and find new ways forward, and to engage in conversations about making assessment more equitable.

Focusing in on queer(y)ing assessment practices – Real-world assessment practices

This section will look at three important and practical ways that teachers can consider GSD-inclusive practices in assessment:

1 Teachers' own assessment practices/designs (e.g., vignettes, etc.).
2 Assessment designed by others including high-stakes assessment.
3 Reporting on big data (e.g., girls/boys).

Whilst it might be impossible to arrive at queer pedagogy for assessment as noted earlier, we can share some examples of que(e)ring assessment pedagogies that primary school teachers can lean into.

Teachers' own assessment practices/designs

Designing and implementing formative and summative assessment is an important part of teachers' everyday work. An important aspect of queer(y)ing assessment is to consider norms about gender and sexuality diversity that might be implicit within assessment tasks and practices. A queer approach encourages teachers to question the 'normalcy' of the patterns of language, to consider what norms are being

Queer(y)ing primary assessment   115

(re)produced about genders and sexualities, and to think about who/what is not included. Following, we provide some practical examples as a beginning point to thinking. As noted before, these are just a starting point for teachers to begin thinking about how to ensure that LGBTIQA+ identities are considered in planning for assessment.

- When using vignettes in primary school, such as those common in mathematics word problems, there is opportunity to reflect on normativities and diversity can be reflected. For instance, we can ensure a variety of family types are represented, rather than just mum/dad families. Similarly, in vignettes using pronouns such as he/him and she/her, we can also use they/them (in the singular) to reflect genderqueer, non-binary, or agender identities.
- Where we include pictorial representations of people, we can think about how we have represented gender, families, and so on, and consider how to include a range of visual representations.
- In relation to grammar, if a student chooses the pronoun 'they' to represent a singular individual, rather than 'he' or 'she', we can recognise that 'they' can be used in the singular (not just for plural). 'They' and 'them' are accepted singular pronouns for individuals, especially if they identify as genderqueer or gender nonconforming (they/them are only two of many pronouns used by individuals who may identify as genderqueer and/or nonconforming, etc.) (Van Horn, 2022, p. 59; Pickering & van Leent, 2024). Other pronouns include 'ze' and 'hir' and 'xi' or just using someone's name only, without the use of generalised pronouns.
- One approach teachers can take when assessing student writing is to ask 'who is privileged and who is othered' in the work and 'reflect on the consequences of such privileging and othering' in order to challenge students to think through the contributions of their writing (Blackburn & Beucher, 2019, p. 38). So, a teacher might recognise the insightful language choices which engage queer understandings about gender and language and how these are often constructed together as hetero-cis-normative in children's writing.

Assessment designed by others including high-stakes assessment

Assessment designed by others including high-stakes assessment typically omits queer identities or ideas. Van Horn (2022, p. 59) states that:

> Sometimes state testing and required pre- and post-assessment data are used as reasons for not including social justice topics, specifically queer literacy. Since there is no question that explicitly asks about queer literacy on a state test, it may not seem as important. When teachers begin to reflect on the taken-for-granted practices though, they will begin to see how queer literacy illuminates what was already there.

National and state testing, for example, the Grade 6 civics and citizenship online demonstration test (National Assessment Program [NAP], 2023), covers topics such as national identity, religious rights, and international working conditions, but not topics about genders or sexualities or diverse families. In queer theory, this is known as performativity. This idea comes from Butler (1990/2007, 1993/2011) and relates to how repeating something over and over again reinforces it as natural and normal and less likely to be questioned. Butler's theory suggests that if we trouble these norms, there is potential for shifts to occur. In other words, as omissions of LGBTIQA+ identities within curricula are questioned and troubled, and considered/included within assessment, possibilities unfold for assessment to be undertaken in more socially just ways.

Reporting on big data (e.g., girls/boys)

Classroom, school, and broader government assessments continue to place children into binary gender boxes of male/female. We return to national testing data that is collected in Australia which only in 2022 revised the Data Standards Manual to replace 'sex characteristic specifications with gender' and they report 'While the responses to be collected has been broadened, only male and female will be reported' (Australian Curriculum, Assessment and Reporting Authority [ACARA], 2022). This pronouncement disregards the range of body diversity and genders that children identify with and now can have recorded on the national testing except they are not included in the reporting of results; a very queer practice, with seemingly a dearth of evidence as to why this information is important to collect. Further, such an approach again reinforces normative notions of gender, providing little support for teachers to question such normativities and, rather, encourages continued binary demarcation of students, and associating particular outcomes with such genders. We note this here to encourage teachers to think beyond and outside the boxes that are performatively (re)constructed through the reporting of data.

Conclusion

Engaging queer theory in education requires ongoing practices that work to challenge assumptions, dismantle biases, and create spaces that celebrate the diversity of human identity.

Note

1 Worthen (2020, p. 25) defines hetero-cis-normativity as 'the system of norms, privilege, and oppression that situates heterosexual cisgender people above all others and thus, places LGBTQ people in a place of systemic disadvantage'. In other words, social power is organised around sexuality and gender, with cisgender and heterosexual identities positioned as 'normal' and natural and those who identify as GSD as abnormal. The author notes that 'hetero-cis-normative thinking is built from norms, stereotypes, and presumptions that often begin with sex assigned at birth (which is frequently confined to a male/female dichotomy) ... [and that] From there, presumptions about gender identity, gender performance/expression, and heterosexuality flow as part of the larger system of hetero-cis-normativity' (pp. 25–26). Worthen makes clear that this normative lens can lead to a view that prejudice against GSD people is acceptable.

References

Australian Curriculum, Assessment and Reporting Authority (ACARA). (2022). *Data standards manual: Student background characteristics.* https://www.acara.edu.au/reporting/student-background-data-collection-for-independent-schools

Australian Human Rights Commission. (2014). *Face the facts: Lesbian, gay, bisexual, trans and intersex people.* Australian Human Rights Commission. https://humanrights.gov.au/our-work/education/face-facts-lesbian-gay-bisexual-trans-and-intersex-people

Blackburn, M. V., & Beucher, B. (2019). Productive tensions in assessment: Troubling sociocritical theories toward an advancement of queer pedagogy. In C. Mayo & N. M. Rodriguez (Eds.), *Queer pedagogies: Theory, praxis, politics* (pp. 23–40). Springer.

Blaise, M. (2009). 'What a girl wants, what a girl needs': Responding to sex, gender, and sexuality in the early childhood classroom. *Journal of Research in Childhood Education, 23*(4), 450–460. https://doi.org/10.1080/02568540909594673

Britzman, D. (1995). Is there a queer pedagogy? Or, stop reading straight. *Educational Theory, 45*(2), 151–165. https://doi.org/10.1111/j.1741-5446.1995.00151.x

Butler, J. (2007). *Gender trouble: Feminism and the subversion of identity.* Routledge (Original work published 1990).

Butler, J. (2011). *Bodies that matter.* Routledge (Original work published 1993).

Callaghan, T., & van Leent, L. (2019). Homophobia in Catholic schools: An exploration of teachers' rights and experiences in Canada and Australia. *Journal of Catholic Education, 22*(3), 36–57. http://dx.doi.org/10.15365/joce.2203032019

Carman, M., Farrugia, C., Bourne, A., Power, J., & Rosenberg, S. (2020). *Research matters: How many people are LGBTIQ? A fact sheet by Rainbow Health Victoria.* Latrobe University. https://www.rainbowhealthvic.org.au/media/pages/research-resources/research-matters-how-many-people-are-lgbtiq/4170611962-1612761890/researchmatters-numbers-lgbtiq.pdf

Connell, R. W. (1992). Citizenship, social justice and curriculum. *International Studies in Sociology of Education, 2*(2), 133–146. https://doi.org/10.1080/0962021920020202

Davies, C., & Robinson, K. H. (2013). Reconceptualising family: Negotiating sexuality in a governmental climate of neoliberalism. *Contemporary Issues in Early Childhood, 14*(1), 39–53. https://doi.org/10.2304/ciec.2014.14.1.39

Ferfolja, T., & Stavrou, E. (2015). Workplace experiences of Australian lesbian and gay teachers: Findings from a national survey. *Canadian Journal of Educational Administration and Policy,* (173), 113–138. https://www.umanitoba.ca/publications/cjeap/pdf_files/qecb7-Ferfolja_Stavrou.pdf

Fisher, C., Waling, A., Kerr, L., Bellamy, R., Ezer, P., Mikolajczak, M., Brown, G., Carman, M., & Lucke, J. (2019). *National survey of secondary students and sexual health 2018: Results of the 6th national survey of Australian secondary students and sexual health.* Australian Research Centre in Sex, Health and Society, La Trobe University. https://www.latrobe.edu.au/__data/assets/pdf_file/0004/1031899/National-Survey-of-Secondary-Students-and-Sexual-Health-2018.pdf

Guerrero, C., Shahnazarian, A., & Brown, M. F. (2017). Queer(y)ing culture through professional learning communities: A reimagining of culturally relevant and responsive pedagogy. *PennGSE Perspectives on Urban Education, 13*(2), 1–12.

Hermann-Wilmarth, J. M., & Ryan, C. (2015). Doing what you can: Considering ways to address LGBT topics in language arts curricula. *Language Arts, 92*(6), 436–443.

Jeffries, M. (2021). *Experiences of gender and sexuality diverse parents in primary schools* [Doctoral thesis, Queensland University of Technology].

Kumashiro, K. K. (2003). Queer ideals in education. *Journal of Homosexuality, 45*(2–4), 365–367. https://doi.org/10.1300/J082v45n02_23

Letts, I. W. J., & Sears, J. T. (Eds.). (1999). *Queering elementary education.* Rowman & Littlefield Publishers, Inc.

Meyer, E. J. (2007). 'But I'm not gay': What straight teachers need to know about queer theory. In W. F. Pinar & N. M. Rodriguez (Eds.), *Queering straight teachers* (pp. 15–32). Peter Lang Publishing.

National Assessment Program (NAP). (2023). *National Assessment Program example test*. Australian Government. https://demo.assessform.edu.au/testattempt/sample/x00109514

Pallotta-Chiarolli, M. (2000). What do they think? Queerly raised and queer-friendly students. *Youth Studies Australia, 19*(4), 34–40.

Pickering, J., & van Leent, L. (2024). Teaching English and the grammatical use of the pronoun: Queer(y)ing the teaching of writing. *The Reading Teacher, 78*, 37–45. https://doi.org/10.1002/trtr.2312

Queensland Curriculum and Assessment Authority (QCAA). (2021). *Principles of quality assessment*. https://www.qcaa.qld.edu.au/about/k-12-policies/student-assessment/understanding-assessment/principles-quality-assessment

Rasmussen, M. L., & Allen, L. (2014). What can a concept do? Rethinking education's queer assemblages. *Discourse: Studies in the Cultural Politics of Education, 35*(3), 433–443. https://doi.org/10.1080/01596306.2014.888846

Renold, E. (2006). 'They won't let us play ... unless you're going out with one of them': Girls, boys and Butler's 'heterosexual matrix' in the primary years. *British Journal of Sociology of Education, 27*(4), 489–509. https://doi.org/10.1080/01425690600803111

Robinson, K. (2005). 'Queerying' gender: Heteronormativity in early childhood education. *Australian Journal of Early Childhood, 30*(2), 19–28. https://doi.org/10.1177/183693910503000206

Thomas-Reid, M. (2021). Queer pedagogical theory. In *Oxford Research Encyclopaedia of Education*. https://doi.org/10.1093/acrefore/9780190264093.013.1398

Van Horn, S. E. (2022). *Towards queer literacy in elementary education: Always becoming allies*. Palgrave Macmillan.

van Leent, L., & Spina, N. (2023). Teachers' representations of genders and sexualities in primary school: The power of curriculum and an institutional ideological code. *Australian Educational Researcher, 50*, 683–700. https://doi.org/10.1007/s13384-022-00515-6

van Leent, L., & Walsh, K. (2020). Sexuality and sexualization in childhood (Australia). In L. Perry & W. Corsaro (Eds.), *Bloomsbury education and childhood studies*. Bloomsbury Publishing. https://doi.org/10.5040/9781350996519.004

Worthen, M. G. F. (2020). *Queers, bis, and straight lies: An intersectional examination of LGBTQ stigma*. Routledge.

11 Embracing translanguaging in designing inclusive assessments with learners of English as an additional language or dialect

Ronan Kelly and Maria Stewart

Introduction

Approximately 40% of the world's school-age population do not have access to education in a language they regularly use or understand (UNESCO, 2016). In many Western countries such as Australia, the United Kingdom, and the USA a significant proportion of school students are multilingual and accessing education while both learning English and learning content through the medium of English. These multilingual, or English as an additional language or dialect (EAL/D), students bring a diverse range of languages, knowledges, and resources to school with them. However, their academic attainment is measured through a narrow monolingual, English-only lens which is misaligned with the reality of their fluid knowledges and abilities across multiple languages (Li & García, 2022; Welply, 2023). These partial assessments of EAL/D students' abilities have serious implications for their opportunities to progress through education systems and contribute to existing deficit perspectives surrounding them. There is an imperative to design more inclusive and valid assessments which fully represent EAL/D students' knowledges and abilities.

In this chapter, we present translanguaging as a theory and pedagogic approach which offers a pathway for teachers to design inclusive school-based assessments for EAL/D learners. We begin by considering who EAL/D learners are and defining how translanguaging represents the reality of their meaning making and communicative practices. Following this, validity and equity issues with current monolingual and monomodal assessment designs are identified and unpacked. The chapter concludes by identifying research-based approaches to embedding translanguaging in assessment designs and evaluating EAL/D learners' assessment artefacts when they contain features of multiple languages and modes.

Who are EAL/D learners?

A range of terminologies have been utilised to describe pupils who do not primarily use the dominant language of their school setting. Given the heterogeneous nature of this group, it is important that educators carefully consider the language *they* use to define those learners (Cunningham, 2019). These students can broadly

DOI: 10.4324/9781003463184-14

include immigrants and refugees, Indigenous students, international students, and children born in the country of their schooling. There have been extensive 'tussles with terminology' in research literature and educational policies around the terms used to describe multilingual learners (Cunningham, 2019, p. 125). One of the most commonly used terms internationally is English as an Additional Language (EAL), referring to those who 'may use one or more languages other than English in their everyday lives' (Bracken et al., 2016, p. 6). Multilingual learners have also been referred to as English Language Learners (ELL), English as a Second Language (ESL), English as a Second or Other Language (ESOL), or Limited English Proficiency (LEP), the latter of which being phased out due to negative connotations (Carder, 2009). In Australia, the term EAL has been expanded to English as an additional language or dialect (EAL/D) to include students who use dialects beyond standard Australian English (Australian Curriculum, Assessment and Reporting Authority [ACARA], 2014). The inclusion of the word *additional* denotes the act of adding to an already-existent language repertoire and perhaps creates a more nuanced understanding of these learners (Bracken et al., 2016). However, the difficulty with the term EAL/D is that it encompasses a hugely diverse range of learners and does not take cognisance of an individual student's sociocultural background across language, culture, race, and migration history among many other factors. It is not surprising then that against this backdrop, assessment practices also fail to acknowledge pupils' prior experiences or their full linguistic repertoires. While noting the inherent issues with any term attempting to represent such a diverse cohort of students, we use EAL/D as a more inclusive and appropriate term than others discussed.

Translanguaging

Translanguaging is a theory and a pedagogic approach which engages with the reality of how multilingual students make meaning and communicate. As a theory, it is defined as the 'act performed by bilinguals of accessing different linguistic features or various modes of what are described as autonomous languages, in order to maximize communicative potential' (García, 2009, p. 140). Rather than switching between several distinct (i.e., named) language systems, it is now widely accepted that multilingual students make meaning and communicate by drawing on all the linguistic and multimodal resources available to them within a single integrated system (Blackledge & Creese, 2010; Canagarajah, 2011; Lewis et al., 2012; Li, 2018). Translanguaging extends beyond linguistic features and refers to a learner's semiotic repertoire which additionally incorporates diverse multimodalities, genres, registers, and symbols (Li, 2018). Translanguaging pedagogy is an approach which supports students to draw on their full semiotic repertoires by using all of the linguistic resources, modes, genres, registers, gestures, and symbols available to them in learning (Conteh, 2019; Flores & Schissel, 2014; García et al., 2017). Translanguaging theory is well accepted by educational researchers and the pedagogy is growing in use, yet Schissel et al. (2021, p. 341) note the 'striking' absence of translanguaging in assessment. If we seek valid and just assessments which are based on the reality of how multilingual students make meaning and communicate, then translanguaging must be embedded in assessment. Before turning to the application of translanguaging in assessment, we first justify the need for it by identifying fairness and validity issues affecting EAL/D students in current assessments.

Issues with current assessments for EAL/D learners

Assessments are based on and perpetuate political and cultural ideologies (Gipps & Stobart, 2009; Solano-Flores, 2011). In many Western countries, such as the United Kingdom (Welply, 2023) and Australia (Scarino, 2014), the curriculum and assessments are conceptualised as monolingual in line with a dominant one nation, one language ideology. In addition, all assessments regardless of discipline intrinsically assess language through content, instructions, and responses. Acknowledging all assessments as language assessments which operate within the bounds of a monolingual ideology has significant implications for EAL/D students' learning, inclusion, and educational opportunities.

When assessments are monolingual, the diverse multilingual knowledges and abilities of EAL/D learners are excluded. If EAL/D learners can only express themselves within the narrow confines of standardised academic English, the assessment results will only partially represent their abilities (Ascenzi-Moreno et al., 2023; Steele et al., 2022). As Li and García (2022, p. 322) state, 'a single numeric score in one named language does not in any way reflect the bilingual and multilingual students' complex understandings'. This instantly poses issues for validity and fairness if assessments do not capture the reality of EAL/D learners' knowledges and abilities.

Monolingual assessments which produce partial and inaccurate results directly contribute to existing narratives of failure and deficit that surround multilingual learners in schools (Ascenzi-Moreno & Seltzer, 2021; Schissel, 2020). This has harmful consequences for EAL/D learners through informing decisions which affect their educational opportunities. For instance, Baker and Wright (2021) highlight how bilingual children are often over-represented in special education and under-represented in gifted and talented programmes due to culturally and linguistically biased assessments. In a different example, after Indigenous Australian EAL/D students' abilities were invalidly represented in monolingual National Assessment Program for Literacy and Numeracy (NAPLAN) tests in 2008, bilingual education programmes in the Northern Territory were blamed for perceived deficiencies and dismantled (Devlin et al., 2017). These two examples demonstrate the lack of consequential validity in current monolingual assessments.

Critiquing a monolingual approach suggests that the alternative is a bilingual approach with direct translation across two languages to check and confirm meaning. However, this would be 'merely the addition of two monolingual assessments' (Ascenzi-Moreno et al., 2023, p. 48). Moreover, research by Lopez and colleagues (2017; see summary in Lopez, 2024) found that EAL/D students will not always perform better when assessed in their first language as the reality is that they fluidly use different languages to express themselves across varying contexts (i.e., translanguaging). Accommodations including bilingual dictionaries or interpreters may also serve to present students' multilingualism as a problem that interferes with an unquestionable monolingual assessment task (Schissel, 2014).

Inclusive assessments which fully engage EAL/D students' multilingual knowledges and abilities are required to bring assessment validity in line with the reality of culturally and linguistically diverse societies in the 21st century (Gorter & Cenoz, 2017; Li & García, 2022; Macqueen et al., 2019). We recognise that monolingual national standardised testing is unlikely to change in the near future and teachers have little influence on changing these assessment types. However, teachers do have agency and the ability to critically review and design school-based assessments for their students. Assessment design which incorporates translanguaging from the beginning and throughout every stage will support teachers to deliver inclusive assessments for EAL/D learners.

Translanguaging and assessment

Research on translanguaging in assessment is at an emergent stage, yet it is a clear 'implementational space' (Flores & Schissel, 2014, p. 454) for developing more inclusive education for EAL/D learners. Here we draw together the emerging evidence of translanguaging assessments in diverse contexts and identify opportunities for teachers of EAL/D learners in schools.

Translingual assessments can take a range of forms; the key distinguishing factor is that EAL/D students' abilities are not evaluated through a single named language in a single mode. Creating translingual assessment tasks which provide EAL/D students with choices and fluidity across modes and languages offers more inclusive opportunities for them to demonstrate their abilities. Achieving this approach first requires a rethinking of assumptions that reading a text in one language necessitates a response in the same language and that only a single mode can be used in this response (Ascenzi-Moreno et al., 2023). The reality of EAL/D students' translanguaging shows that they do not engage with a text using a single language and that they can express responses fluidly across a range of modes including writing, speaking, drawing, and gesturing (Li, 2018). In the context of Australian Aboriginal students with EAL/D, Steele et al. (2022, p. 408) further conceptualise that translingual assessments necessitate a transmodal design which recognises that students' meaning-making across modes is rarely discrete, but 'layered, intwined and infused'. Therefore, providing flexible choices across languages and modes creates space for EAL/D learners to demonstrate their ability by drawing on their full semiotic repertoires.

We first consider how teachers can create tasks and resources which embed translanguaging and, second, how teachers can assess artefacts where students have enacted translanguaging in their responses. This includes multimodal and transmodal assessment designs, supported by community partnerships and machine translation, which can be implemented across curriculum areas including literacy, numeracy, and science.

Designing translingual assessment tasks

For initial assessments with EAL/D students to be inclusive, they must involve diverse modes and both English and a student's first language. Welply (2023) offers a vignette of an EAL/D student who was placed in a lower class set as their initial assessment results, based on a single written mode and separate assessment of English and their first language, indicated low literacy in both English and their first language. The limitations of a monolingual and monomodal approach soon became apparent, as the student demonstrated proficient oral communication and the ability to understand complex concepts rapidly in their curriculum learning. The precedence given to a written-only assessment in evidencing ability meant that the school would not revise their initial assessment and move the student to a higher set. This vignette clearly demonstrates that inclusive assessment which truly represents EAL/D students' abilities needs to embed flexibility across languages and modes. Angelo and Hudson (2020, p. 23) advocate for a 'spiral curriculum approach' where meaning-making progresses from 'oral language-based activities, to literacy activities, to in-depth curriculum area learning' and finally summative assessments. This progressive sequence of activities would offer multiple opportunities for EAL/D students to demonstrate their ability across various modes. The approach could be constructed as transmodal by providing EAL/D students with this suggested sequence but creating opportunities for them to fluidly move between or infuse modes as they progress.

Inclusive translingual assessment approaches extend across school years and discipline areas. In developing literacy assessments, strategies can begin with translating comprehension questions into EAL/D students' first languages (Ascenzi-Moreno, 2021) and creating opportunities for students to retell the text using their first language, English, or a combination of both (Ascenzi-Moreno, 2018). Brown et al. (2023) present a multimodal literacy profile (MLP) as an assessment approach which incorporates a range of multimodal tasks and each one progressively builds on the last to create a holistic profile of an EAL/D student's understanding of a text. Key tasks include prompting students to retell narratives, identify story elements, consider personal and cultural connections, express affective responses, and create imaginative responses building on the story. Students are encouraged to use translanguaging in their responses and choices of modes across all activities include speaking, writing, use of existing classroom objects, creating crafts, sorting visuals, drawing, and using colour to express meaning and emotion. Again, this can be constructed as transmodal by offering EAL/D students the choice to draw on any aspect of their semiotic repertoire during any stage of creating the MLP. When compared alongside traditional English and written only responses, it becomes apparent that this holistic approach is much more likely to accurately represent an EAL/D student's understanding of a text.

Translingual assessments are also possible in numeracy and science curriculum areas. There is research evidence that mathematics assessments where EAL/D students can choose between English or Spanish when reading, listening, and responding better enable them to demonstrate their knowledge, particularly while their English is developing (Lopez et al., 2017). However, a teacher may find it challenging to design such assessments involving only two languages when EAL/D learners in their school have a wide range of linguistic backgrounds. To address this, teachers can focus on creating translingual assessment tasks which afford EAL/D students the autonomy to fluidly choose the languages and modes they use in their responses. Fine and colleagues in the USA (e.g., Fine & Furtak, 2020; Fine et al., 2023) have developed checklists and templates for embedding translanguaging in classroom-based science assessments. Key recommendations from their research include ensuring assessment instructions explicitly state that students can translanguage when responding to the task and modelling or sharing examples of translanguaging to legitimise it both socially and academically.

The growing use of machine translation (MT) in EAL/D (e.g., Beiler & Dewilde, 2020; Kelly & Hou, 2022) can support EAL/D students to engage with translingual assessments. Kelly and Hou's (2022) study across five secondary schools in Northern Ireland unveiled EAL/D students' translanguaging practices with MT and found that they are critical, flexible, and pragmatic users of MT. Incorporating this tool in assessment design can support EAL/D students to clarify language when interpreting tasks and produce deeper and more detailed responses. They may also make use of both written and audio-recording modes on MT apps and combine these with other modes in the classroom. In a high school science classroom in the USA, Fine (2022) describes how EAL/D students successfully used MT to create transcriptions of videos they had produced for an assessment task. The validity of the assessment task remains intact as for EAL/D students to produce the required language in English using MT, they must first have a conceptual understanding which they can express using the features of other languages in their semiotic repertoire.

Partnership between EAL/D students' families and schools through communication and collaboration is critical in developing more inclusive education (Stewart et al., 2022). This directly applies to assessments where Hammond (2014, p. 518) contends that curriculum tasks 'should be recognisable by educators, families, and community stakeholders as being significant and important'. Designing translingual assessments may represent a significant shift in practice, and building a shared understanding and commitment to this new practice with families and communities is more likely to generate success. An initial approach might involve sending a letter to families explaining why a translanguaging approach has been taken and what they can expect in translingual assessments (Fine, 2022). Collaborating with EAL/D students to write these letters would support them to explain this new approach at home and aid their family's understanding. Providing avenues for families to ask questions and give feedback or suggestions would further strengthen the design of inclusive translingual assessments.

Assessing translingual artefacts

Assessment of translingual artefacts requires a clear distinction between conceptual understanding and linguistic proficiency. This distinction can be best achieved through applying a Conceptual Scoring Model where, irrespective of languages and modes, a single rubric is applied to all aspects of a student's work (Ascenzi-Moreno et al., 2023; Bedore et al., 2005). This approach recognises that how EAL/D students demonstrate their conceptual understanding may vary across modes and building a holistic picture is required for a complete and valid assessment. For instance, a student could demonstrate their conceptual understanding of a story through speaking, gestures, acting, images, and drawings, but may not yet be able to showcase the same understanding in writing using only English. Brown et al. (2023) further argue that assessing multimodal coherence including evidence of explicit links, consistent details, or progressive depth across modes will enable teachers to gain a deeper understanding of an EAL/D student's ability. Similarly, when transmodal artefacts represent an infusion of modes, the focus should be placed on the student's overall meaning-making processes and demonstration of conceptual understanding.

Teachers cannot know all the languages that EAL/D students use, so it's relevant to ask how they might understand all of the linguistic aspects of EAL/D learners' translingual assessment artefacts. The recent advances in MT and generative AI offer promising tools in enabling teachers to assess this work. Ascenzi-Moreno et al. (2023) suggest that a monolingual teacher can use MT to make an initial assessment of translingual work and later confirm this in consultation with a bilingual teacher. This may be an ideal approach, but it is difficult to achieve in countries such as Australia or the United Kingdom where there are few bilingual teachers alongside a diverse range of language backgrounds among EAL/D students. When collaboration with a bilingual teacher is not possible, the use of MT makes it possible for monolingual teachers to assess EAL/D students' work. Fine (2022) details a monolingual secondary school teacher's journey towards embedding translingual formative assessments in their science classroom. One example in their study illustrated how two monolingual teachers used MT to support their assessment that a student had understood a science experiment by translating the Spanish *le quita* in the student's work to find that means *to remove* in English (Fine, 2022). This successful example hinged on a specific verb which is likely to produce an accurate and consistent translation; other translations might be less clear. However, a translingual design ensures that if the meaning of a linguistic feature is unclear after using MT, teachers are still able to consider this alongside the other work that an EAL/D student has produced across diverse modes. While MT should not be solely relied upon by teachers, it is a key tool in strengthening inclusive practices within a translingual assessment design. The emergence of generative AI tools (e.g., ChatGPT) which offer translations and have a more dialogic interface than MT is likely to create further opportunities for technology to support the assessment of translingual artefacts.

Conclusion

To create more inclusive assessments for EAL/D students, it is essential that assessments are premised on the reality of culturally and linguistically diverse societies in the 21st century and thus offer opportunities for them to fully represent their diverse knowledges and abilities. Embedding translanguaging in assessment can support this as it produces a more valid and inclusive representation of what EAL/D students know and can do, by engaging their full semiotic repertoire rather than limiting their expression through the narrow lens of a single language or mode. This chapter has offered a way forward by suggesting how translingual assessments which support EAL/D students to use their entire semiotic repertoire can be designed and evaluated. These multimodal or transmodal assessments can be created across disciplines in conjunction with community partnerships and with support from tools including MT and generative AI. It is the teacher who enacts the curriculum and has agency in the design of school-based assessments. Therefore, through embracing a translanguaging approach to assessment, teachers have the opportunity to lead transformational change and ensure more inclusive assessments for EAL/D learners.

References

Angelo, D., & Hudson, C. (2020). From the periphery to the centre: Securing the place at the heart of the TESOL field for First Nations learners of English as an Additional Language/Dialect. *TESOL in Context, 29*(1), 5–35. https://doi.org/10.21153/tesol2020vol29no1art1421

Ascenzi-Moreno, L. (2018). Translanguaging and responsive assessment adaptations. *Language Arts, 95*(6), 355–369. https://doi.org/10.58680/la201829683

Ascenzi-Moreno, L. (2021). Leveraging the 'learning edge': Translanguaging, teacher agency, and assessing emergent bilinguals' reading. In City University of New York – New York State Initiative on Emergent Bilinguals (Ed.), *Translanguaging and transformative teaching for emergent bilingual students* (pp. 207–215). Routledge.

Ascenzi-Moreno, L., García, O., & López, A. A. (2023). Latinx bilingual students' translanguaging and assessment: A unitary approach. In S. Melo-Pfeifer & C. Ollivier (Eds.), *Assessment of plurilingual competence and plurilingual learners in educational settings: Educative issues and empirical approaches* (1st ed.; pp. 48–61). Routledge. https://doi.org/10.4324/9781003177197-4

Ascenzi-Moreno, L., & Seltzer, K. (2021). Always at the bottom: Ideologies in assessment of emergent bilinguals. *Journal of Literacy Research, 53*(4), 468–490. https://doi.org/10.1177/1086296X211052255

Australian Curriculum, Assessment and Reporting Authority (ACARA). (2014). *Meeting the needs of students for whom English is an additional language or dialect.* https://www.australiancurriculum.edu.au/resources/student-diversity/meeting-the-needs-of-students-for-whom-english-is-an-additional-language-or-dialect/

Baker, C., & Wright, W. E. (2021). *Foundations of bilingual education and bilingualism.* Multilingual Matters.

Bedore, L. M., Peña, E. D., García, M., & Cortez, C. (2005). Conceptual versus monolingual scoring. *Language, Speech, and Hearing Services in Schools, 36*(3), 188–200. https://doi.org/10.1044/0161-1461(2005/020)

Beiler, I. R., & Dewilde, J. (2020). Translation as translingual writing practice in English as an additional language. *The Modern Language Journal, 104*(3), 533–549. https://doi.org/10.1111/modl.12660

Blackledge, A., & Creese, A. (2010). *Multilingualism: A critical perspective.* Bloomsbury Publishing.

Bracken, S., Driver, C., & Kadi-Hanifi, K. (2016). *Teaching English as an additional language in secondary schools: Theory and practice* (1st ed.). Routledge. https://doi.org/10.4324/9781315768649

Brown, S., Hao, L., & Zhang, R. (2023). Assessing the multimodal literacy practices of young emergent bilinguals. In K. Raza, D. Reynolds & C. Coombe (Eds.), *Handbook of multilingual TESOL in practice* (pp. 373–401). Springer. https://doi.org/10.1007/978-981-19-9350-3_25

Canagarajah, S. (2011). Translanguaging in the classroom: Emerging issues for research and pedagogy. *Applied Linguistics Review*. https://doi.org/10.1515/9783110239331.1

Carder, M. (2009). ESL or EAL? Programme or 'support'? The baggage that comes with names. *International Schools Journal, 29*(1), 18–25.

Conteh, J. (2019). *The EAL teaching book: Promoting success for multilingual learners.* Learning Matters.

Cunningham, C. (2019). Terminological tussles: Taking issue with 'English as an Additional Language' and 'Languages Other Than English'. *Power and Education, 11*(1), 121–128. https://doi.org/10.1177/1757743818806919

Devlin, B., Disbray, S., Regine, N., & Devlin, F. (2017). *History of bilingual education in the Northern Territory: People, programs and policies.* Springer. https://link.springer.com/book/10.1007/978-981-10-2078-0

Fine, C. G. M. (2022). Translanguaging interpretive power in formative assessment co-design: A catalyst for science teacher agentive shifts. *Journal of Language, Identity & Education, 21*(3), 191–211. https://doi.org/10.1080/15348458.2022.2058858

Fine, C. G. M., & Furtak, E. (2020). The SAEBL checklist: Science classroom assessments that work for emergent bilingual learners. *The Science Teacher, 87*(9), 38–48. https://www.nsta.org/science-teacher/science-teacher-julyaugust-2020/saebl-checklist

Fine, C. G. M., Littich, H., & Getz, M. (2023). The (trans)formative assessment planning template: Explicitly welcome translanguaging during formative assessment in your science classroom. *Science Scope, 46*(31), 29–37. https://www.nsta.org/science-scope/science-scope-januaryfebruary-2023/transformative-assessment-planning-template

Flores, N., & Schissel, J. L. (2014). Dynamic bilingualism as the norm: Envisioning a heteroglossic approach to standards-based reform. *TESOL Quarterly, 48*(3), 454–479. https://doi.org/10.1002/tesq.182

García, O. (2009). Education, multilingualism and translanguaging in the 21st century. In T. Skutnabb-Kangas, R. Phillipson, A. K. Mohanty, & M. Panda (Eds.), *Social justice through multilingual education* (pp. 140–158). Multilingual Matters. https://doi.org/10.21832/9781847691910-011

García, O., Johnson, S. I., & Seltzer, K. (2017). *The translanguaging classroom: Leveraging student bilingualism for learning.* Carson.

Gipps, C., & Stobart, G. (2009). Fairness in assessment. In C. Wyatt-Smith & J. J. Cumming (Eds.), *Educational assessment in the 21st century* (pp. 105–118). Springer.

Gorter, D., & Cenoz, J. (2017). Language education policy and multilingual assessment. *Language and Education, 31*(3), 231–248. https://doi.org/10.1080/09500782.2016.1261892

Hammond, J. (2014). An Australian perspective on standards-based education, teacher knowledge, and students of English as an additional language. *TESOL Quarterly, 48*(3), 507–532. https://doi.org/10.1002/tesq.173

Kelly, R., & Hou, H. (2022). Empowering learners of English as an additional language: Translanguaging with machine translation. *Language and Education, 36*(6), 544–559. https://doi.org/10.1080/09500782.2021.1958834

Lewis, G., Jones, B., & Baker, C. (2012). Translanguaging: Origins and development from school to street and beyond. *Educational Research and Evaluation, 18*(7), 641–654. https://doi.org/10.1080/13803611.2012.718488

Li, W. (2018). Translanguaging as a practical theory of language. *Applied Linguistics, 39*(1), 9–30. https://doi.org/10.1093/applin/amx039

Li, W., & García, O. (2022). Not a first language but one repertoire: Translanguaging as a decolonizing project. *RELC Journal, 53*(2), 313–324. https://doi.org/10.1177/00336882221092841

Lopez, A. A. (2024). Vignette: Using flexible bilingual academic content assessments in the United States. In C. Reilly, F. Chimbutane, J. Clegg, C. Rubagumya, & E. J. Erling (Eds.), *Multilingual learning: Assessment, ideologies and policies in sub-Saharan Africa* (1st ed.; pp. 65–70). Routledge.

Lopez, A. A., Turkan, S., & Guzman-Orth, D. (2017). Conceptualizing the use of translanguaging in initial content assessments for newly arrived emergent bilingual students. *ETS Research Report Series*, *2017*(1), 1–12. https://doi.org/10.1002/ets2.12140

Macqueen, S., Knoch, U., Wigglesworth, G., Nordlinger, R., Singer, R., McNamara, T., & Brickle, R. (2019). The impact of national standardized literacy and numeracy testing on children and teaching staff in remote Australian Indigenous communities. *Language Testing*, *36*(2), 265–287. https://doi.org/10.1177/0265532218775758

Scarino, A. (2014). Situating the challenges in current languages education policy in Australia – Unlearning monolingualism. *International Journal of Multilingualism*, *11*(3), 289–306. https://doi.org/10.1080/14790718.2014.921176

Schissel, J. L. (2014). Classroom use of test accommodations: Issues of access, equity, and conflation. *Current Issues in Language Planning*, *15*(3), 282–295. https://doi.org/10.1080/14664208.2014.915458

Schissel, J. L. (2020). Moving beyond deficit positioning of linguistically diverse test takers: Bi/multilingualism and the essence of validity. In S. Mirhosseini & P. I. De Costa (Eds.), *Sociopolitics of English language testing* (pp. 91–108). Bloomsbury Publishing.

Schissel, J. L., De Korne, H., & López-Gopar, M. (2021). Grappling with translanguaging for teaching and assessment in culturally and linguistically diverse contexts: Teacher perspectives from Oaxaca, Mexico. *International Journal of Bilingual Education and Bilingualism*, *24*(3), 340–356. https://doi.org/10.1080/13670050.2018.1463965

Solano-Flores, G. (2011). Assessing the cultural validity of assessment practices: An introduction. In M. del Rosario Bastera, E. Trumbull, & G. Solano-Flores (Eds.), *Cultural validity in assessment: Addressing linguistic and cultural diversity* (pp. 3–21). Routledge.

Steele, C., Dovchin, S., & Oliver, R. (2022). 'Stop measuring black kids with a white stick': Translanguaging for classroom assessment. *RELC Journal*, *53*(2), 400–415. https://doi.org/10.1177/00336882221086307

Stewart, M., Skinner, B., Hou, H., & Kelly, R. (2022). A systematic literature review of home-school partnership for learners with English as an Additional Language (EAL): A way forward for the UK and Ireland. *Irish Educational Studies*, *43*(2), 301–327. https://doi.org/10.1080/03323315.2022.2074072

UNESCO. (2016). *If you don't understand, how can you learn?* Global education monitoring report: Policy paper 24. https://unesdoc.unesco.org/ark:/48223/pf0000243713

Welply, O. (2023). English as an additional language (EAL): Decolonising provision and practice. *The Curriculum Journal*, *34*(1), 62–82. https://doi.org/10.1002/curj.182

12 Spotlighting rural and remote inclusive assessment

Systemic perspectives from the field

Sarah James and Tracey Sempowicz

Introduction

Inclusive policies and practices are equally important and applicable to the educational outcomes for all students irrespective of where they live and go to school. Administration teams are guided by the Australian Professional Standards for Teachers to 'lead and develop' their schools to maximise student outcomes (Australian Institute for Teaching and School Leadership [AITSL], 2017); inclusive assessment is a conduit through which students can demonstrate and receive feedback on their learning (Australian Curriculum, Assessment and Reporting Authority [ACARA], 2010). While striving for equitable outcomes is the gold standard in inclusive schools today, those in rural and remote (RR) settings experience unique contextual nuances that may impact on inclusive practices and student outcomes. For instance, research identifies that RR schools are often challenged by limited access to educational resources including specialised curriculum materials, technological infrastructure, and learning tools (Lynch et al., 2023). Furthermore, teachers in these areas tend to have fewer opportunities for professional development and networking, which can affect their ability to effectively implement differentiated assessment strategies (Lowe et al., 2024). Geographical isolation from urban centres can influence the logistics of standardised test implementation, like NAPLAN, given sometimes limited or poor internet connectivity for online assessments (Kafa & Eteokleous, 2024). These constraints suggest the need for tailored assessment strategies in RR schools.

In this chapter, two principals from RR schools share what they perceive to be the most significant obstacles to implementing inclusive assessment practices. They describe their schools as 'hard-to-staff' (McPherson et al., 2024), often employing inexperienced teachers (White, 2019) who have limited understanding of differentiated inclusive assessment practices (Duncan et al., 2021). Informal conversations with two school leaders reveal their dedication to tailoring strategies that accommodate the range of student needs and backgrounds. They emphasise the importance of integrating cultural values into their assessment methods, and employing flexible, creative approaches to overcome issues such as limited resources, technological barriers, and professional isolation. Their insights reveal their personal commitment to fostering educational equality in their schools by ensuring that every student can demonstrate their learning in an environment that reflects and respects their individual circumstances *and* the conditions of RR schooling.

Following, we provide a brief outline of the research methods used to collect and analyse data gathered from two participating school leaders. Using a reflexive interview methodology (Pessoa et al., 2019), we represented knowledge which was co-constructed between the researchers and participants. This approach meant that interviews first established the pragmatic 'problems' with inclusive assessment in RR schools. We then investigated the specific responses and strategies that these school leaders used to support and improve student outcomes, with inclusive assessment a foremost consideration. While this research is exploratory and cannot be generalisable to all schools in RR locations, it provides useful insights into just how committed school leaders are to assessment equity and inclusivity in schools.

Study methods

The two participants in this research were recruited using strategic sampling. Ethics approval was obtained from the Queensland University of Technology (QUT) [#8437] to conduct this research. Participants consented to a Zoom interview with the lead researcher during September of 2023 that lasted approximately one hour. The interview questions took the form of provocations that focused on the experiences of the principals regarding inclusive assessment. These provocations were designed to be open and adaptable to suit the participant's comfort level and communication style.

Interviews were recorded and transcribed. These data were analysed via inductive thematic analysis (Braun et al., 2019) that sought to identify the barriers and enablers to inclusive assessment practices in RR schools. This method allowed for the systematic identification and interpretation of themes directly from the data and was effective in highlighting the complexities and contextual specificities faced by educators in RR settings. Under the theme of barriers, seven sub-themes were constructed, including hard-to-staff schools, professional learning, leadership, teacher self-efficacy, cultural competence, language diversity, and trauma. Similarly, four sub-themes were identified under the theme of enablers. These include adjusting assessment, a strengths-based approach to culture and language, connecting to community, and culturally relevant pedagogy. This analysis not only illuminates the challenges of inclusive assessment, but importantly, it also identifies the enabling factors that support effective inclusive assessment strategies. Such strategies include having cultural knowledge, accommodating, recognising, and valuing linguistic diversity, reducing barriers to learning opportunities in flexible ways, using sensitive language, providing advance notice of assessments, offering choice in assessment formats, and ensuring that assessment tasks are culturally relevant and respectful.

Voices from the field

The two participants in this project are Claire and Rachael (pseudonyms). Though at different stages in their careers, both leaders share a passion for educational equity and a deep understanding of the unique challenges and opportunities that define RR education. Claire has extensive RR experience, initially as a curriculum leader in Far-North Queensland for eight years, followed by four years as executive principal of a very remote school. She possesses a deep understanding of inclusive practices and assessment methods, particularly for Aboriginal and Torres Strait Islander students in the communities her schools served. Currently, she works as a consultant with RR schools. Rachael, a teacher-principal in Far-North Queensland, has seven years of diverse teaching experience. She transitioned from a large metropolitan school in Brisbane to her current role in a small rural school with 37 students. Rachael's roles include classroom teacher, middle school leader, ICT coach, literacy coordinator, and acting principal.

Claire and Rachael reflect on their experiences of working in RR schools in Queensland, to share their encounters with inclusive assessment practices. Yet, to understand the intricacies of inclusive assessment design both Claire and Rachael express the need to first understand the unique contextual barriers that challenge the adoption of inclusive assessment, and how they overcame them. It is this empirical contribution that we turn to now.

Pragmatic challenges to delivering inclusive assessment practices

RR schools have become synonymous with the term 'hard-to-staff' and this is due to the limited pool of available teachers in RR locations (McPherson et al., 2024). Also, according to AITSL, Highly Accomplished and Lead teachers are needed to connect learning opportunities to their understanding of students' backgrounds and individual characteristics that impact learning. They also support colleagues, including pre-service teachers, 'to create positive and productive learning environments' which lead to improved learning outcomes for students (AITSL, 2018, p. 7). The stark reality for RR schools, however, is the paucity of experienced teachers with the knowledge and skills required to effectively implement and mentor others in the development of inclusive teaching and assessment strategies. Claire states that high turnover rates amongst her staff routinely disrupt the continuity of inclusive assessment practices. Rachael also observes:

> ... the problem is around that layer of – if you can't even get the quality teacher, then how [are] you going to implement inclusive assessment? That's probably the first systemic layer that affects us, and then it goes into teacher knowledge and capability.

Often, professional development opportunities are suggested as one way to enhance teacher capability (Lowe et al., 2024). Indeed, Claire points out 'we wouldn't expect teachers to be fully prepared for RR teaching from the outset, but we do require them to be receptive to learning and adapting their skills to our unique context'.

Yet, this need for extra/specialist training is also seen as a potential reason that RR teachers experience heightened workload and potential for enhanced burnout and attrition from the profession (Blackmore et al., 2024). Smaller staff numbers and the need to cover multiple subjects or grade levels, and even positions (e.g., Rachael's diverse roles within her school), can leave little time or resources to support developing and implementing inclusive assessment practices. This can lead to assessments that are hastily constructed or not sufficiently tailored to meet the needs of all students (Alonzo et al., 2023; Klenowski, 2014). To overcome this, research has highlighted how important effective school leadership is. The Independent Review into Regional, Rural and Remote Education (Halsey, 2018), more colloquially known as the Halsey review, recommended school leaders are vital to improving student outcomes, including the creation of conducive environments for quality teaching and learning, which encompasses the delivery of inclusive assessment practices. Both Claire and Rachael reflect on this. For example, Claire speaks of the need to follow 'policy and procedure':

> We have been catering for inclusive assessment; we are seeing gains being made by students and I put this progress down to resourcing of the right teacher to the right classroom. At the system level, their teaching needs to meet all of the obligations outlined in the relevant schooling documents, especially around documenting, recording inclusive education practices, assessment policies, and specifically catering for diversification and differentiation. As a principal I lean on the departmental processes and policy in a very practical way with my teachers.

Claire's assertion underscores the fundamental principle that effective implementation of inclusive assessment hinges on the allocation of appropriate resources and support to ensure that every student's needs are met. By emphasising the importance of resourcing the right teacher to the right classroom, Claire highlights the significance of matching educators' expertise and skills with the diverse needs of students. This underscores the critical role of leaders in identifying, recruiting, and retaining teachers who are equipped to implement inclusive assessment practices effectively. Furthermore, Claire's reference to system-level obligations reflects the necessity for leaders to align their practices with broader educational policies and mandates. This entails ensuring that teachers are equipped with the necessary training, resources, and support to document, record, and implement inclusive assessment practices successfully. Claire observes that her school has also 'trained teacher aides to support students with high learning needs across all classes ... [and] are trained in inclusive pedagogy and assessment'. She argues that this is important in ensuring students do not feel overwhelmed and have noticeable progress.

Rachael further discusses differentiation and the adoption of individualised learning plans at her school, explaining

> It was the first thing I brought into the school – we made adjustments for students so that they could access the curriculum at the level that was right for them. We took into account the students' needs and assessments were modified so that the students could have some success.

By prioritising inclusive assessment strategies as the 'first thing' brought into the school, Rachael signals a deliberate shift towards also prioritising the educational needs of all students, including those with diverse abilities and learning needs. This proactive stance sets the tone for a culture of inclusivity within the school community. This approach acknowledges that a one-size-fits-all approach to assessment is inadequate and that accommodations and adjustments may be necessary to support students in achieving success. As a school leader, Rachael's focus on differentiated assessments to allow students to experience success is particularly significant. While inclusive curriculum supports access and participation of all students, inclusive assessment needs to provide multiple ways and opportunities for students to demonstrate their abilities and progress across a teaching period. By modifying assessments to meet individual student needs, school leaders create an environment where students feel valued, supported, and capable of achieving their full potential. Claire confirms that she was able to use the 'experienced special needs teacher' to focus on students with 'individualised support. For instance, a Grade 5 student working at a Grade 1 level received modified assessments to ensure [their] success'.

Both Rachael and Claire identify that it is not only their actions as leaders – to set the tone for inclusivity – that is important, but that teacher efficacy in implementing effective assessment strategies is essential. Indeed, Ekins et al. (2016) propose that low teacher self-efficacy inhibits the uptake of instructional and assessment approaches to support diverse learners. A lack of teacher efficacy, limited education in inclusive practices, and an inadequate understanding of teaching and learning adjustments for students with diverse needs can lead to the marginalisation of some students (Ní Bhroin & King, 2020). Rachael attuned to this provocation discusses that with her focus on 'inclusive practices, differentiation, and appropriate assessment' she needed to

> work with teachers to document and make evidence-based adjustments for students. We supported our teachers in thinking about how to differentiate so that they knew all their students and their abilities. The exposure and experience of teachers when they arrive here is vast; we get a lot of graduates, and I noticed that there is not a lot of knowledge on inclusive approaches and reasonable adjustments for assessment.

Rachael suggested that teacher training and 'a solid induction' is crucial for teachers arriving in RR contexts, and that her school was currently working on improving their induction process for new teachers: 'To get inductions right we are giving new or early career teachers the support with training in relevant skills that address inclusive curriculum, pedagogy, and assessment approaches'.

The significance of effectively implementing inclusive assessment

For Aboriginal and Torres Strait Islander students there is increasing recognition of intergenerational trauma that requires culturally responsive and trauma-informed education approaches to support students' well-being and academic success (Schimke et al., 2022). In addition, pedagogical frameworks aimed at supporting inclusive teaching of Aboriginal and Torres Strait Islander students (e.g., 'eight ways of working'; Yunkaporta, 2010) are being utilised by teachers. The literature suggests, however, that many Indigenous students are learning Standard Australian English (SAE) as a second or additional language which imposes significant cognitive load, impacting on the equitable assessment of students' learning (Nichol & Robinson, 2000).

Claire and Rachael both lead schools with high enrolments of Aboriginal and Torres Strait Islander students, and both agree that teachers must develop cultural and linguistic knowledge relevant to their RR contexts to successfully adopt inclusive assessment approaches.

> All of the students that we're talking about in this conversation are speaking English as a second or third language. So, what we're navigating is English as an additional language and there are two parts to consider. There's a cultural language component about new knowledge and then there's obviously diagnosed or observable learning difficulties that are in the classroom. So, there's two reasons why you might want to have really strong, inclusive education practices and adjusted assessment so that you're either meeting the needs of second language or third language acquisition and/or you're meeting the needs of any diagnosed or observable learning disability that a student might have.
>
> (Claire)

Claire acknowledges that Aboriginal and Torres Strait Islander students are navigating English as an additional language or dialect, which presents challenges in accessing and engaging with academic content, noting 'when we have to use discrete resources we have to modify the assessment task to suit our context and provide some sort of equity for our students'. Research has established that assessments designed for monolingual English learners unfairly judge Aboriginal and Torres Strait Islander English language learners' performance (Freeman et al., 2023). Inclusive assessment strategies are crucial for accommodating students' linguistic diversity (Lloyd et al., 2015). By adjusting assessments for language proficiency levels and providing language acquisition support, RR teachers can ensure Indigenous students are not disadvantaged by language barriers.

Inclusive assessment practices need to be culturally responsive (Gay, 2010), and according to Claire and Rachael, need to recognise and incorporate Indigenous languages, perspectives, and ways of knowing into the assessment process. This cultural responsiveness fosters a sense of belonging and validation for students, enhancing their engagement and academic success. Indeed, Rachael explains that all staff at her school undertake a 'trauma workshop' that 'sheds light on the trauma our kids face, from historical events like the stolen generation to current struggles. Understanding this helps us adapt teaching and assessments to better support our students'. Rachael explains that recognising the trauma of colonisation (Brown et al., 2022), dispossession (Delphine et al., 2024), forced assimilation (Lowe et al., 2021), and ongoing systemic discrimination (Fray et al., 2020) is significant in understanding how trauma affects students' cognitive, emotional, and behavioural functioning, and their ability to engage with learning and assessment.

> I think, acknowledging that even if children of themselves in their own family unit, haven't experienced first-hand, the trauma, they will no doubt experience it vicariously in the form of generational trauma that sits around them. Comprehending this is really important. Sometimes it just means that we have to look more carefully, look differently, be more conscious of reducing barriers to learning, and really create and enable learning opportunities in flexible ways wherever possible.
>
> (Claire)

Inclusive assessment practices in these RR schools aim to mitigate the impact of trauma by ensuring that assessments are fair, culturally responsive, and sensitive to the diverse experiences of students. This may involve using sensitive language (Delphine et al., 2024), providing advance notice of assessments, offering choice and flexibility in assessment formats (DeLuca et al., 2023), and ensuring that assessment tasks are culturally relevant (DeLuca et al., 2023) and respectful (Dillon et al., 2024). Indeed, a strengths-based approach is needed that recognises and builds upon students' resilience, coping strategies, and cultural strengths. For Aboriginal and Torres Strait Islander students, drawing on cultural knowledge, traditions, and community connections can be a source of resilience and empowerment, and by incorporating Indigenous perspectives, histories, and ways of knowing into assessment practices, schools are affirming students' cultural identities and promoting positive self-esteem and self-efficacy.

Concluding thoughts

In conclusion, the discussion of data surrounding pragmatic challenges to delivering inclusive assessment practices in regional and rural (RR) school settings highlights several significant barriers and opportunities for improvement. Despite the challenges presented by limited teacher availability, high teacher turnover rates, and resource constraints, there is a clear recognition among educators, such as Claire and Rachael, of the critical importance of adopting inclusive assessment strategies to support the diverse needs of students, particularly Aboriginal and Torres Strait Islander students in these communities.

This exploratory study emphasises the essential role of effective school leadership in promoting inclusive assessment practices. Claire and Rachael both underscore the importance of aligning policies and procedures with broader educational mandates to ensure that teachers are equipped with the necessary training, resources, and support to implement inclusive assessment practices effectively. Moreover, they highlight the significance of fostering a culture of inclusivity within schools, where adjustments and accommodations are made to meet the unique needs of all students, regardless of background or ability.

Unsurprisingly, given arguments in broader literature about the importance of continuing professional development for teacher capability, one key recommendation emerging from this work is the prioritisation of professional development opportunities for teachers to enhance their knowledge and skills in inclusive assessment practices. According to Claire and Rachael this includes providing training in relevant areas such as cultural competency, trauma-informed approaches, differentiation, and individualised learning plans. By investing in teacher training and induction processes tailored to the specific needs of RR contexts, schools can better support teachers in implementing effective assessment strategies that address the diverse needs of students in RR contexts.

Furthermore, Claire's and Rachael's perspectives of the significance of inclusive assessment in RR schools underscores the importance of adopting culturally responsive approaches to assessment. Recognising the cultural and linguistic diversity of Indigenous students, as well as the impact of intergenerational trauma, is essential in designing assessments that are fair, respectful, and supportive of students' wellbeing. By incorporating Indigenous perspectives, histories, and ways of knowing into assessment practices, educators can create a more inclusive learning environment that validates students' cultural identities and promotes positive academic outcomes.

Considering these recommendations, it is crucial for educational authorities and policymakers to provide ongoing support and resources to RR schools to facilitate the implementation of inclusive assessment practices. This may include funding for professional development initiatives, access to culturally relevant teaching materials and resources, and support for collaborative partnerships with Indigenous communities and Elders. Overall, the adoption of inclusive assessment strategies in RR school contexts is essential for promoting equity, supporting student wellbeing, and enhancing academic outcomes, particularly for Aboriginal and Torres Strait Islander students. By addressing the pragmatic challenges and embracing the recommendations outlined in this discussion, schools can create a more inclusive and supportive learning environment that empowers all students to thrive.

References

Alonzo, D., Baker, S., Knipe, S., & Bottrell, C. (2023). A scoping study relating Australian secondary schooling, educational disadvantage and assessment for learning. *Issues in Educational Research, 33*(3), 874–896.

Australian Curriculum, Assessment and Reporting Authority (ACARA). (2010). *The shape of the Australian Curriculum.* https://docs.acara.edu.au/resources/Shape_of_the_Australian_Curriculum.pdf

Australian Institute for Teaching and School Leadership (AITSL). (2017). *Lead and develop.* https://www.aitsl.edu.au/lead-develop

Australian Institute for Teaching and School Leadership (AITSL). (2018). *Australian Professional Standards for Teachers.* https://www.aitsl.edu.au/docs/default-source/national-policy-framework/australian-professional-standards-for-teachers.pdf

Blackmore, J., Hobbs, L., & Rowlands, J. (2024). Aspiring teachers, financial incentives, and principals' recruitment practices in hard-to-staff schools. *Journal of Education Policy, 39*(2), 233–252. https://doi.org/10.1080/02680939.2023.2193170

Braun, V., Clarke, V., Hayfield, N., & Terry, G. (2019). Thematic analysis. In P. Liamputtong (Ed.), *Handbook of research methods in health social sciences* (pp. 843–860). Springer.

Brown, M., Howard, J., & Walsh, K. (2022). Building trauma informed teachers: A constructivist grounded theory study of remote primary school teachers' experiences with children living with the effects of complex childhood trauma. *Frontiers in Education, 7.* https://doi.org/10.3389/feduc.2022.870537

Delphine, T., Auld, G., Lynch, J., & O'Mara, J. (2024). Neither this nor that: The challenge of social justice for non-Indigenous English teachers in First Nations Australian education contexts. *English in Education, 58*(2), 92–107. https://doi.org/10.1080/04250494.2024.2314581

DeLuca, C., Willis, J., Cowie, B., Harrison, C., & Coombs, A. (2023). *Learning to assess: Cultivating assessment capacity in teacher education* (1st ed.). Springer Nature Singapore.

Dillon, A., Riley, P., Filardi, N., Franklin, A., Horwood, M., McMullan, J., Craven, R. G., & Schellekens, M. (2024). What are the success factors for schools in remote Indigenous communities? *British Educational Research Journal, 50*(3), 944–963. https://doi.org/10.1002/berj.3962

Duncan, J., Punch, R., & Croce, N. (2021). Supporting primary and secondary teachers to deliver inclusive education. *The Australian Journal of Teacher Education, 46*(4), 92–107. https://doi.org/10.14221/ajte.2021v46n4.6

Ekins, A., Savolainen, H., & Engelbrecht, P. (2016). An analysis of English teachers' self-efficacy in relation to SEN and disability and its implications in a changing SEN policy context. *European Journal of Special Needs Education, 31*(2), 236–249.

Fray, L., Gore, J., Harris, J., & North, B. (2020). Key influences on aspirations for higher education of Australian school students in regional and remote locations: A scoping review of empirical research, 1991–2016. *Australian Educational Researcher, 47*(1), 61–93. https://doi.org/10.1007/s13384-019-00332-4

Freeman, L., Staley, B., & Wigglesworth, G. (2023). Assessment equity for remote multilingual Australian Aboriginal students through the lens of Sustainable Development Goals. *International Journal of Speech Language Pathology, 25*(1), 157–161. https://doi.org/10.1080/17549507.2022.2129788

Gay, G. (2010). *Culturally responsive teaching: Theory, research, and practice* (2nd ed.). Teachers College Press.

Halsey, J. (2018). *Independent review into regional, rural and remote education – Final report.* Commonwealth of Australia.

Kafa, A., & Eteokleous, N. (Eds.). (2024). *The power of technology in school leadership during COVID-19: Insights from the field* (1st ed.). Springer.

Klenowski, V. (2014). Towards fairer assessment. *Australian Educational Researcher, 41*, 445–470. https://doi.org/10.1007/s13384-013-0132-x

Lloyd, N. J., Lewthwaite, B. E., Osborne, B., & Boon, H. J. (2015). Effective teaching practices for Aboriginal and Torres Strait Islander students: A review of the literature. *Australian Journal of Teacher Education, 40*(11). https://doi.org/10.14221/ajte.2015v40n11.1

Lowe, K., Tennent, C., Moodie, N., Guenther, J., & Burgess, C. (2021). School-based Indigenous cultural programs and their impact on Australian Indigenous students: A systematic review. *Asia-Pacific Journal of Teacher Education, 49*(1), 78–98. https://doi.org/10.1080/1359866X.2020.1843137

Lowe, K., Thompson, K., Vass, G., & Grice, C. (2024). Transforming schooling practices for First Nations learners: Culturally nourishing schooling in conversation with the theory of practice architectures. *International Journal of Qualitative Studies in Education*, 1–15. https://doi.org/10.1080/09518398.2024.2318265

Lynch, J., Auld, G., O'Mara, J., & Cloonan, A. (2023). Teachers' everyday work-for-change: Implementing curriculum policy in 'disadvantaged' schools. *Journal of Education Policy*, *39*(4), 564–582. https://doi.org/10.1080/02680939.2023.2245794

McPherson, A., Lampert, J., & Burnett, B. (2024). A summary of initiatives to address teacher shortages in hard-to-staff schools in the Anglosphere. *Asia-Pacific Journal of Teacher Education*, *52*(3), 332–349. https://doi.org/10.1080/1359866X.2024.2323936

Ní Bhroin, Ó, & King, F. (2020). Teacher education for inclusive education: A framework for developing collaboration for the inclusion of students with support plans. *European Journal of Teacher Education*, *43*(1), 38–63. https://doi.org/10.1080/02619768.2019.1691993

Nichol, R., & Robinson, J. (2000). Pedagogical challenges in making mathematics relevant for Indigenous Australians. *International Journal of Mathematics Education in Science and Technology*, *31*(4), 495–504. https://doi.org/10.1080/002073900412606

Pessoa, A. S. G., Harper, E., Santos, I. S., & Gracino, M. C. S. (2019). Using reflexive interviewing to foster deep understanding of research participants' perspectives. *International Journal of Qualitative Methods*, *18*. https://doi.org/10.1177/1609406918825026

Schimke, D., Krishnamoorthy, G., Ayre, K., Berger, E., & Rees, B. (2022). Multi-tiered culturally responsive behavior support: A qualitative study of trauma-informed education in an Australian primary school. *Frontiers in Education*, *7*. https://doi.org/10.3389/feduc.2022.866266

White, S. (2019). *Recruiting, retaining and supporting early career teachers for rural schools*. Springer.

Yunkaporta, T. (2010). Our ways of learning in Aboriginal languages. In J. Hobson, K. Lowe, S. Poetsch, & M. Walsh (Eds.), *Re-awakening languages: Theory and practice in the revitalisation of Australia's Indigenous languages* (pp. 37–49). Sydney University Press.

Part III
Future practice

13 Inclusive classroom assessment and social justice

Karen Dooley, Annette Woods, and Martin Mills

Introduction

During the past few decades, the principle of inclusivity has been written into education policy on scales from the global to the local. While the inclusive education movement is widely associated with dis/ability, proponents have reiterated that multiple and intersecting forms of social difference fall within its purview, for instance, class; sex, gender, and sexuality; religion; and race, ethnicity, and language (Mac Ruairc, 2020). As inclusivity has become established in policy, proponents have expressed disappointment about classroom enactment (Mavropoulou et al., 2021). It is that problem to which this volume speaks: the previous chapters describe approaches for making school and classroom-based assessment more inclusive. In this final chapter, we use a social justice lens to propose some directions for future research and practice. We begin by considering the relationship between inclusive education and social justice. We then conclude with comments about teaching as a profession and the possibilities and challenges of achieving a context where socially just assessment practices are a reality.

Social justice and inclusive education

Social justice and inclusive education are increasingly linked in education policy. Perhaps the beginning point for this can be seen as 1948, when education was codified as one of a set of universal human rights and construed as a social justice remedy for inequalities. This inclusion was an attempt to address social dynamics like those that had precipitated conflict and brutality during the first half of the century (Grant & Gibson, 2010). As written in Article 26 of the Universal Declaration of Human Rights, education is to be free and compulsory at elementary level, directed at full human development and respect for human rights, and subject to prior parental right to choose the form of their children's education (United Nations, 1948). Aspects of this right have since been embedded in global goals for education, most recently, Sustainable Development Goal 4 (SDG 4) which was formulated to complete and transcend earlier global goals for education, namely, the Education for All and Millenium Development Goals. SDG 4 envisages, inter alia, *quality* education for all by 2030 that is *inclusive* and *equitable* (UNESCO, 2015).

DOI: 10.4324/9781003463184-17

So, inclusion and social justice have been inter-related in written education policy at least. However, inclusivity has been embraced by policymakers at a time when some proponents have grappled with sociological questions of how, and to what extent, schooling is currently able to enable social justice. Further, questions have been asked about whether schooling is 'worth being included into' and whether everyone wants, or should be compelled to want, to be 'included' (Anderson & Boyle, 2020). One popular response sees inclusive education as an agent of social justice to the extent that it enables a fairer distribution of educational outcomes linked to life chances, in what Nancy Fraser (2009) has called redistributive social justice approaches. But redistributive approaches to justice have themselves been subject to critique for their failure to acknowledge the importance of cultural and political justice (Fraser, 2009; see also Keddie, 2017 for further discussion).

By way of example, consider one US elementary school's attempt at *inclusive* reform described by Waitoller and Kozleski (2015). Green Valley school served a high-poverty high-diversity neighbourhood and provided mainstream, pull-out, and segregated approaches for students with disability. To ensure all students received a *quality* programme and more *equitable* outcomes, students at Green Valley were regularly assessed with reading skills measures. Consistent with the performative ethos of neoliberal reform, district benchmarks were displayed around the school, as were data walls recording each teacher's performance. This neoliberal redistributive approach to inclusivity was exclusionary in that it misrecognised diverse cultural knowledge, and misrepresented student capabilities in relation to their own learning. Reading scores became ability profiles: 'intensive' kids ('red' on a traffic light system), 'strategic' kids (yellow), and 'at-benchmark' kids (green) (p. 18). The profiles determined who was allowed to participate in political and philosophical conversations in language arts and who had to work on their reading skills instead, and in this way positioned certain children in certain ways and other children in other ways.

Like much educational research, the Green Valley study used the multidimensional theory of justice of political scientist Nancy Fraser (1997, 2009, 2014) to provide insights into the consequential implications of educational policy. That theory posits three dimensions of justice: the *distributive* (economic), the *recognitive* (cultural), and the *representative* (political). As with the redistributive project at Green Valley, remedies can be *affirmative* by remediating inequitable outcomes. But these same remedies can cause recognitive injustice as occurred at Green Valley – and with implications for distribution of meaning-making about social issues. Remedies can also be *transformative* by precluding inequity, for instance, through the flexible assessment practices of Universal Design for Learning (Waitoller & Kozleski, 2015).

The research at Green Valley used an interpretation of Fraser's theory specified for inclusive education (Waitoller & Kozleski, 2015). With this, it is possible to describe inclusivity as struggles for *distribution* of access to quality learning opportunities and of participation in such; *recognition* through valorisation of all student differences in curriculum, pedagogy, and assessment; and opportunities for students to *represent* themselves in decisions about inclusivity. Broadly speaking, this interpretation of Fraser's theory resonates with those of education researchers whose work is not conducted under the banner of inclusive education (Cazden, 2012). We now use the theory to explore approaches to inclusive assessment described in this volume.

Approaches to inclusive assessment

Given constraints of space, our analyses here are illustrative rather than exhaustive. They identify the array of approaches to inclusive assessment represented in this volume. There are several examples in the volume showing how assessment barriers can be eliminated in *recognition* of students' characteristics to *redistribute* access to institutionalised curriculum and outcomes. These address:

- How neurotypical teachers might misrecognise the thinking of neurodivergent students when designing assessment tasks in science and technology (Granone & Knudsen, Chapter 5).
- Strategies for differentiating Arts assessment for diverse classes through choice of text, adjustment to physical processes, and the use of assistive technologies (Clark-Fookes, Chapter 6).
- The potential of assistive technology in science assessment for students with diagnosed cognitive, social-emotional, physical, and sensory disabilities (Teh & Davis, Chapter 7).
- Peculiarities of visual, procedural, and linguistic barriers in geography assessments (Adams et al., Chapter 8).
- Ways of creating and assessing translingual, transmodal artefacts with students who speak academic English as an additional language or dialect (Kelly & Stewart, Chapter 11).

Furthermore, Assessment for Learning (AfL) is explored in several chapters which:

- Describe customisation of AfL to enable students with and without diagnosed cognitive and social-emotional disabilities to develop and display historical thinking (Henderson et al., Chapter 2).
- Show how teachers of English Language Arts can occasion learning by inviting all students to exercise agency in assessment events in the shadow of summative and high-stakes assessment events (Arnold & Holden, Chapter 3).
- Describe an interactive routine by which teachers might assess mathematical thinking for learning to create equitable instructional environments for all (Challen & Strong, Chapter 4).

In sociological terms (Luke, 2009/2019), all these approaches rest on analyses which locate the problem of exclusive assessment variously in the languages and modes legitimised for assessment purposes in school fields or in the rules of interaction of teacher and student during assessment. Accordingly, they adjust those aspects of the field to better recognise differences of student habitus (dispositions and schemes for classifying the world) in classroom assessment. These strategies of recognitive justice may require alteration to teacher habitus, including new classificatory schemes for identifying the characteristics of student habitus, along with the technical expertise to design inclusive assessment. This is a particular challenge in rural and remote Australia where teachers may be more likely to have less experience than in more highly populated areas and to be living in an unfamiliar community which may require some specialist teaching capabilities (James & Sempowicz, Chapter 12).

The other two chapters in the volume suggest approaches to assessment that rest on some other analyses of the problem of exclusivity. They:

- Map out how assessment *for*, *as*, and *of* Indigenous place-based learning enables students to engage with Country as Teacher; can involve Indigenous students in the design of assessments; and develop students' meta-awareness of the implications of assessment (Armour et al., Chapter 9).
- Raise consciousness of ways in which high-stakes assessment positions teachers to binarise gender (e.g., producing girl/boy performance data) and provide suggestions for challenging hetero-cis normative assumptions, with decision-making input from students (van Leent & Jeffries, Chapter 10).

These approaches to inclusive assessment pursue *recognitive* and *representative* justice both for their own sake and in the interest of *distributing* outcomes justly. In sociological terms (Luke, 2009/2019), they identify sources of exclusion in the knowledge legitimised in assessment and in the discriminatory social and cultural work of assessment itself. Accordingly, remedies involve altering the structures of knowledge legitimised by assessment and enabling student awareness and critique of discrimination in social fields.

Working within a sociological model of justice in education (Luke, 2009/2019), we have identified an array of approaches to inclusive assessment reform in this volume that turn on different descriptions of the source of exclusion. We turn now to future practice and research.

Looking ahead

In this chapter, we have drawn on Fraser's multidimensional model of social justice to consider some of the ways in which assessment can manifest normative versions of children and young people and learning that foreground white, middle-class notions of such constructs (Compton-Lilly et al., 2020, p. 386). Drawing on the work of Fraser and other sociologists interested in the ways that social and cultural dimensions of schooling practices – learning, teaching, and assessing – position children and young people according to the intersections of, for example, class, race, sexuality, gender, socio-economic status, language, accent, and culture, much of the work reviewed here takes forward the human dimensions of social justice as they play out in institutions such as education. This is a productive approach as it allows for both analysis of systems, but also for forward-facing alternatives to be imagined that go beyond one-dimensional approaches that centre redistributive *or* recognitive *or* representational social justice.

Critiques of assessment for cultural bias have a long history, foregrounding the ways in which assessments manifest certain knowledges and ways of doing as universal, ignoring the fact that they are instead cultural artefacts. The impacts of these normative views do not apply to all children equally. Those already socially disadvantaged are most likely to be measured as lacking when the standard of assessment fits their middle-class peers. So, when inclusive assessment has focused on the unpacking of cultural biases, it is language or textual resources of assessment that are usually centred. Where inclusivity has focused on diverse learners, thus centring learners and their different abilities, inclusive assessment has often centred people and human relations. Both of these approaches can provide important insights. However, in looking to the future, shifting contexts, not least of which those that relate to the burgeoning digital landscape of education, which includes a shift to digital ways of representing learning for assessment, requires that the pursuit of inclusive assessment must consider a shift in focus from people and language or text, towards the material and spatial dimensions of assessment.

To explain, where a child who has had limited engagement with a keyboard or iPad is judged against one who has engaged with smart technology from an early age as part of national testing schemes such as Australia's NAPLAN[1] and the result is represented as the capacity to produce written text rather than the capacity to keyboard or use an iPad, the ideal of inclusive assessment will remain forever out of reach. Inclusive assessment requires shifts to not only the human components of learning and the textual or language resources used but also requires the material and spatial elements of learning to be taken into consideration. In full circle, this returns our thinking to moving beyond only considering recognitive social justice, to instead balance the redistributive and representative dimensions of a socially just education reliant on inclusive assessment, pedagogy, and curriculum.

We now briefly turn to a silence in the book. For the approaches to AfL suggested here to take effect at scale, consideration has to be given to the current constructions of teachers and their work. Acknowledging this silence is not a criticism of the chapters here, but a recognition that if the important messages contained within them are to have purchase, we need professionals who are adept at challenging dominant constructions of teachers' work. In recent times we have seen significant moves towards a view of teachers as technicians, expected to implement curriculum, pedagogy, *and* assessment practices determined by others (see Acuña, 2024; Ball, 2003; Connell, 2009). This view of teachers' work is based on a presumption that the teaching profession needs 'to be told what to do as it has lost the capacity to determine a course of action for itself' (Ellis, 2011, p. 9). This needs to be resisted if inclusion at a system or local level is to be a reality.

While pedagogy is perhaps where teachers have the most freedom to subvert this paradigm, what this book shows is that teachers can and do shape assessment to meet the needs of students. However, for such practices to become widespread, teachers require significant assessment literacy and a solid grounding in the principles of social justice. This in turn requires an understanding of the teaching profession as an intellectual enterprise – one which requires teachers to critically engage with and contribute to the body of knowledge in their professional field (Evans, 2008). This book provides an engaging resource for pre-service teachers, practising teachers, and teacher educators with which to do this in relation to what a socially just assessment regime could look like if teachers were able to exercise scholarly professionalism.

Such scholarly professionalism has been discussed widely elsewhere (see, e.g., BERA/RSA, 2013; Evans, 2008; Sachs, 2016). However, as this book illustrates, providing an inclusive assessment regime cannot occur without teachers' critical engagement with the justice principles of distribution, recognition, and representation. A concern with the 'distribution' of disciplinary knowledges is at the heart of Part I of this book. Teachers need to consider how what Michael Young (2008) calls 'powerful knowledges' are distributed. These are the knowledges that carry cultural capital and provide access to the realms of the privileged. Denying students from marginalised backgrounds access to these will lead to the reproduction of inequalities through the schooling system. What the authors do in this section of the book is demonstrate that this is not simply a matter of transmission of knowledge, but also one of ensuring that higher order thinking, engaging in intellectual enterprises, and developing understandings of knowledge as constructed are likewise given distributive consideration.

While concerns with recognition are certainly present in Part I, it is in Part II where they are foregrounded. AfL cannot ignore cultural justice and what young people bring to the classroom in terms of their own knowledges and the knowledges residing in the local community – what Moll (see, e.g., Moll, 2019) calls 'funds of knowledge'. Euro/Anglocentric, masculinist, heteronormative curricula have worked to silence important non-dominant cultural knowledges and erase young people from marginalised backgrounds out of existence. What these chapters do is stress that Indigeneity, diverse genders and sexualities, ethnicities, first language, and rurality matter in relation to assessment. These matter of course for young people from marginalised backgrounds, but as Connell (1993) has argued, a socially just education ensures that *all* students engage with such knowledges. Balancing the provision of powerful knowledges alongside a funds of knowledge approach requires significant professional judgement on the part of the teacher.

Across several of the chapters in the book the importance of political justice – or representation – is evident. Young people's voices are regularly ignored in the construction of assessment items; and so too, the voices of their communities. As Fraser (2014) has argued, a lack of input into key decisions affecting one's life inhibits people's opportunities to make justice claims in relation to distribution and recognition, and is in itself also an injustice. As the chapters in this book that address voice and representation demonstrate, educationalists have long underestimated young people's abilities to contribute meaningfully to their own education. Such contributions can come through spaces to propose projects on issues affecting them and their communities (including the global community), through access to diverse knowledges not possessed by their teachers and/or by asking questions from diverse standpoints. Ownership of assessment by students encourages learning and teaching that can take young people (and sometimes teachers) into hitherto unknown and unexpected territory.

We are pleased to have been invited to provide this concluding response to the chapters in this book. While curriculum, pedagogy, and assessment are inextricably linked, when considering socially just practices in schooling the focus is commonly on curriculum and pedagogy. However, as this book demonstrates, assessment is equally important. Ignoring it will prevent schools from becoming places where social injustices affecting young people's educational experiences and future life opportunities can be averted. At the same time, we need to stay committed to promoting teaching as a scholarly activity requiring a deep engagement with the latest research in education.

Note

1 NAPLAN = National Assessment Program—Literacy and Numeracy. It is a programme of standardised cohort testing administered to Australian school students in Grades 3, 5, 7, and 9.

References

Acuña, F. (2024). Governing teachers' subjectivity in neoliberal times: The fabrication of the bonsai teacher. *Journal of Education Policy*, *39*(2), 171–190.

Anderson, J., & Boyle, C. (2020). Including into what? Reigniting the 'good education' debate in an age of diversity. In C. Boyle, T. Anderson, A. Page, & S. Mavropoulou (Eds.), *Inclusive education: Global issues and controversies* (pp. 15–34). Brill.

Ball, S. J. (2003). The teacher's soul and the terrors of performativity. *Journal of Education Policy*, *18*(2), 215–228.

BERA/RSA. (2013). *Research and teacher education: The BERA-RSA inquiry. Policy and practice within the United Kingdom*. British Educational Research Association.

Cazden, C. (2012). A framework for social justice in education. *International Journal of Educational Psychology*, *1*(3), 179–198. https://doi.org/10.4471/ijep.2012.11

Compton-Lilly, C., Dixon, K., Janks, H., & Woods, A. (2020). Summative literacy assessments and how they imagine children: An international comparison. In C. Martin (Ed.), *Handbook of research on formative assessment in pre-K through elementary classrooms* (pp. 368–390). IGI Global Publishing. https://doi.org/10.4018/978-1-7998-0323-2.ch018

Connell, R. (1993). *Schools and social justice*. Temple University Press.

Connell, R. (2009). Good teachers on dangerous ground: Towards a new view of teacher quality and professionalism. *Critical Studies in Education*, *50*(3), 213–229.

Ellis, V. (Ed.). (2011). *Learning and teaching in secondary schools* (4th ed.). Learning Matters.

Evans, L. (2008). Professionalism, professionality and the development of education professionals. *British Journal of Education Studies*, *56*(1), 20–38.

Fraser, N. (1997). From redistribution to recognition? Dilemmas of justice in a 'postsocialist' age. In N. Fraser (Ed.), *Justice interruptus: Critical reflections on the postsocialist condition* (pp. 11–39). Taylor & Francis.

Fraser, N. (2009). *Scales of justice: Reimagining political space in a globalizing world*. Columbia University Press.

Fraser, N. (2014). Publicity, subjection, critique: A reply to my critics. In K. Nash (Ed.), *Transnationalizing the public sphere* (pp. 129–156). Polity Press.

Grant, C. A., & Gibson, M. L. (2010). 'These are revolutionary times': Human rights, social justice and popular protest. In T. K. Chapman, & N. Hobble (Eds.), *Social justice pedagogy across the curriculum: The practice of freedom* (pp. 9–35). Routledge.

Keddie, A. (2017). Schooling and social justice through the lenses of Nancy Fraser. In S. Ball (Ed.), *Education policy* (pp. 146–167). Routledge.

Luke, A. (2019). Race and language as capital: A sociological template for language education reform. In A. Luke (Ed.), *Educational policy, narrative and discourse* (pp. 190–216). Routledge. (Original work published 2009)

Mac Ruairc, G. (2020). Headspace: School leaders working towards inclusive schools. In C. Boyle, T. Anderson, A. Page, & S. Mavropoulou (Eds.), *Inclusive education: Global issues and controversies* (pp. 58–70). Brill.

Mavropoulou, G., Mann, G., & Carrington, S. (2021). The divide between inclusive education policy and programs in Australia and the way forward. *Journal of Policy and Practice in Intellectual Disabilities*, *18*(1), 44–52.

Moll, L. (2019). Elaborating funds of knowledge: Community-oriented practices in international contexts. *Literacy Research: Theory, Method, and Practice*, *68*(1), 130–138. https://doi.org/10.1177/2381336919870805

Sachs, J. (2016). Teacher professionalism: Why are we still talking about it? *Teachers and Teaching*, *22*(4), 413–425.

UNESCO. (2015). Education 2030 Framework for Action to be formally adopted and launched. *UNESCO News*. https://www.unesco.org/en/articles/education-2030-framework-action-be-formally-adopted-and-launched

United Nations. (1948). *Universal Declaration of Human Rights*. https://www.un.org/en/about-us/universal-declaration-of-human-rights

Waitoller, F. R., & Kozleski, E. B. (2015). No stone left unturned: Exploring the convergence of New Capitalism in inclusive education the U.S. *Education Policy Analysis Archives*, *23*(37), 1–33. https://doi.org/10.14507/epaa.v23.1779

Young, M. (2008). *Bringing knowledge back in: From social constructivism to social realism in the sociology of education*. Routledge.

Index

Note: *Italicized* page references refer to figures, **bold** references refer to tables, and page references with "n" refer to endnotes.

Aboriginal and Torres Strait Islander: English language learners' performance 134; peoples 99, 104–105; students 99, 131, 134–135
accessibility 53, **77**, 84; assessment 69; in assessment tasks and processes 68; to learning opportunities 73; linguistic 84, 90; procedural 84, 88, 90; in science education 76, 77; of science knowledge for diverse learners 74–75; visual 84, 90
Adams, S. 8
adaptive educational software 8, 75
adjustments 44; assistive technologies for 76–77, **77**; classroom 76–77, **77**; in context of arts 67; equitable 73; evidence-based 133; in film classroom 67; mid-term 78–79; to physical processes 67; summative 79; to summative assessments 75; in teaching and assessment methods 73; teaching and learning 133
agency 5–6, 27–30, 33, 36, 64, 67, 69, 122, 126
Ajjawi, R. 29
Alberta, Canada 32–35
Angelo, D. 10, 123
anxiety 7, 17, **23**, 34, 42–45, 74
Armour, D. 9
Arnold, J. 6, 17
artificial intelligence (AI) 81
artistry 62–63, 64, 66, 69
arts assessment: formative assessment in 63–64; inclusive practices in 62–70; overview 62; summative assessment in 64–70; tensions in 62–63
Arts classrooms 64, 68

arts education 63, 65, 67, 70
arts educators 62, 63–65, 68–70
Ascenzi-Moreno, L. 125
assessment: accessibility 69; for cultural bias 145; as event 27–30, *28*, 31–36; Indigenous place-based approaches to 98, 99, 101, 103–106; as invitation 27–30, *28*, 31–36; methods 73; monolingual 121–122; as occasion 27–30, *28*, 31–36; ownership of 147; peer 31–32; in school environment 51; in school science 73–81; and student learning considerations **23**; tasks and processes 68; *see also* arts assessment; formative assessment; summative assessments
Assessment as Learning 100–101
Assessment for Learning (AfL) 5, 6, 15–24, 73, 100–101, 143; accessible and inclusive history classrooms 19–22; co-constructed success criteria 30–31; conceptual framework 27–29, *28*; defined 15–16; engagement with the past 22; engagement with sources 20–21; in English Language Arts (ELA) 27–36; event–occasion–invitation framework 27–29, *28*; historical thinking 15–24; inclusivity with 16–17; interdependent practices 27; mathematics in 40, 41–42; peer assessment 31–32; processes 16; and reasoning 17–19; routine 7, 43; strategies 19; TADPOLE analysis 20–21; TEEL analysis 20–21; work with sources 21
Assessment of Learning 100–101
assessment practices 33, 36, 70; complexities of 27; and Country-centred knowledges 99; and curriculum 112;

150 *Index*

inclusive 131–134, 135–136; Indigenous perspectives within 98; Indigenous place-based approaches in 99; queer(y)ing 112–116; school-based 111; teachers' 114–115
Assessment Reform Group 15
assistive technologies 5, 67–68; AI integration in 81; case study 77–79; for classroom adjustments 76–77, **77**; defined 75–76; for diverse learners 73–81; initial implementation 77–78; mid-term adjustments 78–79; opportunities in 80–81; summative adjustments 79; in summative science assessments 76
attention deficit hyperactivity disorder (ADHD) **23**, 50, 74
augmented reality (AR) 81
Australian Curriculum (AC) 19, 40, 84, 98; Aboriginal and Torres Strait Islander Histories and Cultures 99
Australian Curriculum, Assessment and Reporting Authority (ACARA) 84–85, 97, 98
Australian Curriculum: History 7–10 17–19
Australian Human Rights Commission 109
Australian Institute for Teaching and School Leadership (AITSL) 17, 131
Australian Professional Standards for Teachers 99, 129
authentic assessment 103
autism spectrum disorder (ASD) 7, **23**, 52, 74
autonomy 5, 20–21, 24, 124
availability 52–53, 135

backward mapping 19
Baker, C. 121
Bartholomaeus, P. 97
Bearman, M. 29
belonging, sense of 5, 7, 42, 44, 99, 109, 111, 135
Bishop, A. J. 50
Boyle, M. 83
bridging 5, 59, 74
Bring Your Own Device (BYOD) policy 78
Britzman, D. 110
Brookhart, S. M. 36
Brown, S. 123, 125
Butler, J. 116

Caldis, S. 83
Challen, C. 6
chunking guides 19
Clark-Fookes, T. 7

classroom: adjustments 76–77, **77**; conversations about mathematics 41; culture 45, 47; vignette 39–40
climate change in Torres Strait Islands 103–106
co-constructed success criteria 30–31
cognitive disabilities 74, 78
cognitive diversity 51
collaboration 52, 74, 124–125
collective knowing/knowledge 97
collective learning 4–5
Common Core State Standards for Mathematical Practice, United States 40
compartmentalisation 65
complexity thinking 3, 28
computational thinking 57–58
conceptual scoring model 10, 124
Connell, R. W. 112, 146
continuous change 3
control 52–53
Country 101, **104**, 105–106; -centred knowledges and assessment practices 99; and cultural practices 104; different tracts of 99; effective custodians of 101; for Indigenous peoples 104; Indigenous place-based assessment 102; learning from and with 100–101; relationship with other entities 100; ways of being (ontology) 99; ways of knowing 99
Country as Teacher 98, 100, 101, 104, 144
Country/place 99, 102, **104**
C-Pen 75, 79
criteria compliance 63–64
cross-curriculum priority (CCP) 100, 101, 104, **104**
cultural competence 10, 130
culturally and linguistically diverse (CALD) 42, 73, 122, 125
culture 98, 102, 104, 133, 136; classroom 45, 47; -fair assessment 100; Indigenous 102; place-based education (PBE) 102; strengths-based approach to 130; transcend 62; ways of being as 111
curriculum descriptors 104–106

Daily Discourse (DD) 5, 6–7, 39–48; in action 44–47; classroom vignette 39–40; evaluation of process 47; goals for 45; in mathematics 43–47; as routine 43; usefulness 43–44
dance 67
Data Standards Manual 116
Davis, B. 28–29, 33

Index   151

Davis, James P. 8
De La Paz, S. 18
DeLuca, C. 17
dialogical exchange 54, 57–59
didactic classrooms 40, 47–48
differentiation 19, 66–69, 133, 136; adjusting physical processes 67; choice of texts 67; constraints in assessment design 69–70; limits of assistive technology 67–69; use of Gen AI 68–69
disabilities: cognitive 74, 78; diverse learners with 74–75; intellectual 50, 74; physical 74–75, 79; sensory 75; social-emotional 74
disciplinary knowledge 15–16, 31, 146
diverse bodies/genders/sexualities 109–112; in assessment policy 111–112; in education 110–111
diverse learners: accessibility of science knowledge for 74–75; assistive technologies for 73–81; case study 77–79; defined 73; with disability 74–75; needs of 73; planning support for 75–76
diversity 3, 5; cognitive 51; gender and sexuality 109–111, 113–114; genders 109–116; human 109; language/linguistic 130, 134, 136; of learners and learning conditions 4; of students' actual learning levels 32
Dooley, K. 11
DreamBox Learning 8, 75
dyslexia 8, 74, 75, 78

early childhood education (ECE) 52
early childhood education and care (ECEC) 7; analysis 53–55; data collection 53–55; dialogical assessment of mathematics in 53–55; ethics 53–55; observation 51; participants 53–55; technology in 53–55; transcription from institution 55–57
Education for All 141
Education Perfect 76
Ekins, A. 133
engagement with the past 22
engagement with sources 20–21
English as an Additional Language (EAL) 120
English as an additional language or dialect (EAL/D) 5, 10, 69, 119–126; Australian Aboriginal students with 122; defined 119–120; inclusive assessments for 122, 125–126; issues with current assessments for 121–122; machine translation (MT) in 124; overview 119; translanguaging 120–121; translanguaging and assessment 122–125; translingual artefacts 124–125; translingual assessment tasks 123–124
English as a Second Language (ESL) 120
English as a Second or Other Language (ESOL) 120
English Language Arts (ELA): AfL in 27–36; conceptual framework 27–29; illustrative examples from 29–35; overview 27
English Language Learners (ELL) 120
equitable adjustments 73
equity 40, 43, 46–48, 70, 136, 142; for diverse learners with physical disabilities 75; issues 119; in schools 130; for students 92
ethical assessment 103
Eurocentrism 97
event, assessment 27–30, 28, 31–36
evidence-based adjustments 133

fealty 20, 22
feedback 8, 16, 64, 66, 103, 124, 129; anonymous 78; conference 21; constructive 21; peer 28, 31, 32; real-time 81; teacher 27
feudalism 18, 22
Feuerstein, R. 51
film and media 67, 69
Fine, C. G. M. 124–125
first-order concepts 18, 19, 22
formalized testing 34–35
formative assessment 5, 15, 41, 44; in the arts 63–64; criteria compliance 63–64; feedback 64
Fraser, Nancy 142, 146
funds of knowledge 40, 146

García, O. 121
gender 4–5, 92, 116n1; -based barriers 9, 92; binary 110, 116, 144; diversity 109–116, 146; equality 85–86; inequality 87–88; queer(y)ing 113
gender-based barriers 9, 92
gender or sexuality diverse (GSD) 109–111, 113–114, 116n1
General Comment No. 4 (GC 4) 83
Generative artificial intelligence (Gen AI) 66, 68–69, 125
geographical assessment 83–92; context 84; method of analysis 84; overview

83–84; pre-service teacher 84–88; structural barriers 90–92; visual, procedural, and linguistic barriers 88–90
Geographies of Wellbeing 84, 87
geography: discipline 83; education 83–84; Grade 10 90, 92
gifted and talented programmes 73, 121
grade 10–12 34–35
Graham, L. 8–9, 28–29, 84, 86, 88, 90, 92
Granone, F. 7
Guerrero, C. 113

Hammond, J. 124
hard-to-staff schools 129–130, 131
Haugenes, M. 52
Haywood, H. C. 59
Head of Student Services (HoSS) 77, 78
helping learning 15
Henderson, Deborah 6
hetero-cis-normativity 110, 116n1
heterosexuality 110, 116n1
high-stakes assessment 34, 115–116
historical thinking 15–24
Hodgen, J. 41
Hogan, S. L. 64
Hogarth, M. 98
Holden, M. 6
Hou, H. 124
Howie, D. R. 51, 58–59
Hudson, C. 10, 123
human development index (HDI) 85
human-Earthkin relationships 97

identities 42, 92, 98–99, 102; cisgender 116n1; diversity 3, 5; gender 111; as GSD 109; heterosexual 110, 116n1; as Indigenous peoples 106; intersectionality of 111; LGBTIQA+ 109, 111, 113, 115, 116; sexuality 111
implementational space 122
inclusion: defined 4, 83; in education 4, 51, 83; in mathematics 42–43; in Norwegian context 51
inclusive assessment 3–11, 122, 125–126, 129–136; approaches to 143–144; collective learning 4–5; and complexity 3; and contextualising systems 4; and continuous change 3; defined 4; and diversity 3; translanguaging in designing 5
inclusive education 4, 50–51, 83, 122, 124, 132, 134, 141–142

inclusive practices: in arts assessment 62–70; and geographical assessment 83–92
inclusive research 50–59; approaches 52–53; case study 53–55; concept of 52; defined 51–52; dialogical exchange 57–59; in ECEC 53–55; overview 50–51; realisation of 52–53; results 55–57; teachers' competence 57–59
inclusivity with AfL 16–17
Index of Community Socio-Educational Advantage (ICSEA) 19, 24n1
Indigenous communities 5, 10, 102, 136
Indigenous country 3
Indigenous culture 102
Indigenous education 98
Indigenous/ethnic minorities 73
Indigenous peoples 98, 99, 102, 104, 106
Indigenous perspectives 83, 97–99, 102, 103, 135, 136
Indigenous place-based assessment *see* place-based education (PBE)
Indigenous students 98, 99, 102, 103, 120, 134, 136, 144
Indigenous ways of being/knowing/doing 99
intellectual disabilities 50, 74
interests 33, 52, 67, 106
invitation, assessment 27–30, *28*, 31–36

James, Sarah 10
Jeffries, Michelle 9
Johnson, K. 52–53
justification 40, 42–43, 47, 48, 85, 87

Kelly, R. 10, 124
kindergarten 32–33
Kleeman, G. 83
Klenowski, V. 16
knowledge: collective 97; Country-centred 99; cultural 99, 102, 130, 135, 142, 146; disciplinary 15–16, 31, 146; funds of 40, 146; science 74–75
Knudsen, G. 7
Kozleski, E. B. 142
Kumashiro, K. K. 110

Langer, S. K. 65
leadership 86, 111, 130, 132, 136
learning: as an active and social process 16; and assessment in school science 73–81; collective 4–5; considerations **23**; from and with Country 100–101; difficulties 50, 134; helping 15; intentions 27; mathematical 50, 53; opportunities 4,

28, 35, 70, 73, 130, 131, 142; science 8, 75, 77; Standard Australian English (SAE) 134; students' 5, 16, 34, 134; *see also* Assessment for Learning (AfL)
Lee, P. 22
Letts, I. W. J. 110
LGBTIQA+ 109–111, 113, 115–116
LGBTQI+ people 73
Li, W. 121
Limited English Proficiency (LEP) 120
linguistic accessibility 84, 90, 92
Loan and Training Officers (LTOs) 90
Lopez, A. A. 121
Lubbe, H. 17

machine translation (MT) 124–126
Marshall, B. 41
mathematical learning 50, 53
mathematics 39–48, 50–51; anxiety 42; in Assessment for Learning (AfL) 40, 41–42; classroom conversations about 41; DD in 43–47; inclusion in 42–43; overview 40; students as constructors and creators of 40
Mather, Mark 16–19, 24
Meta Quest 3 81
Michaels, S. 46
mid-term adjustments 78–79
Millenium Development Goals 141
mindset capabilities 5
MIO observation tool 54, 57
Moll, L. 146
monolingual assessments 121–122
Monte-Sano, C. 18
multilingual learners 119, 120–122
multimodal literacy profile (MLP) 123
music 67, 69

National Assessment Program for Literacy and Numeracy (NAPLAN) 121, 129, 145, 147n1
National Council of Teachers of Mathematics (NCTM) 43
Nationally Consistent Collection of Data on School Students and Disability (NCCD) 8, 19, **23**, 74, 75, 76, 78
neurodiversity 3, 5, 50–53, 143
Nokes, J. D. 18
Norway 51–52
Norwegian Agency for Shared Services in Education and Research (Sikt) 54
Norwegian Inclusive Community Report 51
number sequence *54*, 58

observation 51–52, 54, 57
occasion, assessment 27–30, *28*, 31–36
O'Connor, M. C. 46
optimism 8, 66
Østby, M. 52
ownership 35, 52, 147

Padlet 78
partnerships 122, 124, 126, 136
peer assessment 5–6, 28, 31–32
physical disabilities 74–75, 79
place-based education (PBE) 5, 9, 97–107; assessment 98–99; Australian education context 97–98; authentic assessment 103; climate change in Torres Strait Islands 103–106; conceptual framework *101*, 101–102; Country/place 102; culture 102; defined 97; ethical assessment 103; Indigenous ways of being/knowing/doing 99; learning from and with Country 100–101; peoples 102; policy 98–99; positionality in Indigenous education 98; student interest/design 103; Western 97
pre-service teacher 3, 16, 84–88, 131; analysis of tasks constructed by 86–88; assessment design 85–86; assessment for 84–85
problem-solving 6–7, 47; endeavours 4; skills 40, 50
procedural: accessibility 84, 88, 90; barriers 88–90
procedural concepts *see* second-order concepts

qualifiers 66
Queensland Curriculum and Assessment Authority (QCAA) 85, 88, 111
Queensland University of Technology (QUT) 84, 130
queer pedagogy 110
queer theory 110–111, 116
queer(y)ing primary assessment 109–116; approaches/practices 113, 114–116; diverse bodies/genders/sexualities 109–112; gender and sexuality normativities 113; high-stakes assessment 115–116; literature 112–114; reporting on big data 116; teachers' own assessment practices/designs 114–115; warning from literature 114

Index

reasoning 24, 40, 43; and historical thinking 17–19; opportunities for 42; skills 15, 43, 47–48, 50; spatial 83
redistributive social justice 142, 145
reflection 21, 30, 63, 84, 85, 88, 103, 107; on assistive technologies 79–80
Regional, Rural and Remote Education 132
Robinson, K. 110
routine 6, 20, 143; AfL 7, 43; DD as 43; stages 44
'Rugged Robot' 53
rural and remote (RR) assessment 10, 129–136; challenges 131–134; field study 131; implementation of inclusive assessment 134–135; overview 129–130; study methods 130

Schissel, J. L. 120
school science, assessment 73–81
science 105, 106; classroom-based assessments 124; classroom 76, 124, 125; knowledge 74–75; placed-based approaches 9; school 73–81; summative assessments 76; teachers 73
science education 73–76
science learning 8, 75, 77
Sears, J. T. 110
second-order concepts 15, 18, 19, 22
self-assessment 5, 6, 21, 27
semiotic repertoire 120, 122–124, 126
Sempowicz, Tracey 10
sense of belonging 5, 7, 42, 44, 99, 109, 111, 135
sensitive language 130, 135
sensory disabilities 75
Separating Mixtures and Renewable Resources (ACARA) 76
serfs 20, 22
sexuality, identities 111; *see also* gender or sexuality diverse (GSD)
Sheehan, M. 15
Shemilt, D. J. 24
Shepard, L. A. 36
Smart Sparrow 75
social-emotional disabilities 74
social justice 73, 110, 112, 115; and inclusive classroom assessment 141–147; and inclusive education 141–143; principles of 146; redistributive 142
source-based inquiry 15, 24
sources: engagement with 20–21, 24; work with 21
South-East Queensland, Australia 30–32

spatial understanding 50–59; case study 53–57; dialogical assessment 53–57; dialogical exchange 57–59; inclusive research 51–53; overview 50–51; *see also* early childhood education and care (ECEC)
speech and language impairments 74
speech-to-text software 68, 75–76, 79, 80
Spillman, D. 9, 100–101
Stahl, S. A. 18
Standard Australian English (SAE) 120, 134
Steele, C. 122
Stewart, Maria 10
Stile Education 76
Stobart, G. 16, 19
strengths-based approach 9, 100, 102, 106, 130, 135
Strong, S. 6
student agency 5, 27, 29, 36
student-centred assessment 103
students' learning 5, 16, 34, 134
success criteria 5, 27–29, 30–31, 36, 78
Sumara, D. J. 28–29, 33
summative adjustments 79
summative assessments 5, 75, 76; in the arts 64–70; criteria construction 65–66; differentiation 66–69; enabling constraints in assessment design 69–70; optimism 66; value measure 64–65
Sustainable Development Goal 4 (SDG 4) 141

TADPOLE 20–21, 24n2
Taylor, T. 24
teachers: assessment practices 114–115; assessment practices/designs 114–115; competence 57–59; pre-service 3, 16, 84–88, 131; science 73, 74
technology: assistive 67–68, 73, 75–76; in ECEC 53–55; *see also* inclusive research
TEEL 20–21, 24, 24n3
Teh, Nicholas K. 8
Thomas-Reid, M. 9, 113–114
Torres Strait Islander peoples 104, 105
translanguaging 119, 120–121
translanguaging in designing inclusive assessment 5, 119–126
translingual artefacts 124–125

translingual assessment 123–124
trauma-informed approaches 5, 134, 136

UNESCO 63
United Nations (UN) Convention on the Rights of Persons with Disabilities (CRPD) 4, 83
United Nations Human Rights Committee (UNHCR) 104
United States 42, 43; Common Core State Standards for Mathematical Practice in 40
Universal Declaration of Human Rights 141
Universal Design for Learning (UDL) 5, 34, 36
University of Stavanger 53

Van Horn, S. E. 115
van Leent, Lisa 9
virtual laboratories 76

virtual reality (VR) 81
visual 87, 115; accessibility 84, 90; aids **23**, 79; barriers 88–99; complexities 84; data interpretation 75; disabilities 67; impaired learners 76; information and in science 75; representations of scientific concepts 80; stimuli 83
VR Chemistry Lab app 81

Waitoller, F. R. 142
Walmsley, J. 52–53
Warnich, P. 17
Welply, O. 123
White, D. Y. 45–46
Wiliam, D. 16
work with sources 21
Worthen, M. G. F. 116n1
Wright, W. E. 121

Young, C. 24
Young, M. 146

Printed in the United States
by Baker & Taylor Publisher Services